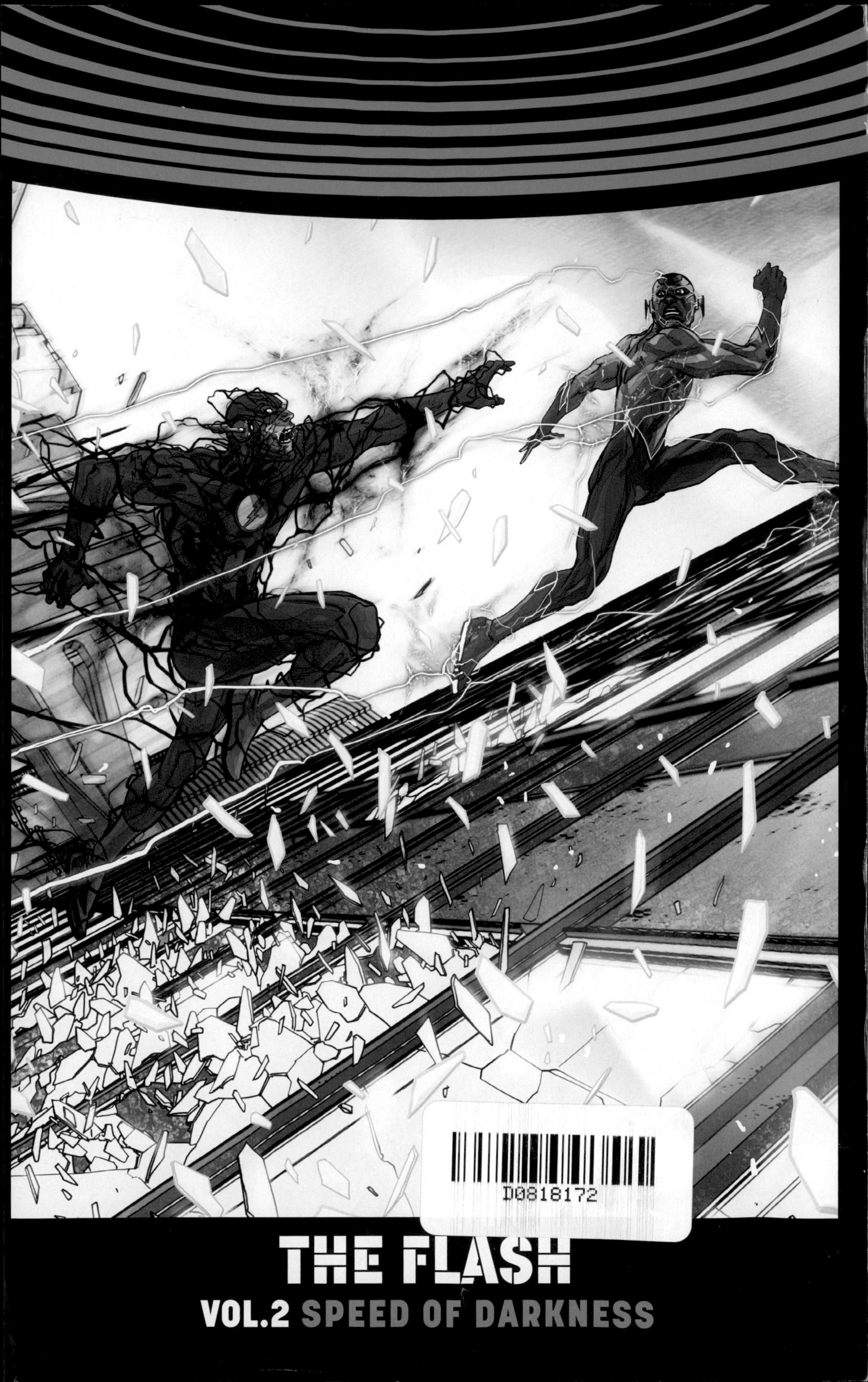

THE FLASH

VOL.2 SPEED OF DARKNESS

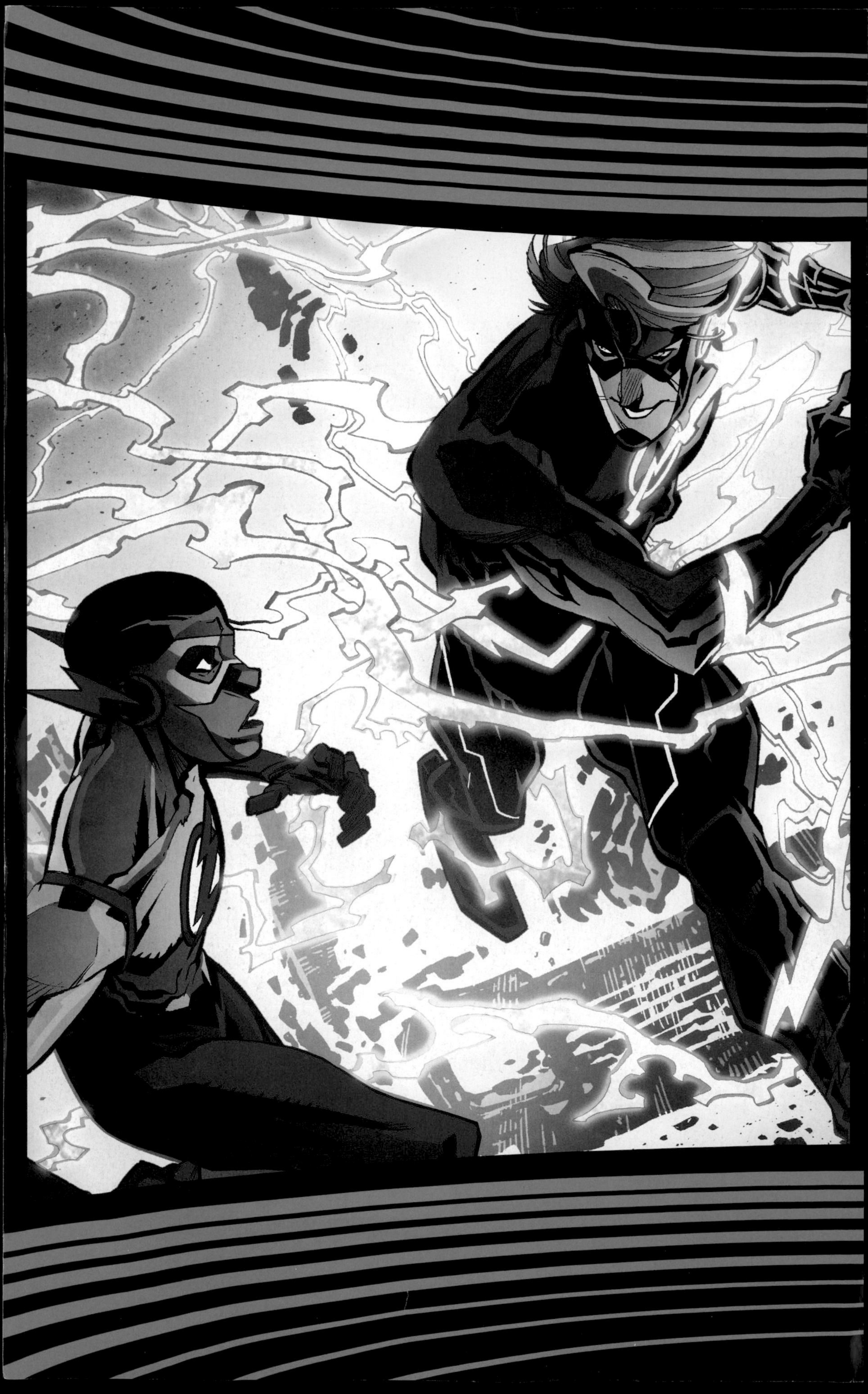

THE FLASH

VOL.2 SPEED OF DARKNESS

JOSHUA WILLIAMSON
writer

DAVIDE GIANFELICE * **JORGE CORONA** * **NEIL GOOGE**
FELIPE WATANABE * OCLAIR ALBERT
artists

IVAN PLASCENCIA * **CHRIS SOTOMAYOR**
colorists

STEVE WANDS
letterer

CARMINE DI GIANDOMENICO
series and collection cover artist

BRIAN CUNNINGHAM Editor - Original Series ✷ **AMEDEO TURTURRO DIEGO LOPEZ** Assistant Editors - Original Series
JEB WOODARD Group Editor - Collected Editions ✷ **ERIKA ROTHBERG** Editor - Collected Edition
STEVE COOK Design Director - Books ✷ **MONIQUE GRUSPE** Publication Design

BOB HARRAS Senior VP - Editor-in-Chief, DC Comics

DIANE NELSON President ✷ **DAN DiDIO** Publisher ✷ **JIM LEE** Publisher ✷ **GEOFF JOHNS** President & Chief Creative Officer
AMIT DESAI Executive VP - Business & Marketing Strategy, Direct to Consumer & Global Franchise Management ✷ **SAM ADES** Senior VP - Direct to Consumer
BOBBIE CHASE VP - Talent Development ✷ **MARK CHIARELLO** Senior VP - Art, Design & Collected Editions
JOHN CUNNINGHAM Senior VP - Sales & Trade Marketing ✷ **ANNE DePIES** Senior VP - Business Strategy, Finance & Administration
DON FALLETTI VP - Manufacturing Operations ✷ **LAWRENCE GANEM** VP - Editorial Administration & Talent Relations
ALISON GILL Senior VP - Manufacturing & Operations ✷ **HANK KANALZ** Senior VP - Editorial Strategy & Administration
JAY KOGAN VP - Legal Affairs ✷ **THOMAS LOFTUS** VP - Business Affairs
JACK MAHAN VP - Business Affairs ✷ **NICK J. NAPOLITANO** VP - Manufacturing Administration
EDDIE SCANNELL VP - Consumer Marketing ✷ **COURTNEY SIMMONS** Senior VP - Publicity & Communications
JIM (SKI) SOKOLOWSKI VP - Comic Book Specialty Sales & Trade Marketing ✷ **NANCY SPEARS** VP - Mass, Book, Digital Sales & Trade Marketing

THE FLASH VOL. 2: SPEED OF DARKNESS

Published by DC Comics. Compilation and all new material Copyright © 2017 DC Comics. All Rights Reserved.
Originally published in single magazine form in THE FLASH 9-13. Copyright © 2016 DC Comics.
All Rights Reserved. All characters, their distinctive likenesses and related elements featured in this publication are trademarks of DC Comics.
The stories, characters and incidents featured in this publication are entirely fictional.
DC Comics does not read or accept unsolicited submissions of ideas, stories or artwork

DC Comics, 2900 West Alameda Ave., Burbank, CA 91505.
Printed by LSC Communications, Salem, VA, USA. 4/14/17.
First Printing. ISBN: 978-1-4012-6893-0

Library of Congress Cataloging-in-Publication Data is available.

PEFC Certified

Printed on paper from
sustainably managed
forests, controlled
sources

PEFC/29-31-337   www.pefc.org

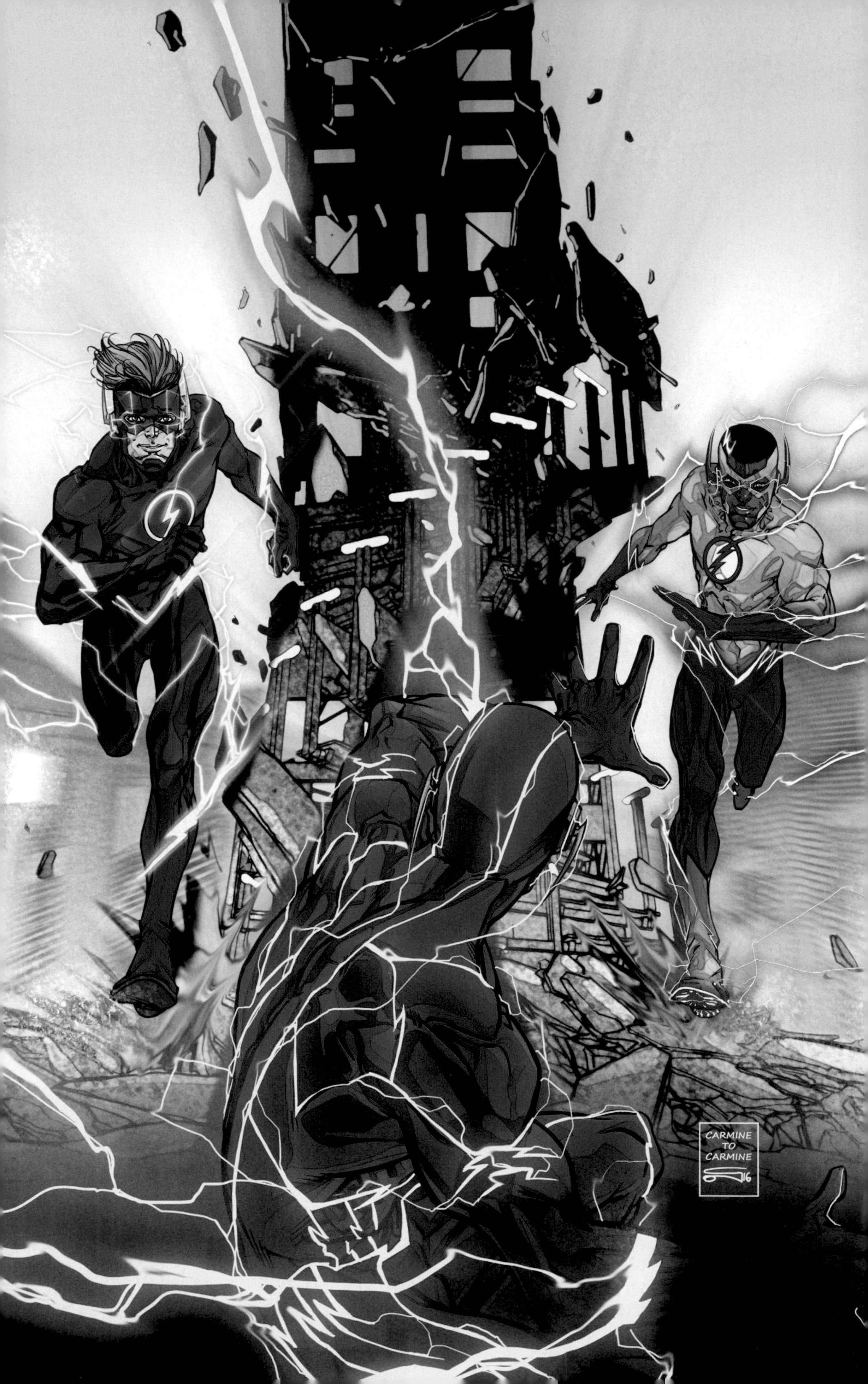
CARMINE
TO
CARMINE

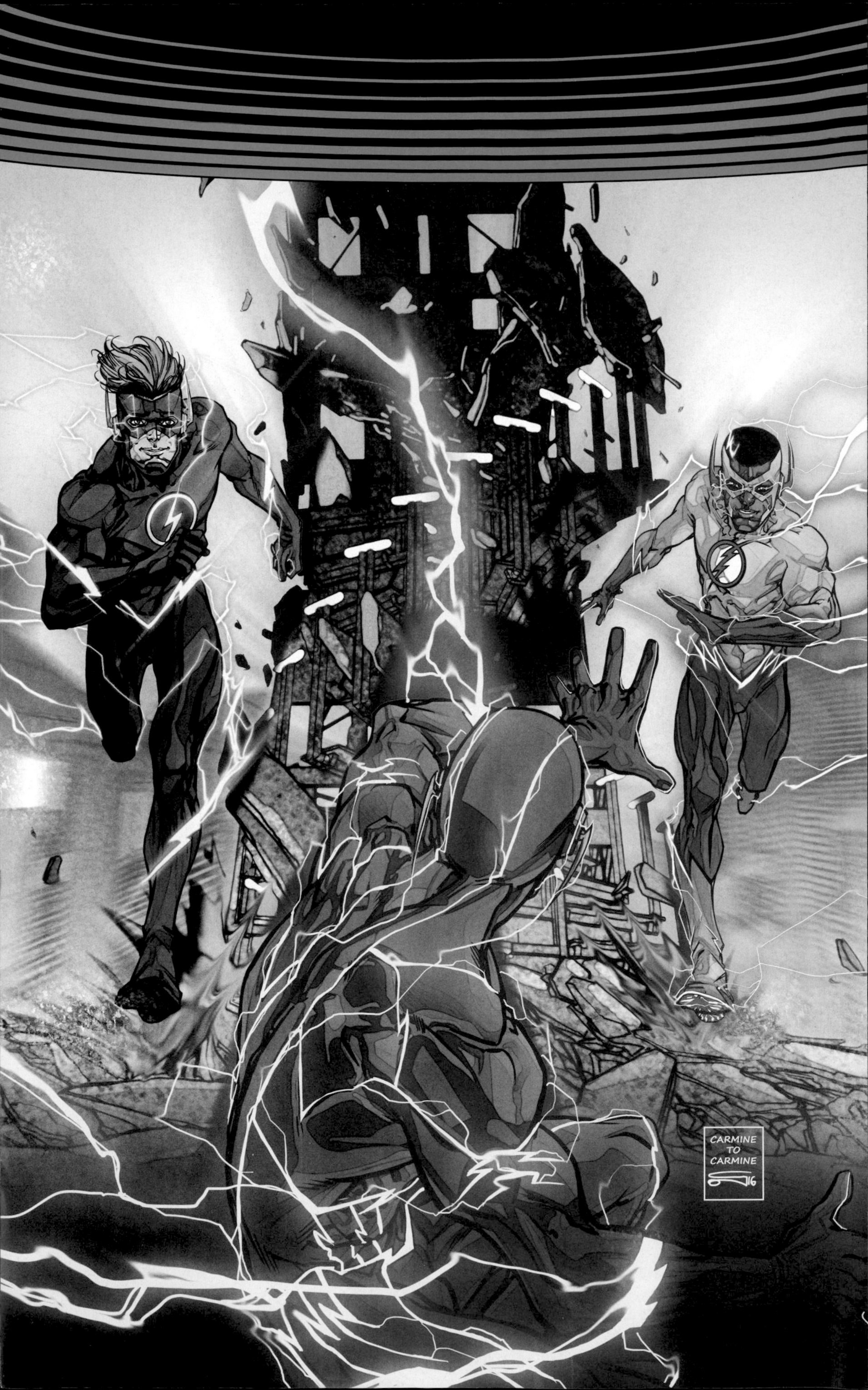
CARMINE
TO
CARMINE

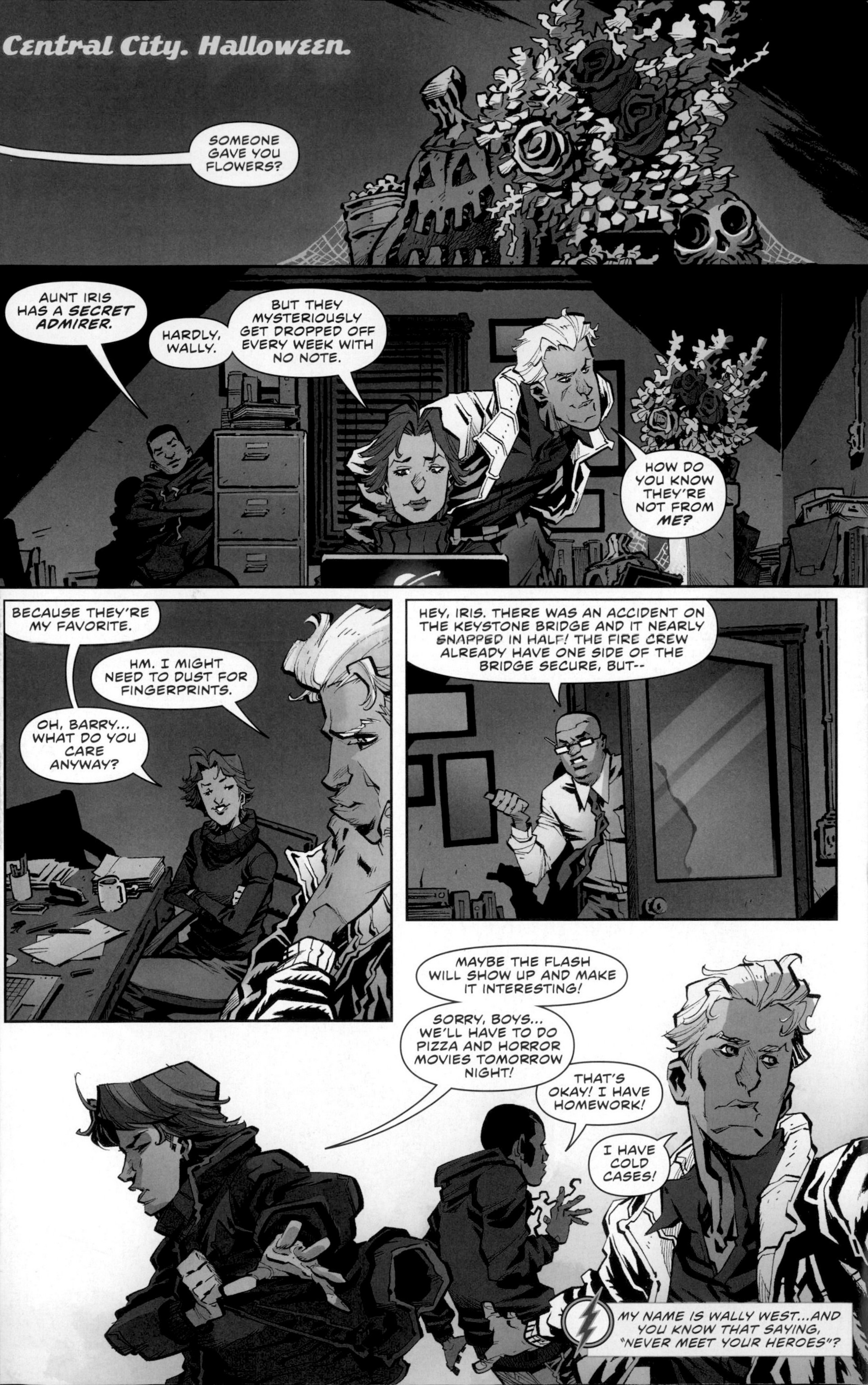
Central City. Halloween.
SOMEONE GAVE YOU FLOWERS?
AUNT IRIS HAS A SECRET ADMIRER.
HARDLY, WALLY.
BUT THEY MYSTERIOUSLY GET DROPPED OFF EVERY WEEK WITH NO NOTE.
HOW DO YOU KNOW THEY'RE NOT FROM ME?
BECAUSE THEY'RE MY FAVORITE.
HM. I MIGHT NEED TO DUST FOR FINGERPRINTS.
OH, BARRY... WHAT DO YOU CARE ANYWAY?
HEY, IRIS. THERE WAS AN ACCIDENT ON THE KEYSTONE BRIDGE AND IT NEARLY SNAPPED IN HALF! THE FIRE CREW ALREADY HAVE ONE SIDE OF THE BRIDGE SECURE, BUT--
MAYBE THE FLASH WILL SHOW UP AND MAKE IT INTERESTING!
SORRY, BOYS... WE'LL HAVE TO DO PIZZA AND HORROR MOVIES TOMORROW NIGHT!
THAT'S OKAY! I HAVE HOMEWORK!
I HAVE COLD CASES!
MY NAME IS WALLY WEST...AND YOU KNOW THAT SAYING, "NEVER MEET YOUR HEROES"?

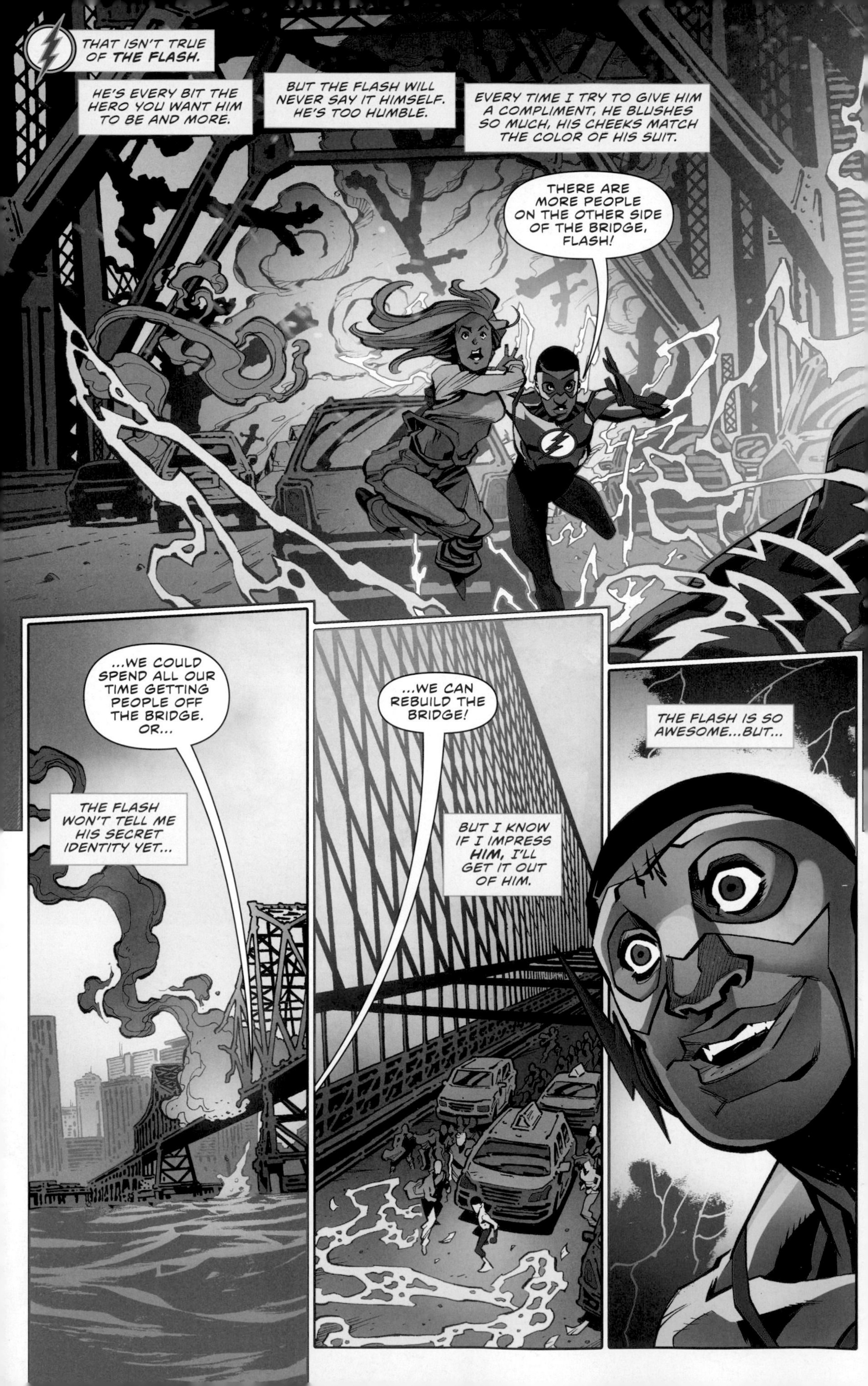
THAT ISN'T TRUE OF THE FLASH.
HE'S EVERY BIT THE HERO YOU WANT HIM TO BE AND MORE.
BUT THE FLASH WILL NEVER SAY IT HIMSELF. HE'S TOO HUMBLE.
EVERY TIME I TRY TO GIVE HIM A COMPLIMENT, HE BLUSHES SO MUCH, HIS CHEEKS MATCH THE COLOR OF HIS SUIT.
THERE ARE MORE PEOPLE ON THE OTHER SIDE OF THE BRIDGE, FLASH!
...WE COULD SPEND ALL OUR TIME GETTING PEOPLE OFF THE BRIDGE. OR...
THE FLASH WON'T TELL ME HIS SECRET IDENTITY YET...
...WE CAN REBUILD THE BRIDGE!
BUT I KNOW IF I IMPRESS HIM, I'LL GET IT OUT OF HIM.
THE FLASH IS SO AWESOME...BUT...

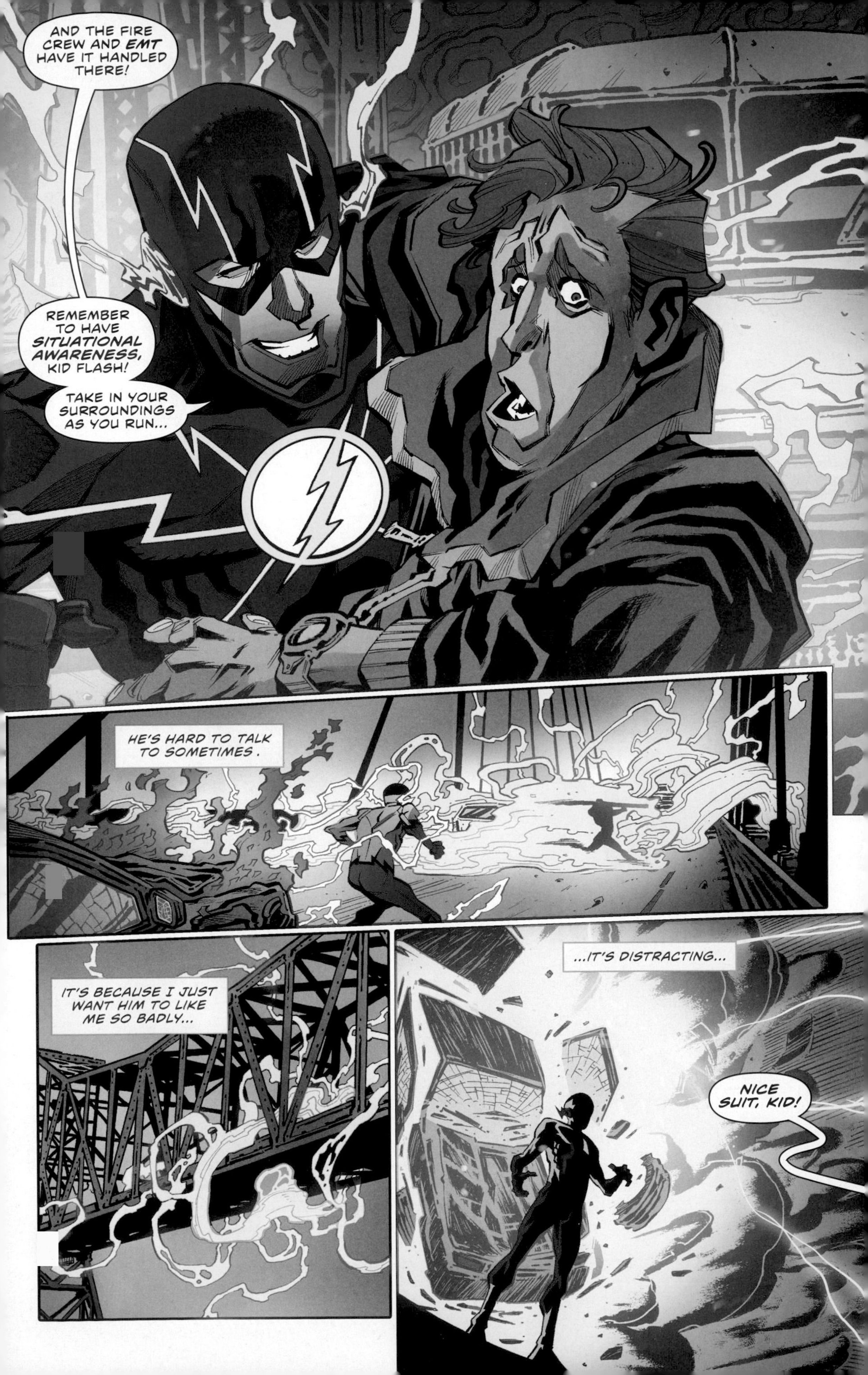
AND THE FIRE CREW AND EMT HAVE IT HANDLED THERE!
REMEMBER TO HAVE SITUATIONAL AWARENESS, KID FLASH!
TAKE IN YOUR SURROUNDINGS AS YOU RUN...
HE'S HARD TO TALK TO SOMETIMES.
IT'S BECAUSE I JUST WANT HIM TO LIKE ME SO BADLY...
...IT'S DISTRACTING...
NICE SUIT, KID!

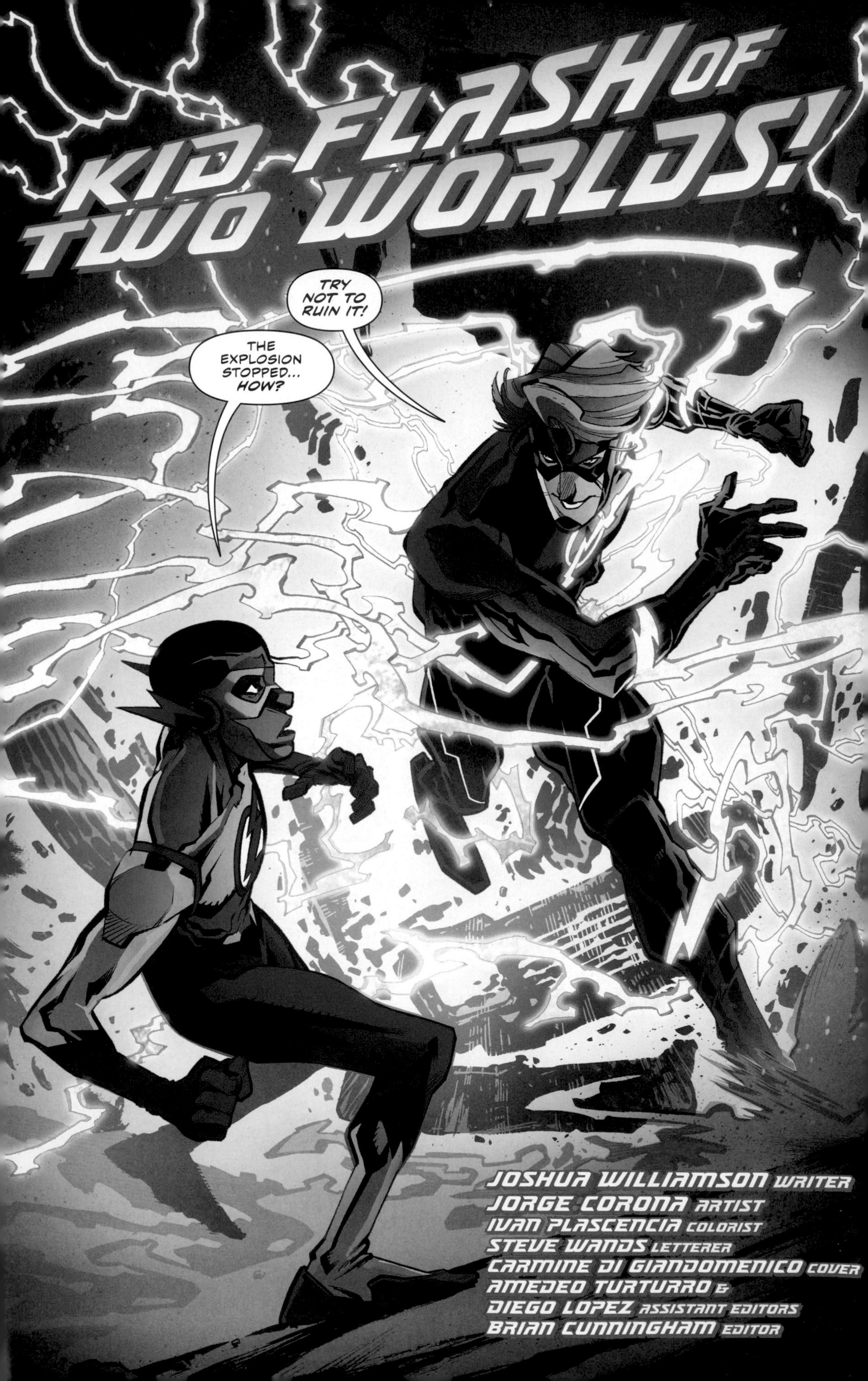

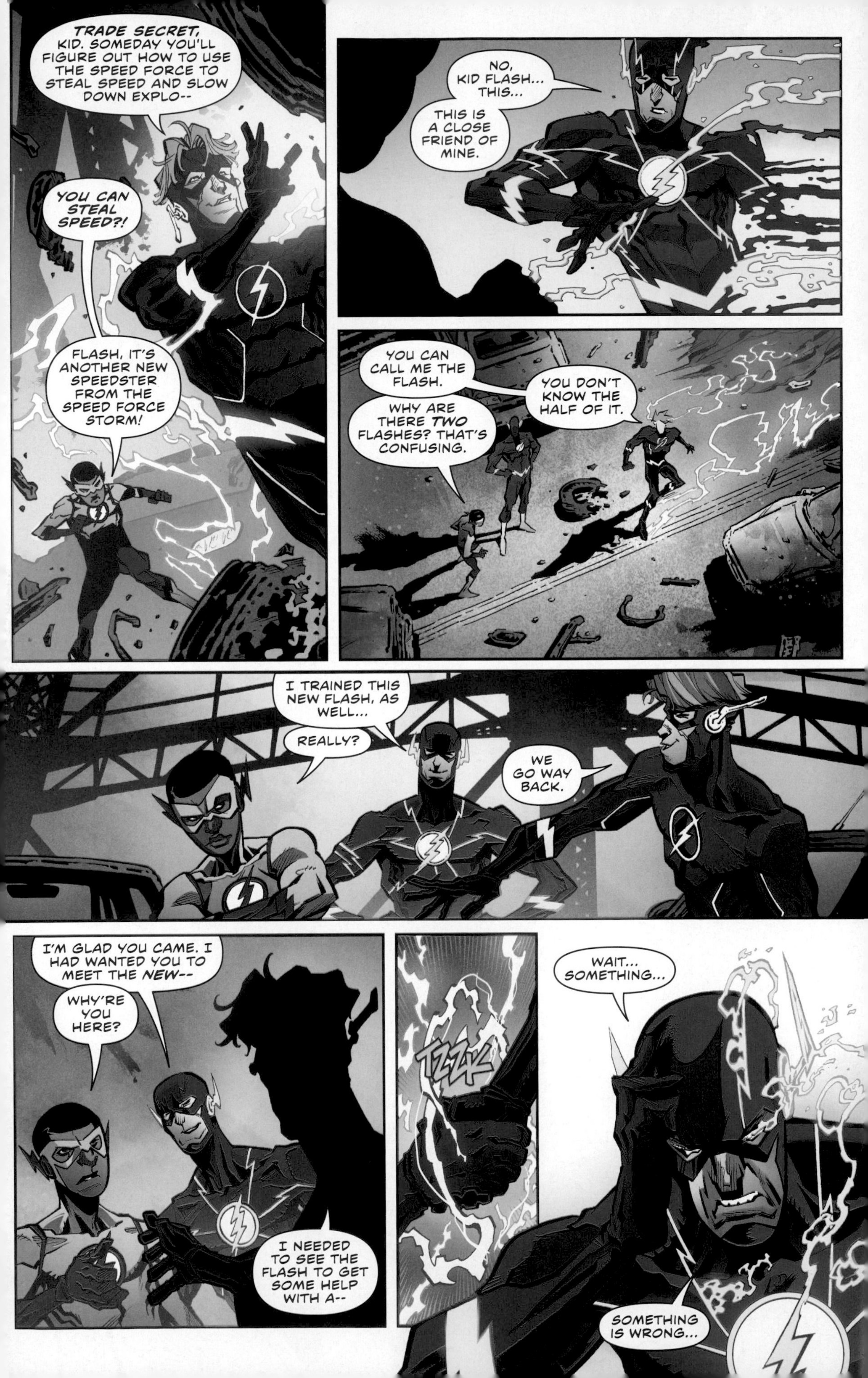
TRADE SECRET, KID. SOMEDAY YOU'LL FIGURE OUT HOW TO USE THE SPEED FORCE TO STEAL SPEED AND SLOW DOWN EXPLO--
YOU CAN STEAL SPEED?!
FLASH, IT'S ANOTHER NEW SPEEDSTER FROM THE SPEED FORCE STORM!
NO, KID FLASH... THIS...
THIS IS A CLOSE FRIEND OF MINE.
YOU CAN CALL ME THE FLASH.
WHY ARE THERE TWO FLASHES? THAT'S CONFUSING.
YOU DON'T KNOW THE HALF OF IT.
I TRAINED THIS NEW FLASH, AS WELL...
REALLY?
WE GO WAY BACK.
I'M GLAD YOU CAME. I HAD WANTED YOU TO MEET THE NEW--
WHY'RE YOU HERE?
I NEEDED TO SEE THE FLASH TO GET SOME HELP WITH A--
TZZK
WAIT... SOMETHING...
SOMETHING IS WRONG...

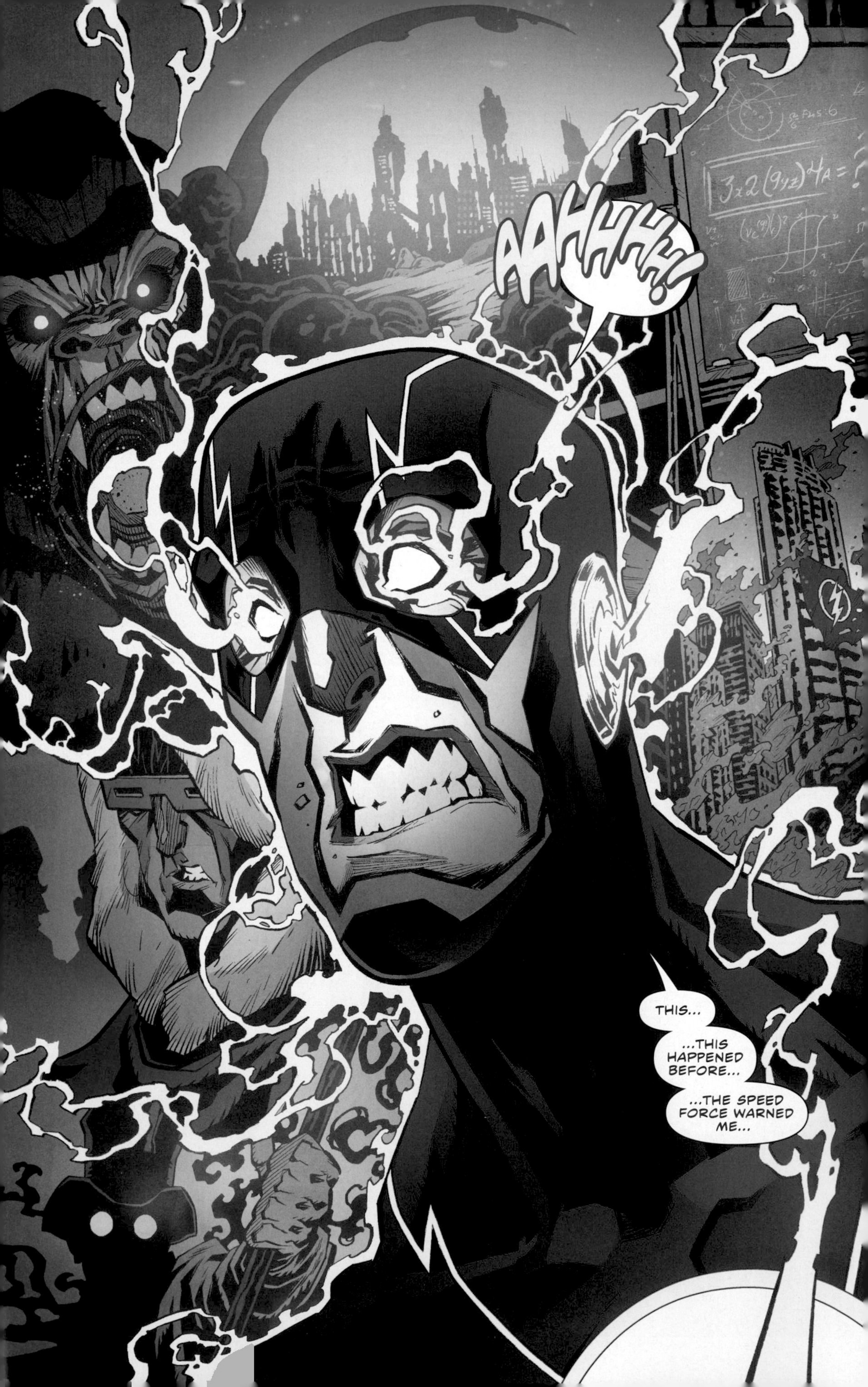
AAHHHH!
THIS...
...THIS HAPPENED BEFORE...
...THE SPEED FORCE WARNED ME...

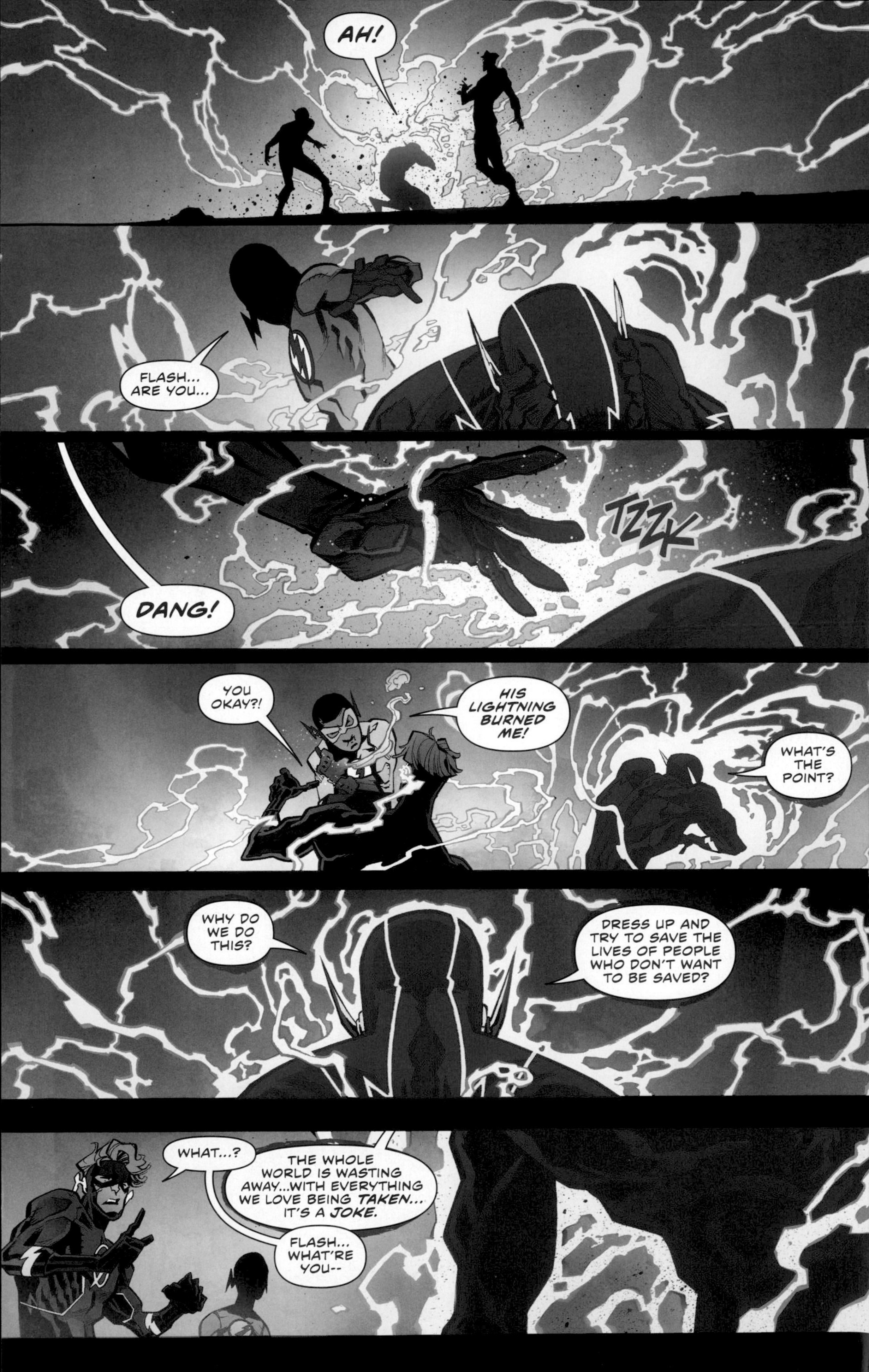
AH!
FLASH... ARE YOU...
TZZK
DANG!
YOU OKAY?!
HIS LIGHTNING BURNED ME!
WHAT'S THE POINT?
WHY DO WE DO THIS?
DRESS UP AND TRY TO SAVE THE LIVES OF PEOPLE WHO DON'T WANT TO BE SAVED?
WHAT...?
THE WHOLE WORLD IS WASTING AWAY...WITH EVERYTHING WE LOVE BEING TAKEN... IT'S A JOKE.
FLASH... WHAT'RE YOU--

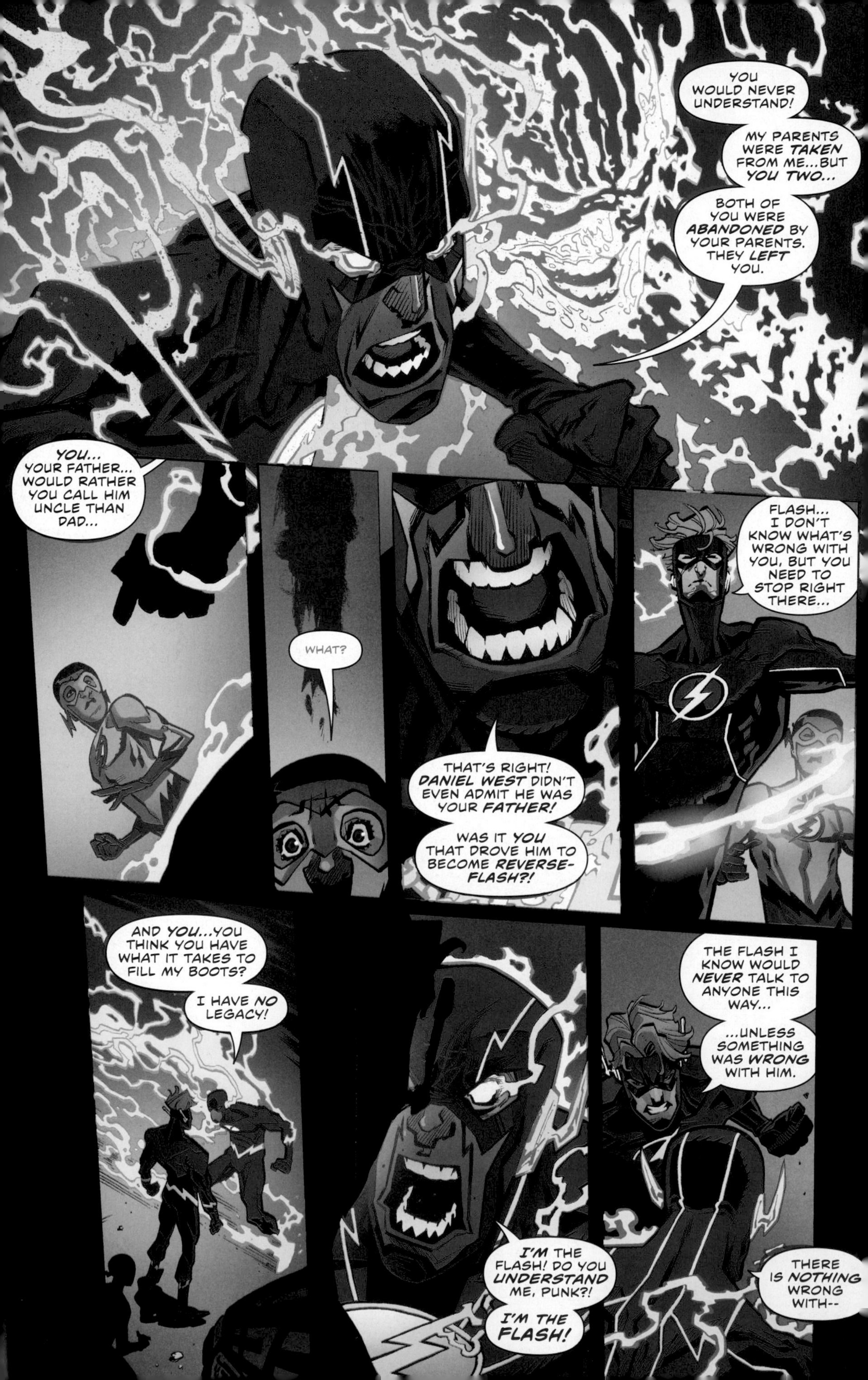
YOU WOULD NEVER UNDERSTAND!
MY PARENTS WERE TAKEN FROM ME...BUT YOU TWO...
BOTH OF YOU WERE ABANDONED BY YOUR PARENTS. THEY LEFT YOU.
YOU... YOUR FATHER... WOULD RATHER YOU CALL HIM UNCLE THAN DAD...
WHAT?
THAT'S RIGHT! DANIEL WEST DIDN'T EVEN ADMIT HE WAS YOUR FATHER!
WAS IT YOU THAT DROVE HIM TO BECOME REVERSE-FLASH?!
FLASH... I DON'T KNOW WHAT'S WRONG WITH YOU, BUT YOU NEED TO STOP RIGHT THERE...
AND YOU...YOU THINK YOU HAVE WHAT IT TAKES TO FILL MY BOOTS?
I HAVE NO LEGACY!
I'M THE FLASH! DO YOU UNDERSTAND ME, PUNK?!
I'M THE FLASH!
THE FLASH I KNOW WOULD NEVER TALK TO ANYONE THIS WAY...
...UNLESS SOMETHING WAS WRONG WITH HIM.
THERE IS NOTHING WRONG WITH--

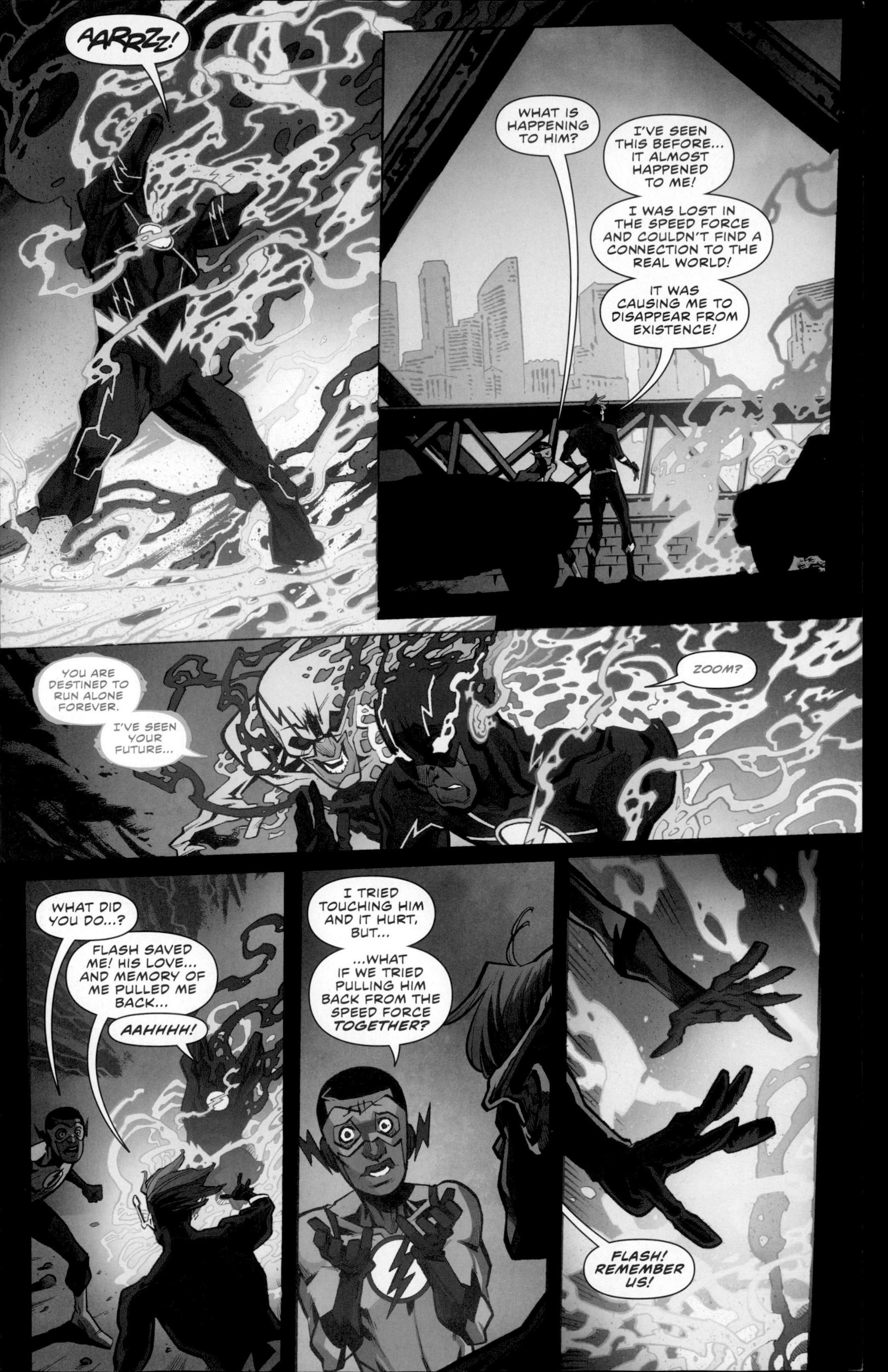
AARRZZ!
WHAT IS HAPPENING TO HIM?
I'VE SEEN THIS BEFORE... IT ALMOST HAPPENED TO ME!
I WAS LOST IN THE SPEED FORCE AND COULDN'T FIND A CONNECTION TO THE REAL WORLD!
IT WAS CAUSING ME TO DISAPPEAR FROM EXISTENCE!
YOU ARE DESTINED TO RUN ALONE FOREVER.
I'VE SEEN YOUR FUTURE...
ZOOM?
WHAT DID YOU DO...?
FLASH SAVED ME! HIS LOVE... AND MEMORY OF ME PULLED ME BACK...
AAHHHH!
I TRIED TOUCHING HIM AND IT HURT, BUT...
...WHAT IF WE TRIED PULLING HIM BACK FROM THE SPEED FORCE TOGETHER?
FLASH! REMEMBER US!

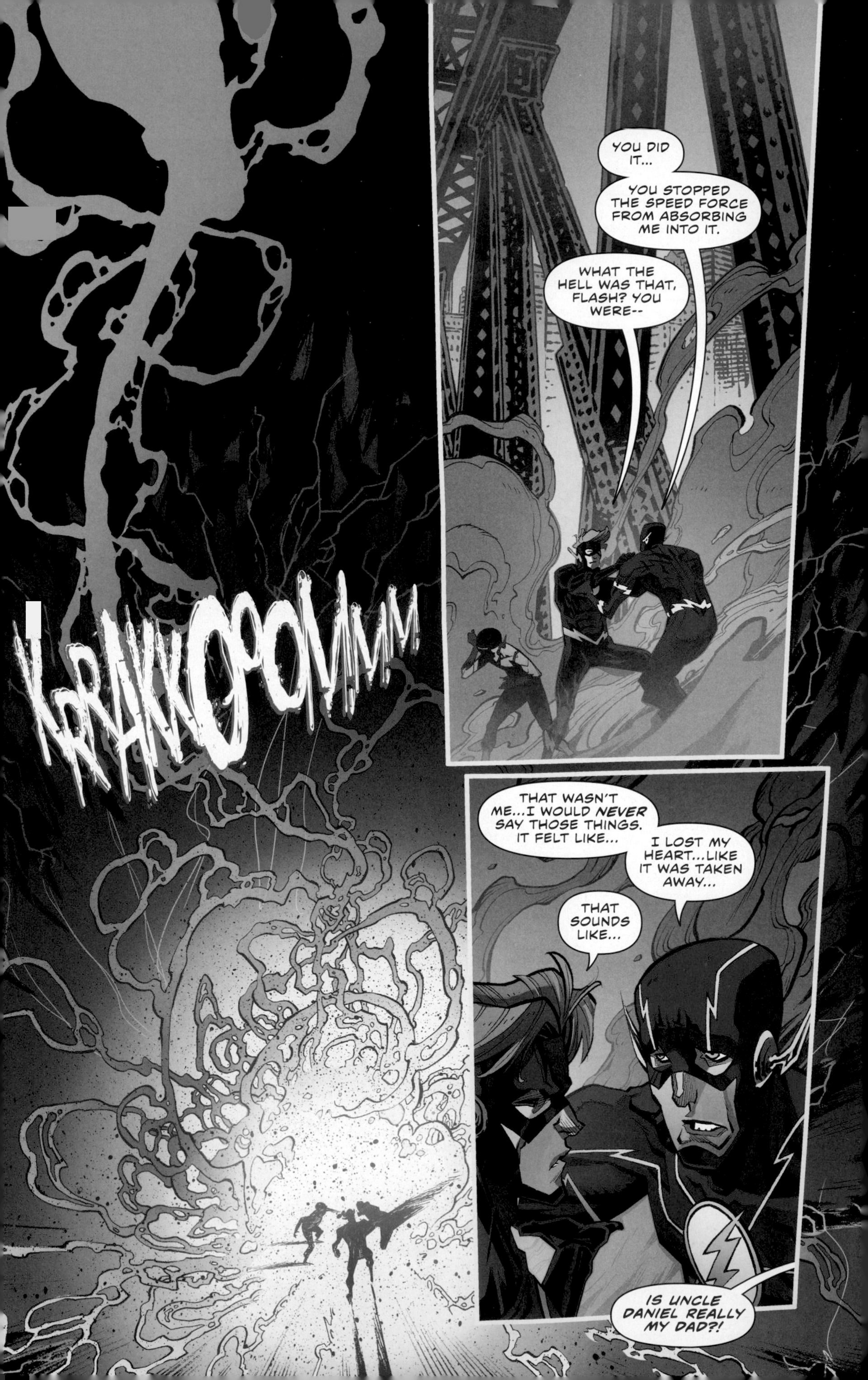
KRAKKOOOMMM
YOU DID IT...
YOU STOPPED THE SPEED FORCE FROM ABSORBING ME INTO IT.
WHAT THE HELL WAS THAT, FLASH? YOU WERE--
THAT WASN'T ME...I WOULD NEVER SAY THOSE THINGS. IT FELT LIKE...
I LOST MY HEART...LIKE IT WAS TAKEN AWAY...
THAT SOUNDS LIKE...
IS UNCLE DANIEL REALLY MY DAD?!

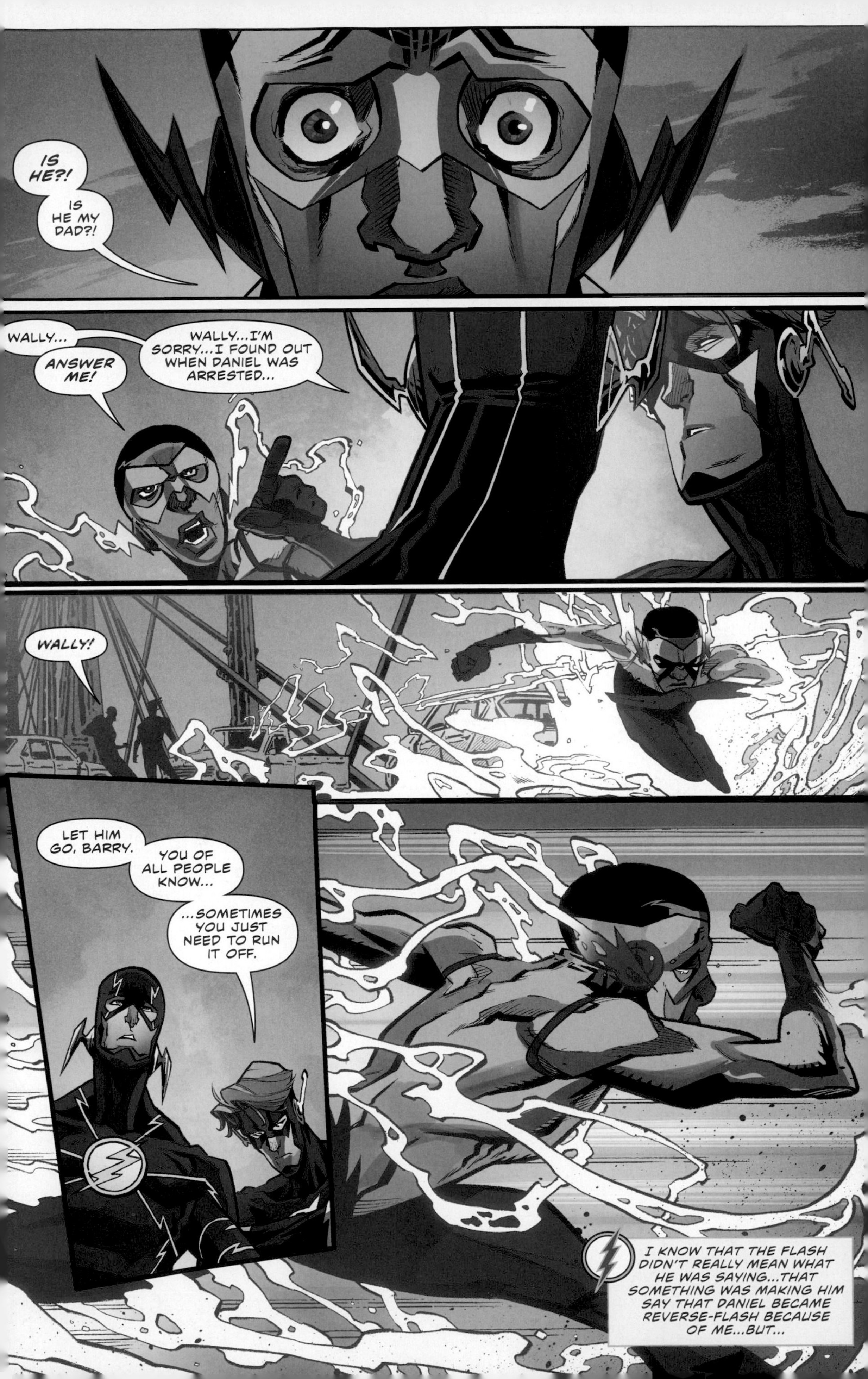
IS HE?!
IS HE MY DAD?!
WALLY...
ANSWER ME!
WALLY...I'M SORRY...I FOUND OUT WHEN DANIEL WAS ARRESTED...
WALLY!
LET HIM GO, BARRY.
YOU OF ALL PEOPLE KNOW...
...SOMETIMES YOU JUST NEED TO RUN IT OFF.
I KNOW THAT THE FLASH DIDN'T REALLY MEAN WHAT HE WAS SAYING...THAT SOMETHING WAS MAKING HIM SAY THAT DANIEL BECAME REVERSE-FLASH BECAUSE OF ME...BUT...

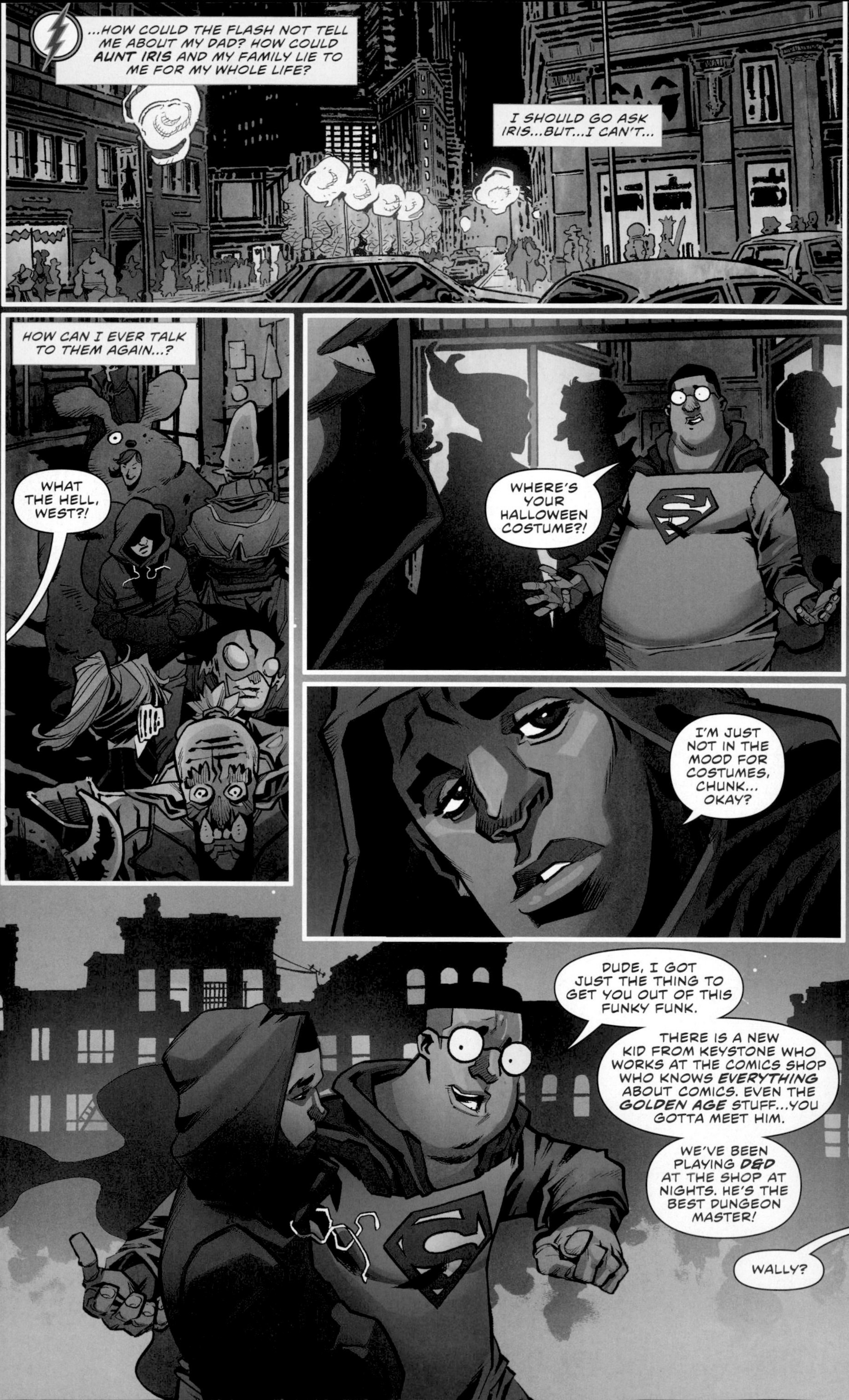
...HOW COULD THE FLASH NOT TELL ME ABOUT MY DAD? HOW COULD AUNT IRIS AND MY FAMILY LIE TO ME FOR MY WHOLE LIFE?
I SHOULD GO ASK IRIS...BUT...I CAN'T...
HOW CAN I EVER TALK TO THEM AGAIN...?
WHAT THE HELL, WEST?!
WHERE'S YOUR HALLOWEEN COSTUME?!
I'M JUST NOT IN THE MOOD FOR COSTUMES, CHUNK... OKAY?
DUDE, I GOT JUST THE THING TO GET YOU OUT OF THIS FUNKY FUNK.
THERE IS A NEW KID FROM KEYSTONE WHO WORKS AT THE COMICS SHOP WHO KNOWS EVERYTHING ABOUT COMICS. EVEN THE GOLDEN AGE STUFF...YOU GOTTA MEET HIM.
WE'VE BEEN PLAYING D&D AT THE SHOP AT NIGHTS. HE'S THE BEST DUNGEON MASTER!
WALLY?

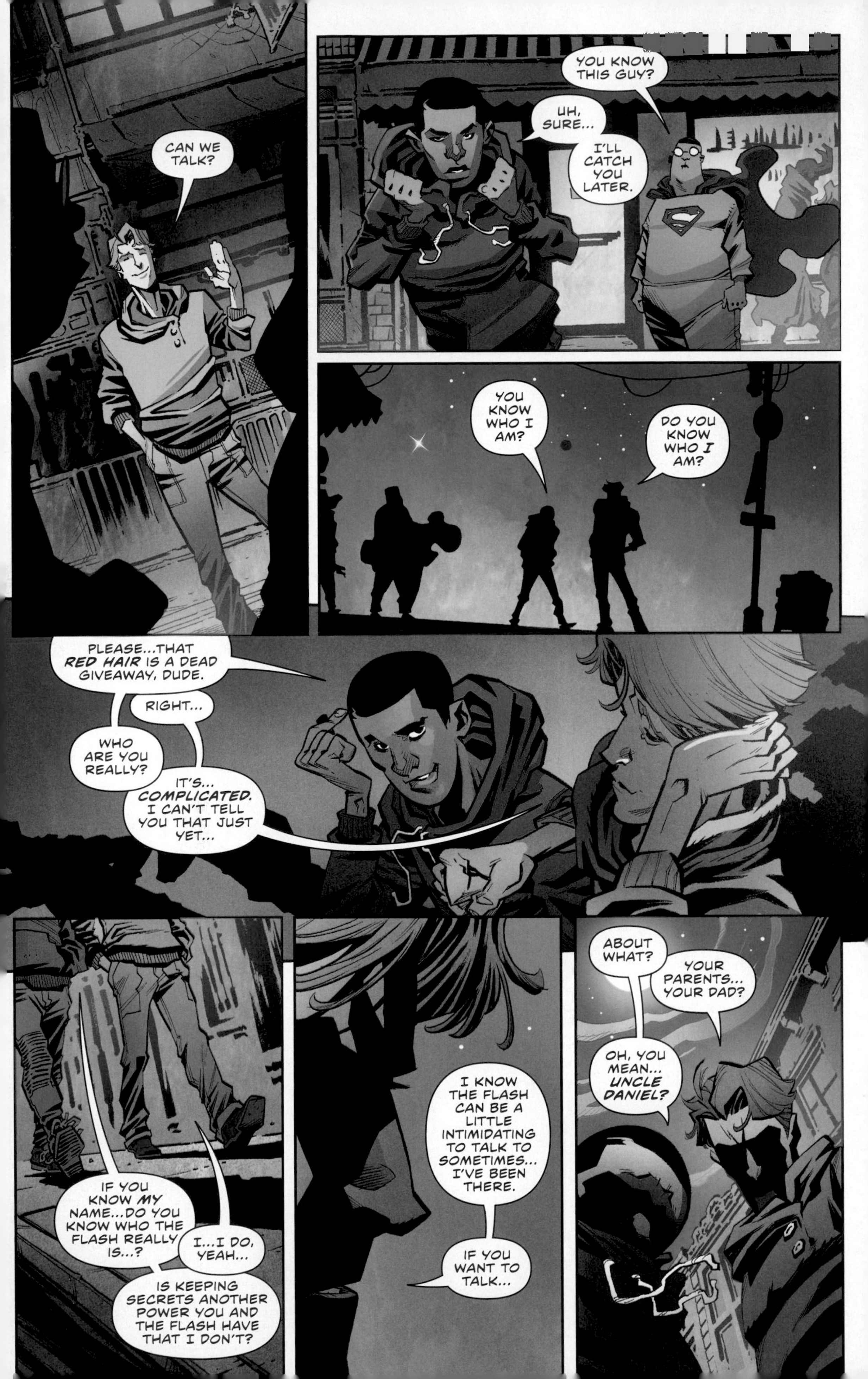
CAN WE TALK?
YOU KNOW THIS GUY?
UH, SURE...
I'LL CATCH YOU LATER.
YOU KNOW WHO I AM?
DO YOU KNOW WHO *I* AM?
PLEASE...THAT *RED HAIR* IS A DEAD GIVEAWAY, DUDE.
RIGHT...
WHO ARE YOU REALLY?
IT'S... *COMPLICATED.* I CAN'T TELL YOU THAT JUST YET...
IF YOU KNOW *MY* NAME...DO YOU KNOW WHO THE FLASH REALLY IS...?
I...I DO, YEAH...
IS KEEPING SECRETS ANOTHER POWER YOU AND THE FLASH HAVE THAT I DON'T?
I KNOW THE FLASH CAN BE A LITTLE INTIMIDATING TO TALK TO SOMETIMES... I'VE BEEN THERE.
IF YOU WANT TO TALK...
ABOUT WHAT?
YOUR PARENTS... YOUR DAD?
OH, YOU MEAN... *UNCLE DANIEL?*

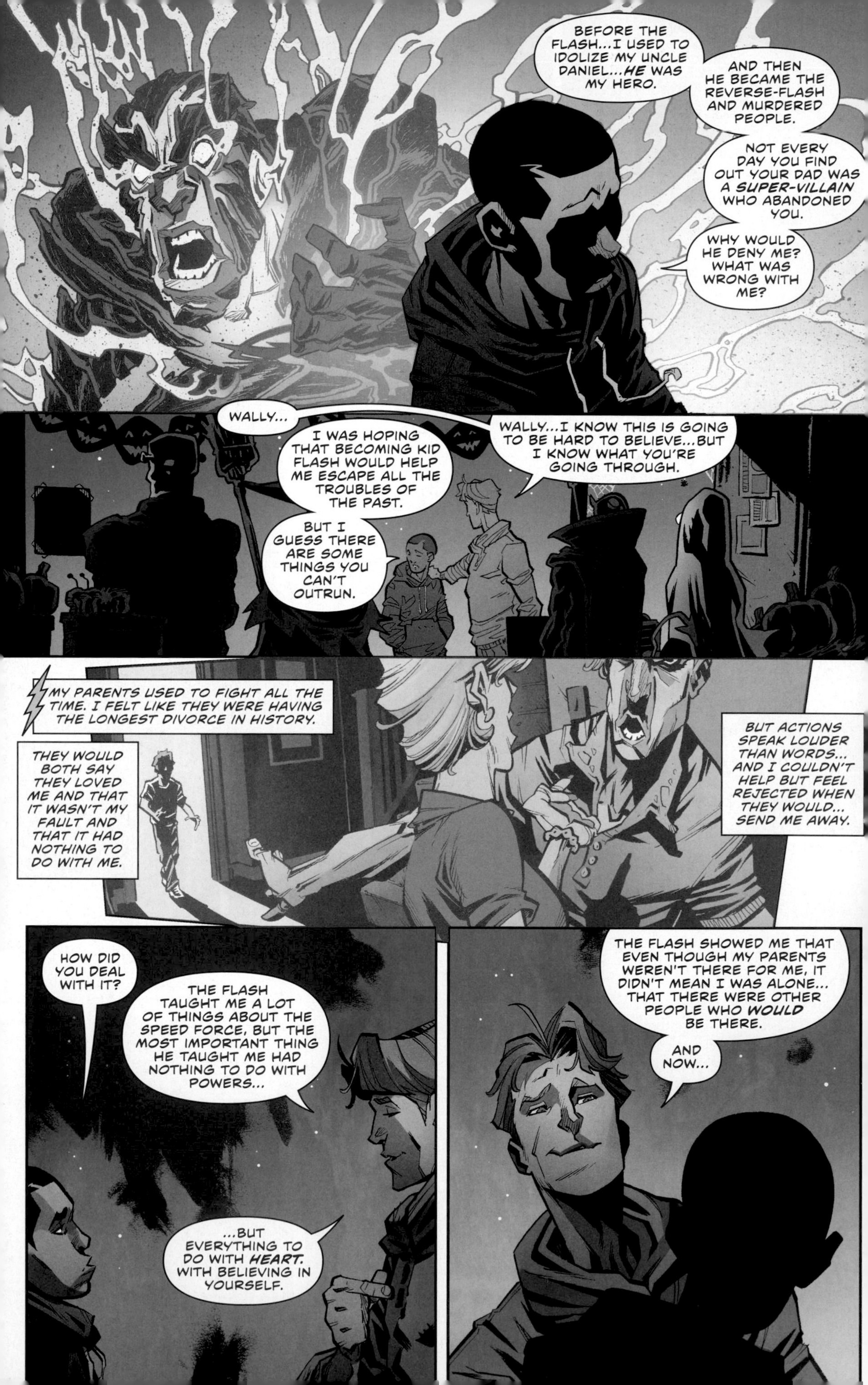
BEFORE THE FLASH...I USED TO IDOLIZE MY UNCLE DANIEL...HE WAS MY HERO.
AND THEN HE BECAME THE REVERSE-FLASH AND MURDERED PEOPLE.
NOT EVERY DAY YOU FIND OUT YOUR DAD WAS A SUPER-VILLAIN WHO ABANDONED YOU.
WHY WOULD HE DENY ME? WHAT WAS WRONG WITH ME?
WALLY...
I WAS HOPING THAT BECOMING KID FLASH WOULD HELP ME ESCAPE ALL THE TROUBLES OF THE PAST.
BUT I GUESS THERE ARE SOME THINGS YOU CAN'T OUTRUN.
WALLY...I KNOW THIS IS GOING TO BE HARD TO BELIEVE...BUT I KNOW WHAT YOU'RE GOING THROUGH.
MY PARENTS USED TO FIGHT ALL THE TIME. I FELT LIKE THEY WERE HAVING THE LONGEST DIVORCE IN HISTORY.
THEY WOULD BOTH SAY THEY LOVED ME AND THAT IT WASN'T MY FAULT AND THAT IT HAD NOTHING TO DO WITH ME.
BUT ACTIONS SPEAK LOUDER THAN WORDS... AND I COULDN'T HELP BUT FEEL REJECTED WHEN THEY WOULD... SEND ME AWAY.
HOW DID YOU DEAL WITH IT?
THE FLASH TAUGHT ME A LOT OF THINGS ABOUT THE SPEED FORCE, BUT THE MOST IMPORTANT THING HE TAUGHT ME HAD NOTHING TO DO WITH POWERS...
...BUT EVERYTHING TO DO WITH HEART. WITH BELIEVING IN YOURSELF.
THE FLASH SHOWED ME THAT EVEN THOUGH MY PARENTS WEREN'T THERE FOR ME, IT DIDN'T MEAN I WAS ALONE... THAT THERE WERE OTHER PEOPLE WHO WOULD BE THERE.
AND NOW...

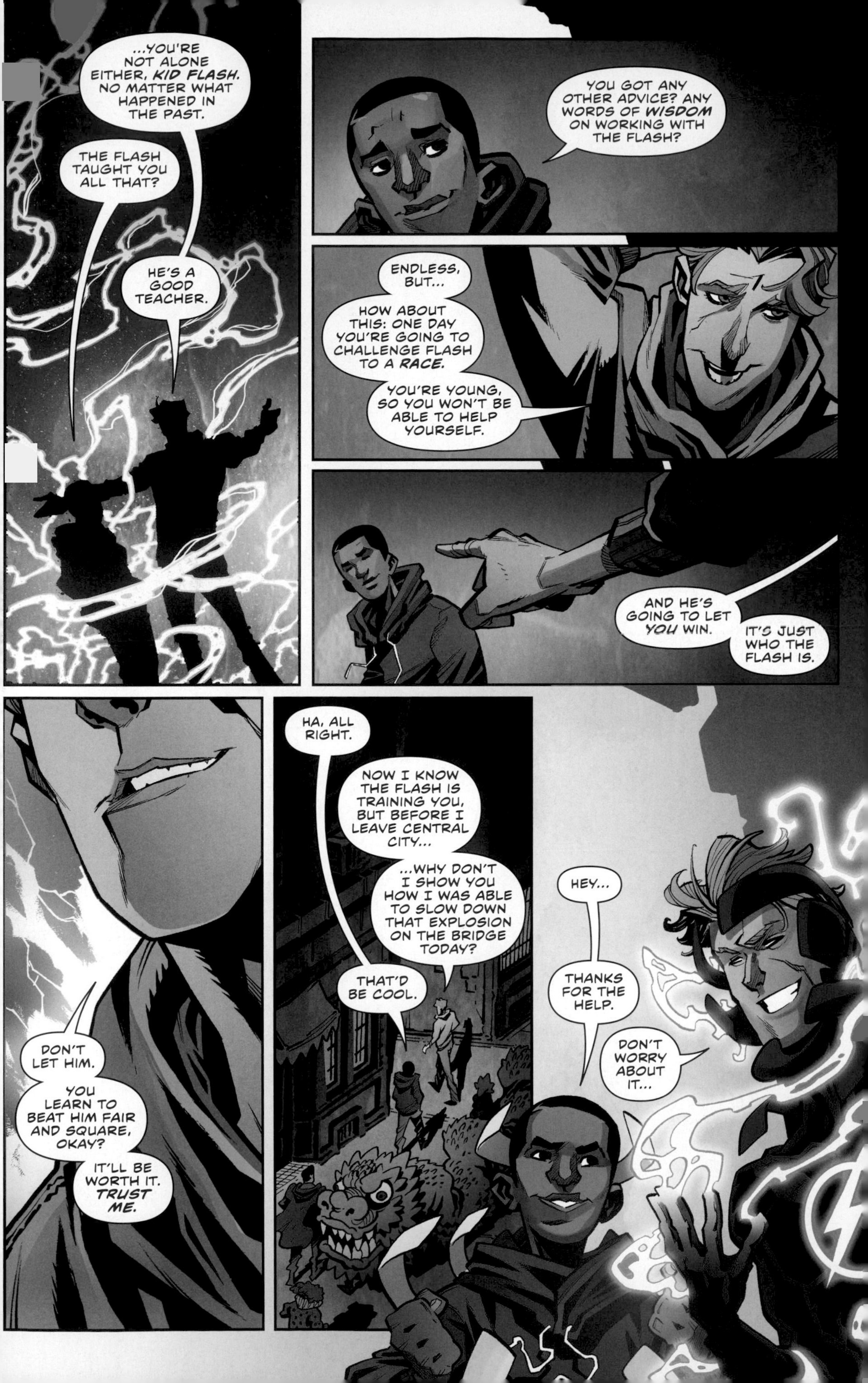

...YOU'RE NOT ALONE EITHER, KID FLASH. NO MATTER WHAT HAPPENED IN THE PAST.
THE FLASH TAUGHT YOU ALL THAT?
HE'S A GOOD TEACHER.
YOU GOT ANY OTHER ADVICE? ANY WORDS OF WISDOM ON WORKING WITH THE FLASH?
ENDLESS, BUT...
HOW ABOUT THIS: ONE DAY YOU'RE GOING TO CHALLENGE FLASH TO A RACE.
YOU'RE YOUNG, SO YOU WON'T BE ABLE TO HELP YOURSELF.
AND HE'S GOING TO LET YOU WIN.
IT'S JUST WHO THE FLASH IS.
DON'T LET HIM.
YOU LEARN TO BEAT HIM FAIR AND SQUARE, OKAY?
IT'LL BE WORTH IT. TRUST ME.
HA, ALL RIGHT.
NOW I KNOW THE FLASH IS TRAINING YOU, BUT BEFORE I LEAVE CENTRAL CITY...
...WHY DON'T I SHOW YOU HOW I WAS ABLE TO SLOW DOWN THAT EXPLOSION ON THE BRIDGE TODAY?
THAT'D BE COOL.
HEY...
THANKS FOR THE HELP.
DON'T WORRY ABOUT IT...

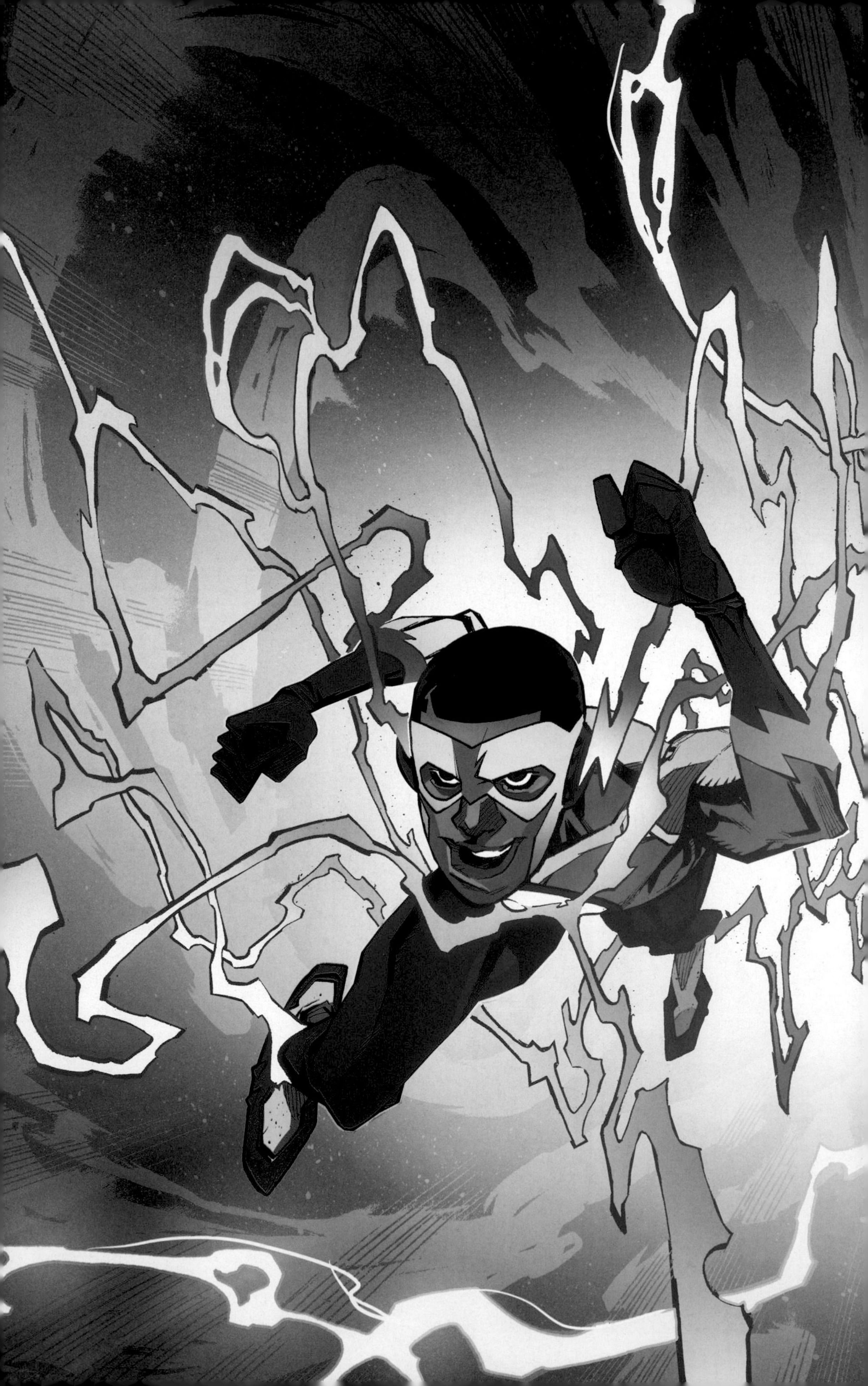

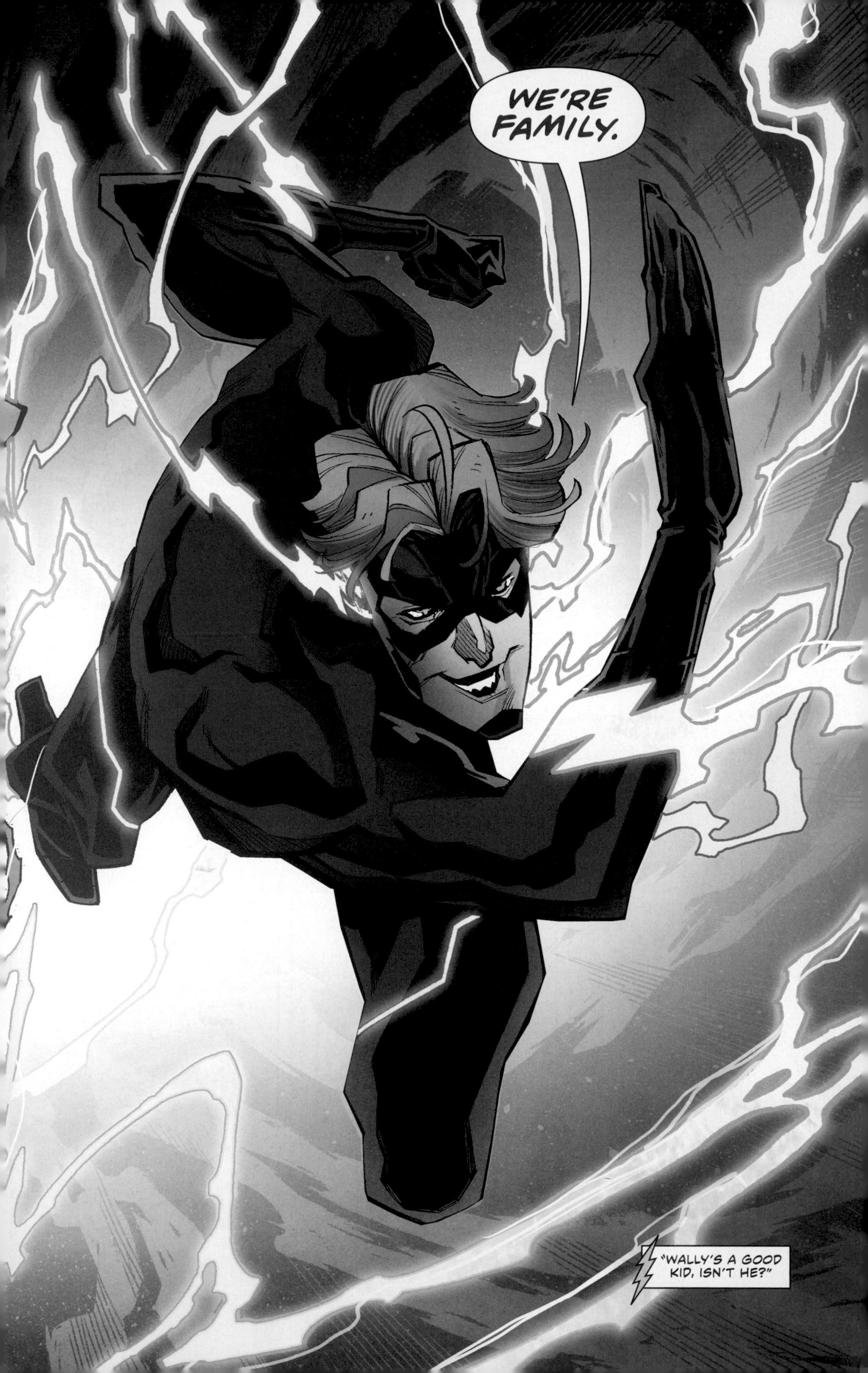
WE'RE FAMILY.
"WALLY'S A GOOD KID, ISN'T HE?"

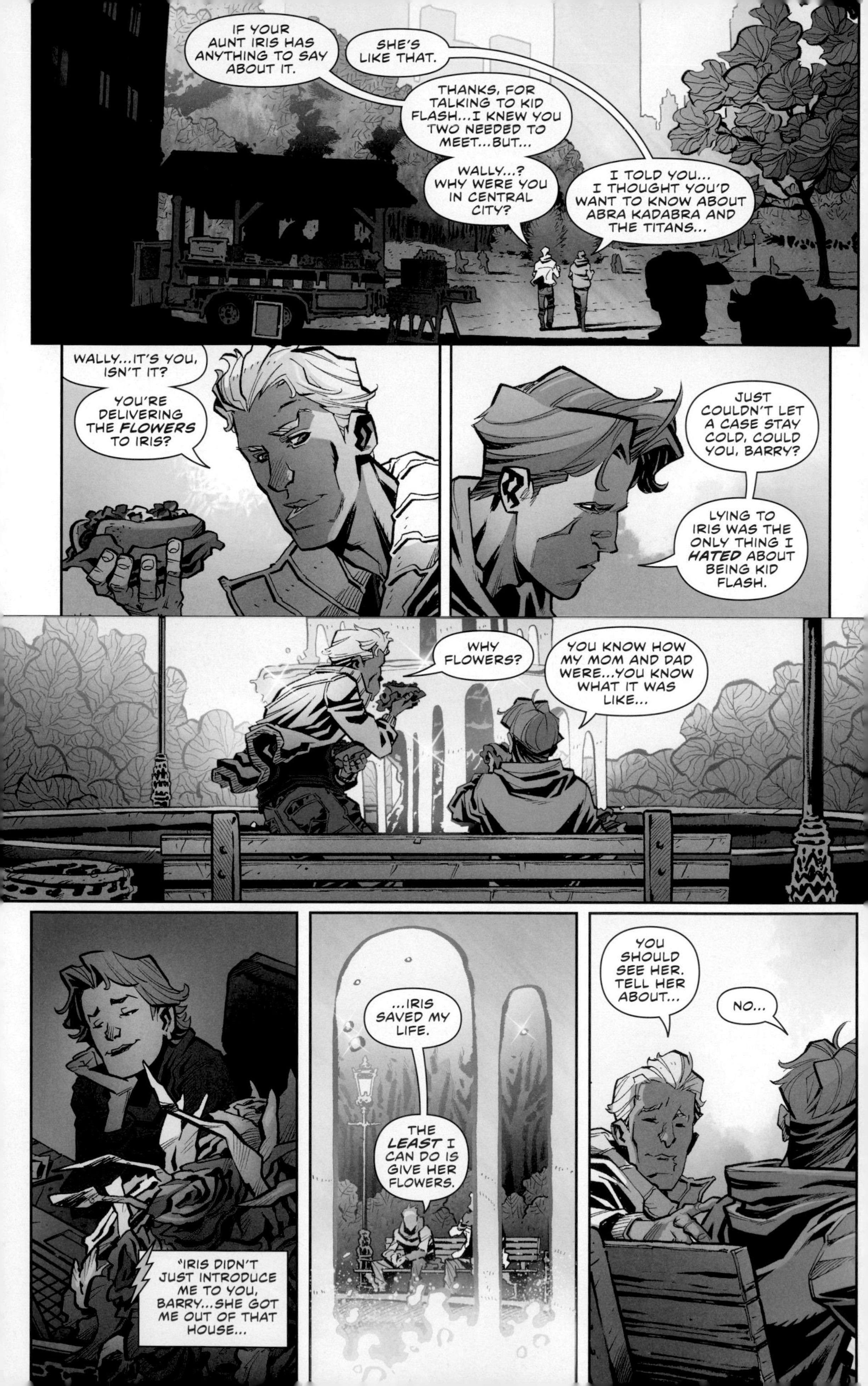
IF YOUR AUNT IRIS HAS ANYTHING TO SAY ABOUT IT.
SHE'S LIKE THAT.
THANKS, FOR TALKING TO KID FLASH...I KNEW YOU TWO NEEDED TO MEET...BUT...
WALLY...? WHY WERE YOU IN CENTRAL CITY?
I TOLD YOU... I THOUGHT YOU'D WANT TO KNOW ABOUT ABRA KADABRA AND THE TITANS...
WALLY...IT'S YOU, ISN'T IT?
YOU'RE DELIVERING THE *FLOWERS* TO IRIS?
JUST COULDN'T LET A CASE STAY COLD, COULD YOU, BARRY?
LYING TO IRIS WAS THE ONLY THING I *HATED* ABOUT BEING KID FLASH.
WHY FLOWERS?
YOU KNOW HOW MY MOM AND DAD WERE...YOU KNOW WHAT IT WAS LIKE...
"IRIS DIDN'T JUST INTRODUCE ME TO YOU, BARRY...SHE GOT ME OUT OF THAT HOUSE...
...IRIS SAVED MY LIFE.
THE *LEAST* I CAN DO IS GIVE HER FLOWERS.
YOU SHOULD SEE HER. TELL HER ABOUT...
NO...

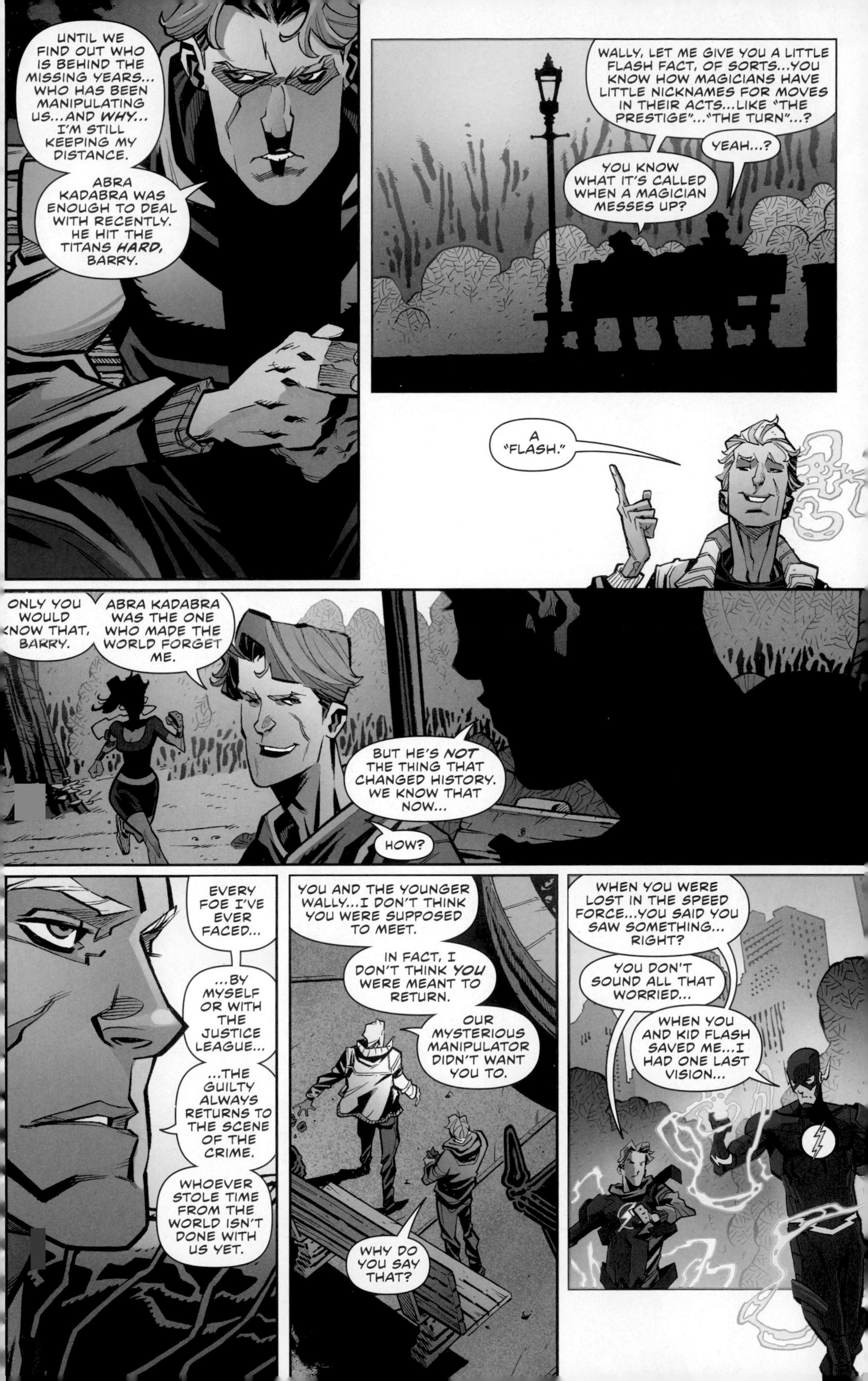
UNTIL WE FIND OUT WHO IS BEHIND THE MISSING YEARS... WHO HAS BEEN MANIPULATING US...AND WHY... I'M STILL KEEPING MY DISTANCE.
ABRA KADABRA WAS ENOUGH TO DEAL WITH RECENTLY. HE HIT THE TITANS HARD, BARRY.
WALLY, LET ME GIVE YOU A LITTLE FLASH FACT, OF SORTS...YOU KNOW HOW MAGICIANS HAVE LITTLE NICKNAMES FOR MOVES IN THEIR ACTS...LIKE "THE PRESTIGE"..."THE TURN"...?
YEAH...?
YOU KNOW WHAT IT'S CALLED WHEN A MAGICIAN MESSES UP?
A "FLASH."
ONLY YOU WOULD KNOW THAT, BARRY.
ABRA KADABRA WAS THE ONE WHO MADE THE WORLD FORGET ME.
BUT HE'S NOT THE THING THAT CHANGED HISTORY. WE KNOW THAT NOW...
HOW?
EVERY FOE I'VE EVER FACED...
...BY MYSELF OR WITH THE JUSTICE LEAGUE...
...THE GUILTY ALWAYS RETURNS TO THE SCENE OF THE CRIME.
WHOEVER STOLE TIME FROM THE WORLD ISN'T DONE WITH US YET.
YOU AND THE YOUNGER WALLY...I DON'T THINK YOU WERE SUPPOSED TO MEET.
IN FACT, I DON'T THINK YOU WERE MEANT TO RETURN.
OUR MYSTERIOUS MANIPULATOR DIDN'T WANT YOU TO.
WHY DO YOU SAY THAT?
WHEN YOU WERE LOST IN THE SPEED FORCE...YOU SAID YOU SAW SOMETHING... RIGHT?
YOU DON'T SOUND ALL THAT WORRIED...
WHEN YOU AND KID FLASH SAVED ME...I HAD ONE LAST VISION...

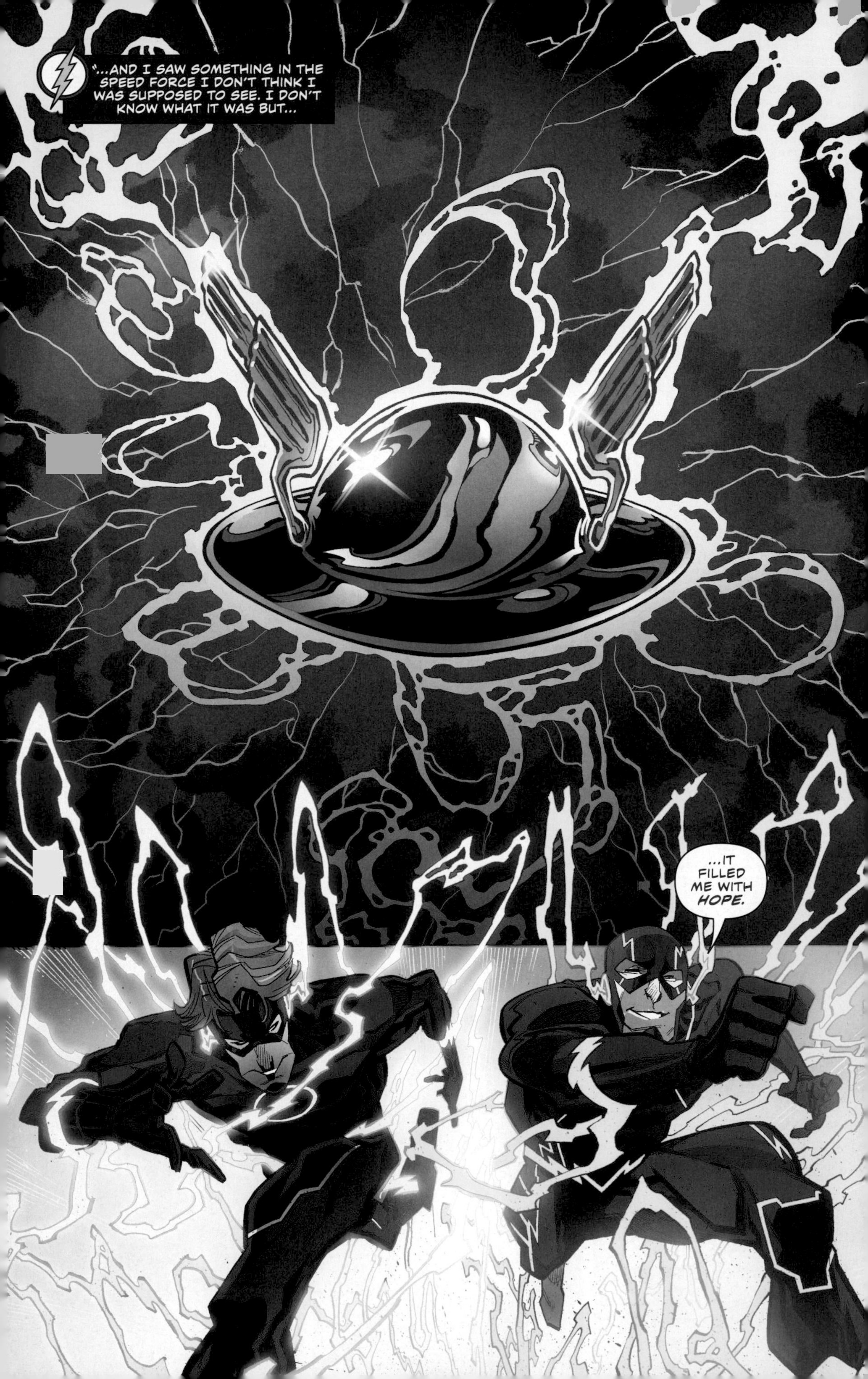
"...AND I SAW SOMETHING IN THE SPEED FORCE I DON'T THINK I WAS SUPPOSED TO SEE. I DON'T KNOW WHAT IT WAS BUT...
...IT FILLED ME WITH *HOPE.*

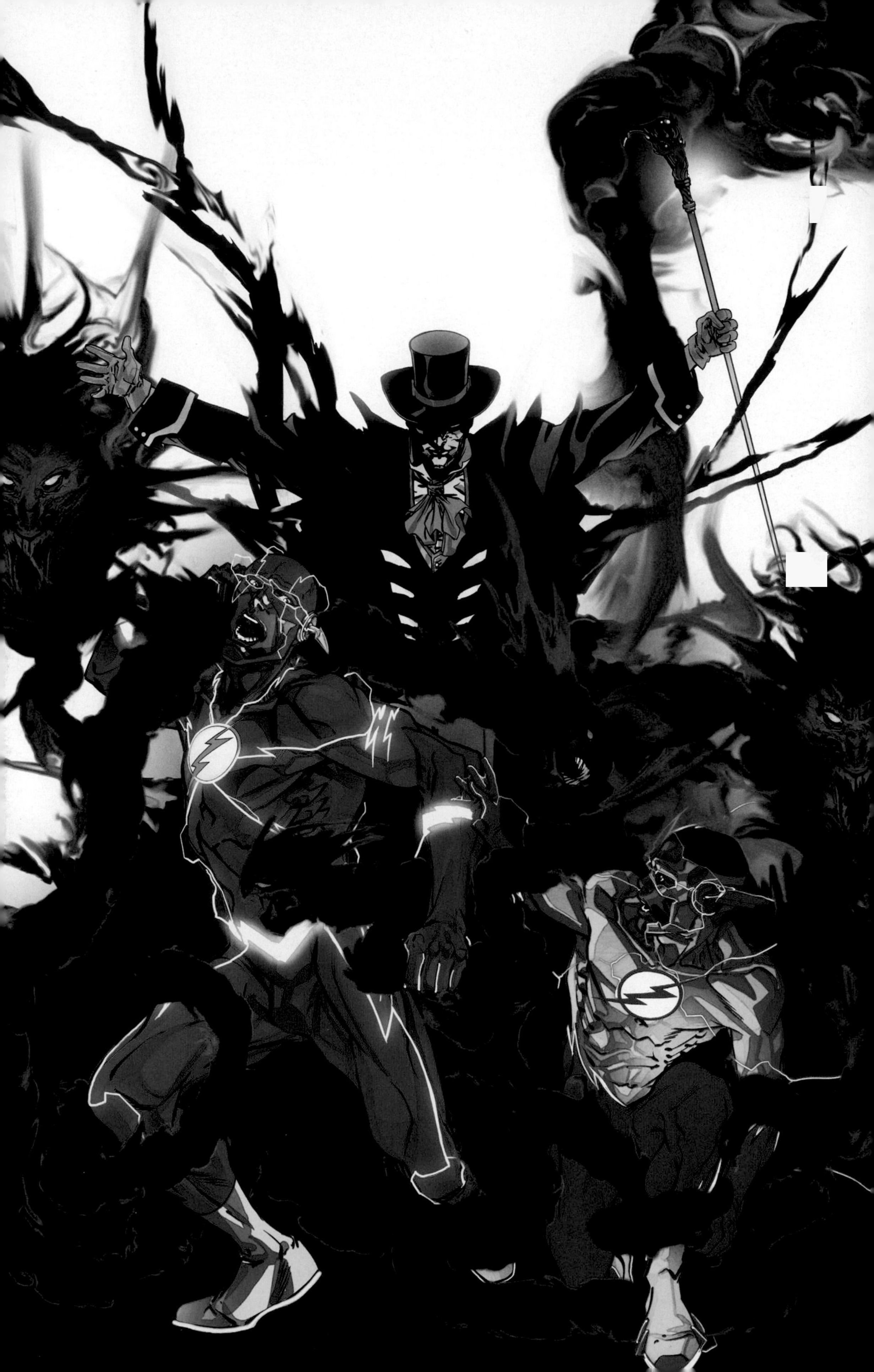

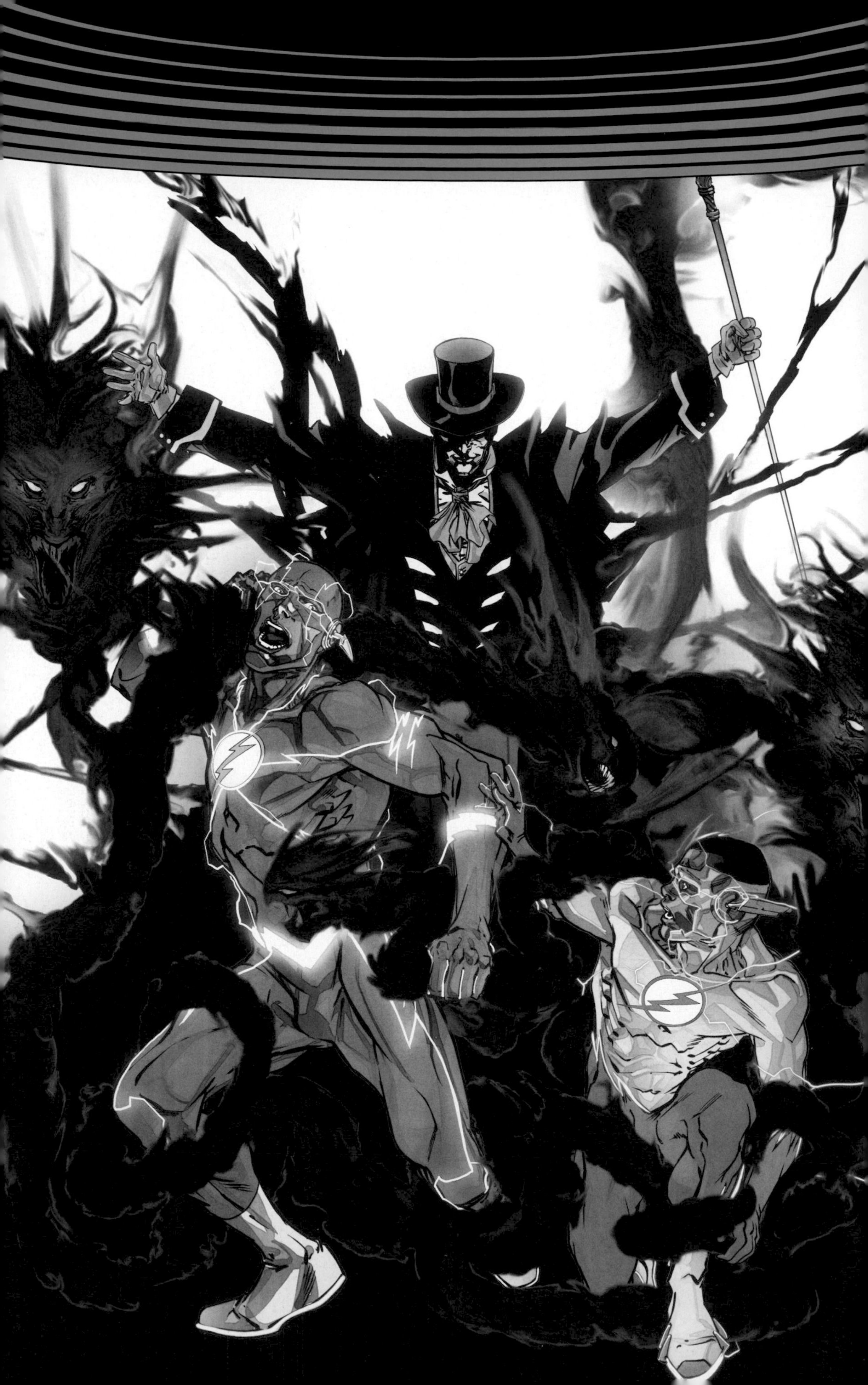

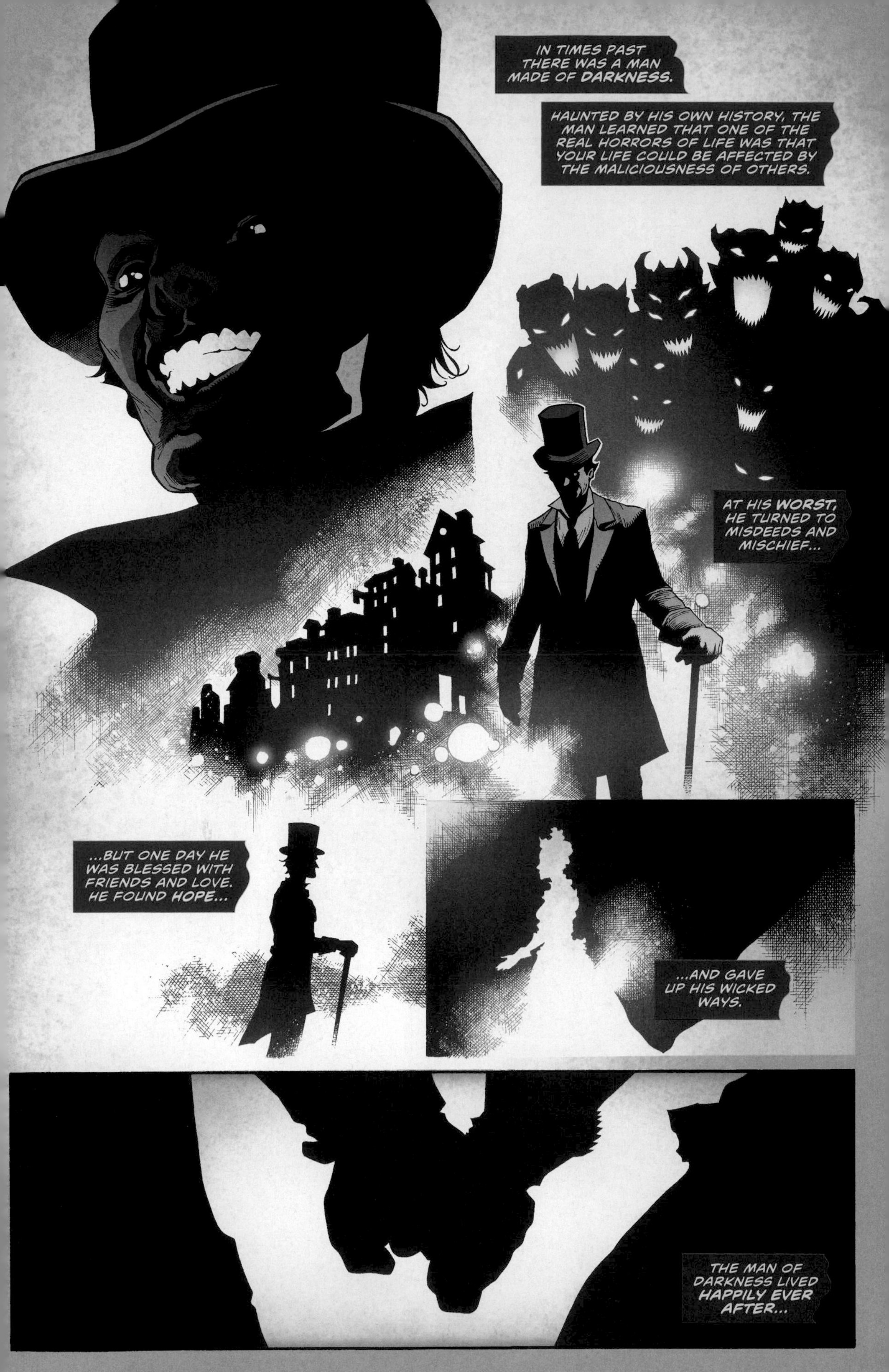
IN TIMES PAST THERE WAS A MAN MADE OF DARKNESS.
HAUNTED BY HIS OWN HISTORY, THE MAN LEARNED THAT ONE OF THE REAL HORRORS OF LIFE WAS THAT YOUR LIFE COULD BE AFFECTED BY THE MALICIOUSNESS OF OTHERS.
AT HIS WORST, HE TURNED TO MISDEEDS AND MISCHIEF...
...BUT ONE DAY HE WAS BLESSED WITH FRIENDS AND LOVE. HE FOUND HOPE...
...AND GAVE UP HIS WICKED WAYS.
THE MAN OF DARKNESS LIVED HAPPILY EVER AFTER...

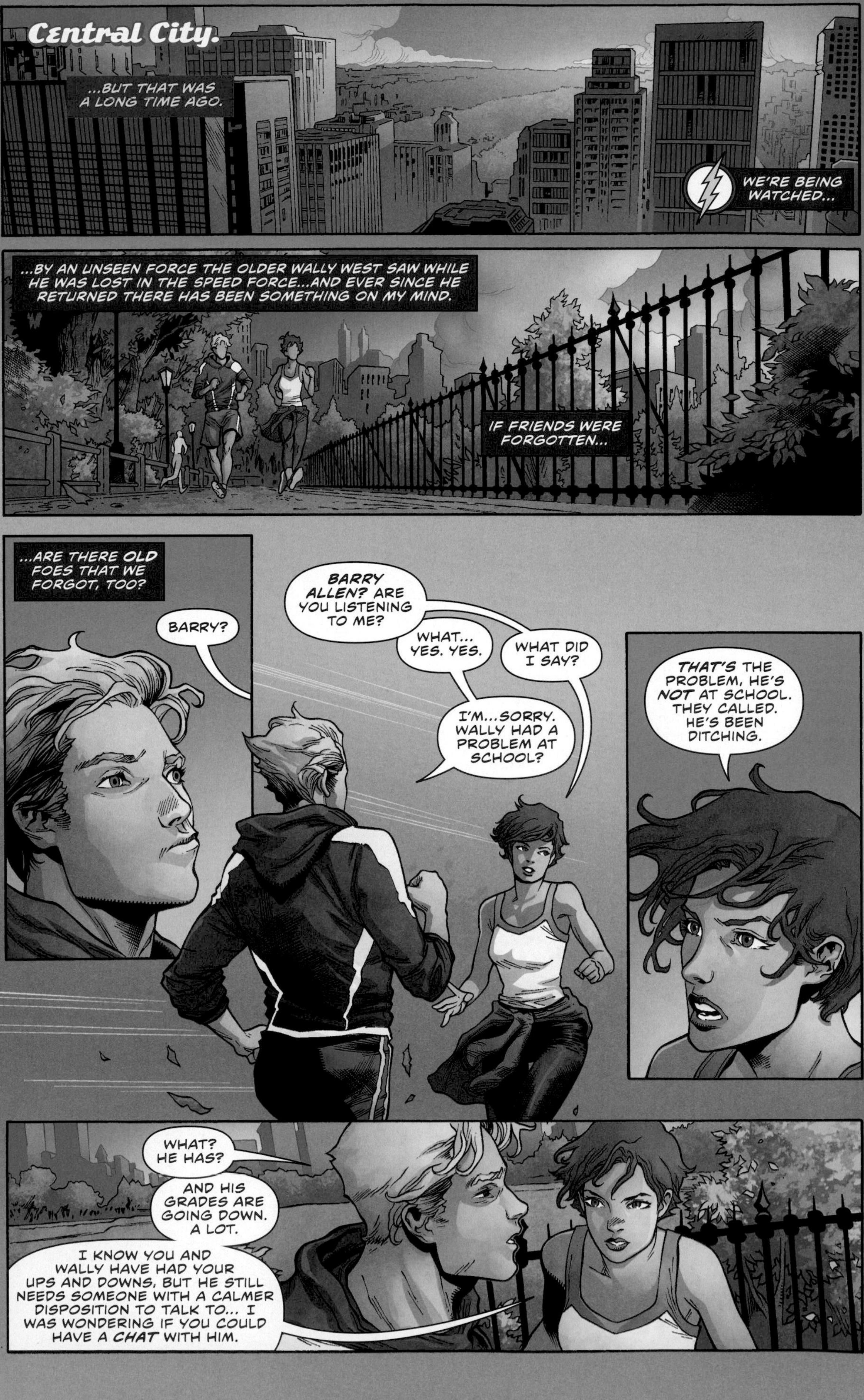
Central City.
...BUT THAT WAS A LONG TIME AGO.
WE'RE BEING WATCHED...
...BY AN UNSEEN FORCE THE OLDER WALLY WEST SAW WHILE HE WAS LOST IN THE SPEED FORCE...AND EVER SINCE HE RETURNED THERE HAS BEEN SOMETHING ON MY MIND.
IF FRIENDS WERE FORGOTTEN...
...ARE THERE OLD FOES THAT WE FORGOT, TOO?
BARRY?
BARRY ALLEN? ARE YOU LISTENING TO ME?
WHAT... YES. YES.
WHAT DID I SAY?
I'M...SORRY. WALLY HAD A PROBLEM AT SCHOOL?
THAT'S THE PROBLEM, HE'S NOT AT SCHOOL. THEY CALLED. HE'S BEEN DITCHING.
WHAT? HE HAS?
AND HIS GRADES ARE GOING DOWN. A LOT.
I KNOW YOU AND WALLY HAVE HAD YOUR UPS AND DOWNS, BUT HE STILL NEEDS SOMEONE WITH A CALMER DISPOSITION TO TALK TO... I WAS WONDERING IF YOU COULD HAVE A CHAT WITH HIM.

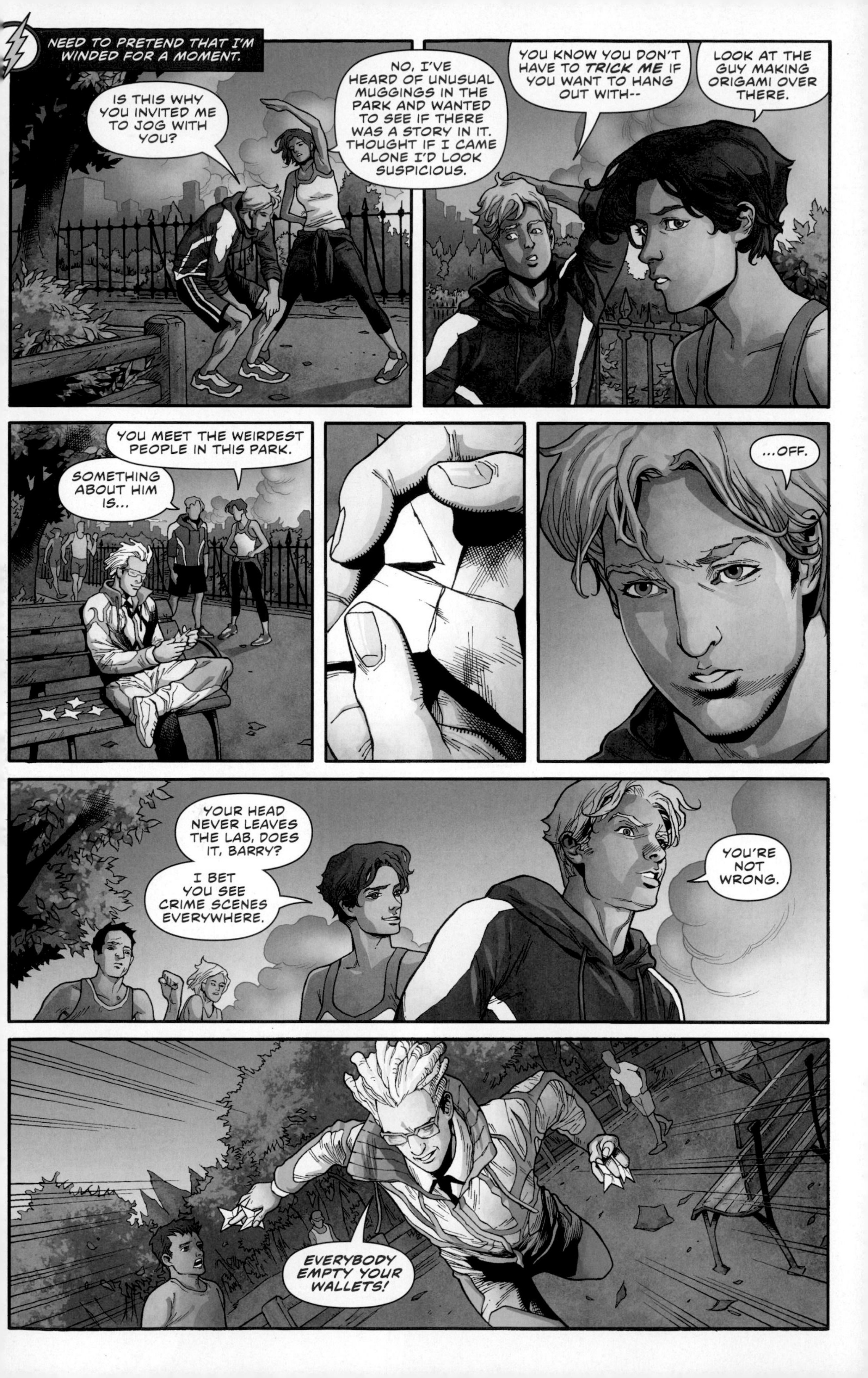
NEED TO PRETEND THAT I'M WINDED FOR A MOMENT.
IS THIS WHY YOU INVITED ME TO JOG WITH YOU?
NO, I'VE HEARD OF UNUSUAL MUGGINGS IN THE PARK AND WANTED TO SEE IF THERE WAS A STORY IN IT. THOUGHT IF I CAME ALONE I'D LOOK SUSPICIOUS.
YOU KNOW YOU DON'T HAVE TO TRICK ME IF YOU WANT TO HANG OUT WITH--
LOOK AT THE GUY MAKING ORIGAMI OVER THERE.
YOU MEET THE WEIRDEST PEOPLE IN THIS PARK.
SOMETHING ABOUT HIM IS...
...OFF.
YOUR HEAD NEVER LEAVES THE LAB, DOES IT, BARRY?
I BET YOU SEE CRIME SCENES EVERYWHERE.
YOU'RE NOT WRONG.
EVERYBODY EMPTY YOUR WALLETS!

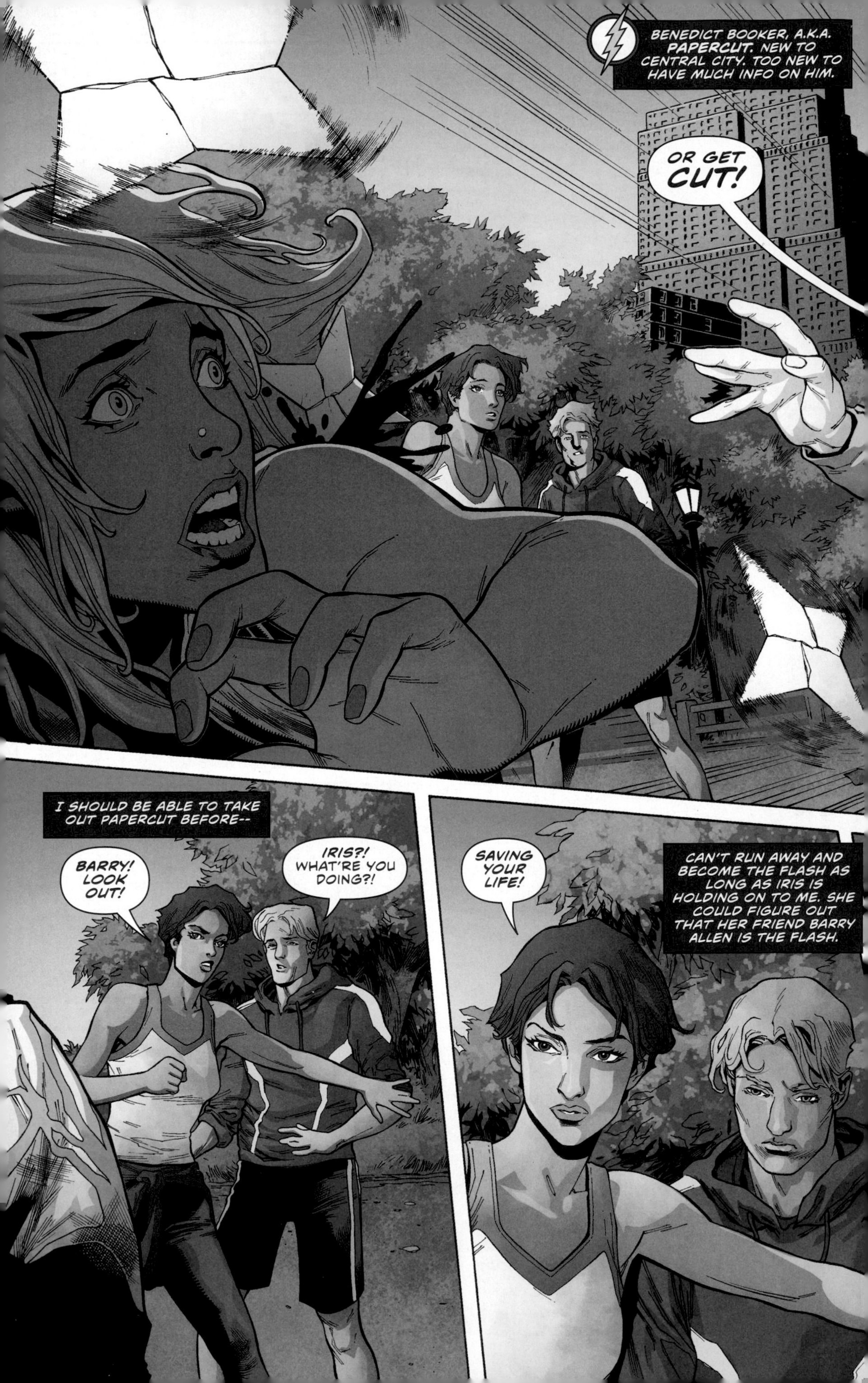
BENEDICT BOOKER, A.K.A. PAPERCUT. NEW TO CENTRAL CITY. TOO NEW TO HAVE MUCH INFO ON HIM.
OR GET CUT!
I SHOULD BE ABLE TO TAKE OUT PAPERCUT BEFORE--
BARRY! LOOK OUT!
IRIS?! WHAT'RE YOU DOING?!
SAVING YOUR LIFE!
CAN'T RUN AWAY AND BECOME THE FLASH AS LONG AS IRIS IS HOLDING ON TO ME. SHE COULD FIGURE OUT THAT HER FRIEND BARRY ALLEN IS THE FLASH.

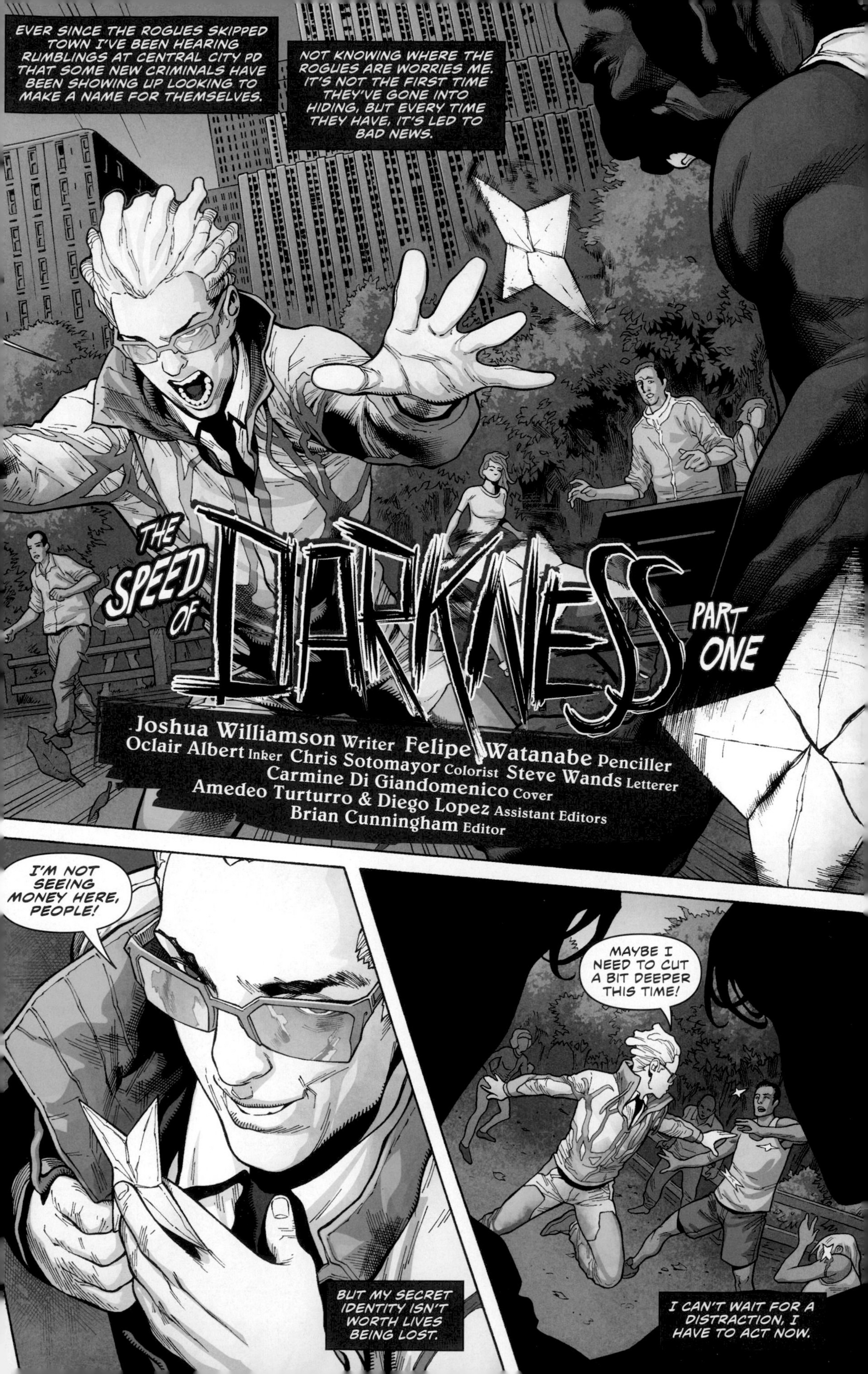
EVER SINCE THE ROGUES SKIPPED TOWN I'VE BEEN HEARING RUMBLINGS AT CENTRAL CITY PD THAT SOME NEW CRIMINALS HAVE BEEN SHOWING UP LOOKING TO MAKE A NAME FOR THEMSELVES.
NOT KNOWING WHERE THE ROGUES ARE WORRIES ME. IT'S NOT THE FIRST TIME THEY'VE GONE INTO HIDING, BUT EVERY TIME THEY HAVE, IT'S LED TO BAD NEWS.
THE SPEED OF DARKNESS PART ONE
Joshua Williamson Writer Felipe Watanabe Penciller
Oclair Albert Inker Chris Sotomayor Colorist Steve Wands Letterer
Carmine Di Giandomenico Cover
Amedeo Turturro & Diego Lopez Assistant Editors
Brian Cunningham Editor
I'M NOT SEEING MONEY HERE, PEOPLE!
BUT MY SECRET IDENTITY ISN'T WORTH LIVES BEING LOST.
MAYBE I NEED TO CUT A BIT DEEPER THIS TIME!
I CAN'T WAIT FOR A DISTRACTION. I HAVE TO ACT NOW.

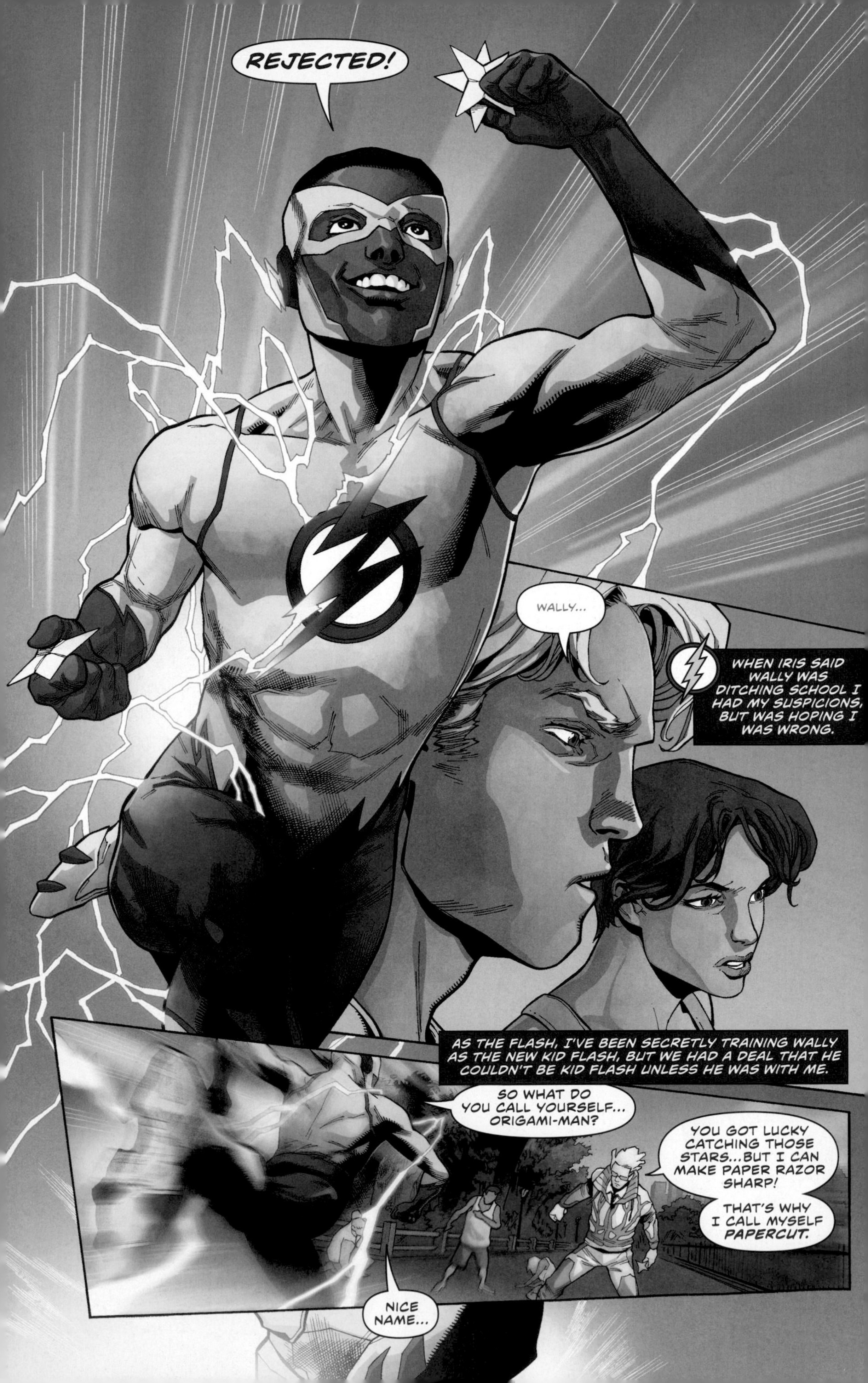
REJECTED!
WALLY...
WHEN IRIS SAID WALLY WAS DITCHING SCHOOL I HAD MY SUSPICIONS, BUT WAS HOPING I WAS WRONG.
AS THE FLASH, I'VE BEEN SECRETLY TRAINING WALLY AS THE NEW KID FLASH, BUT WE HAD A DEAL THAT HE COULDN'T BE KID FLASH UNLESS HE WAS WITH ME.
SO WHAT DO YOU CALL YOURSELF... ORIGAMI-MAN?
YOU GOT LUCKY CATCHING THOSE STARS...BUT I CAN MAKE PAPER RAZOR SHARP!
THAT'S WHY I CALL MYSELF PAPERCUT.
NICE NAME...

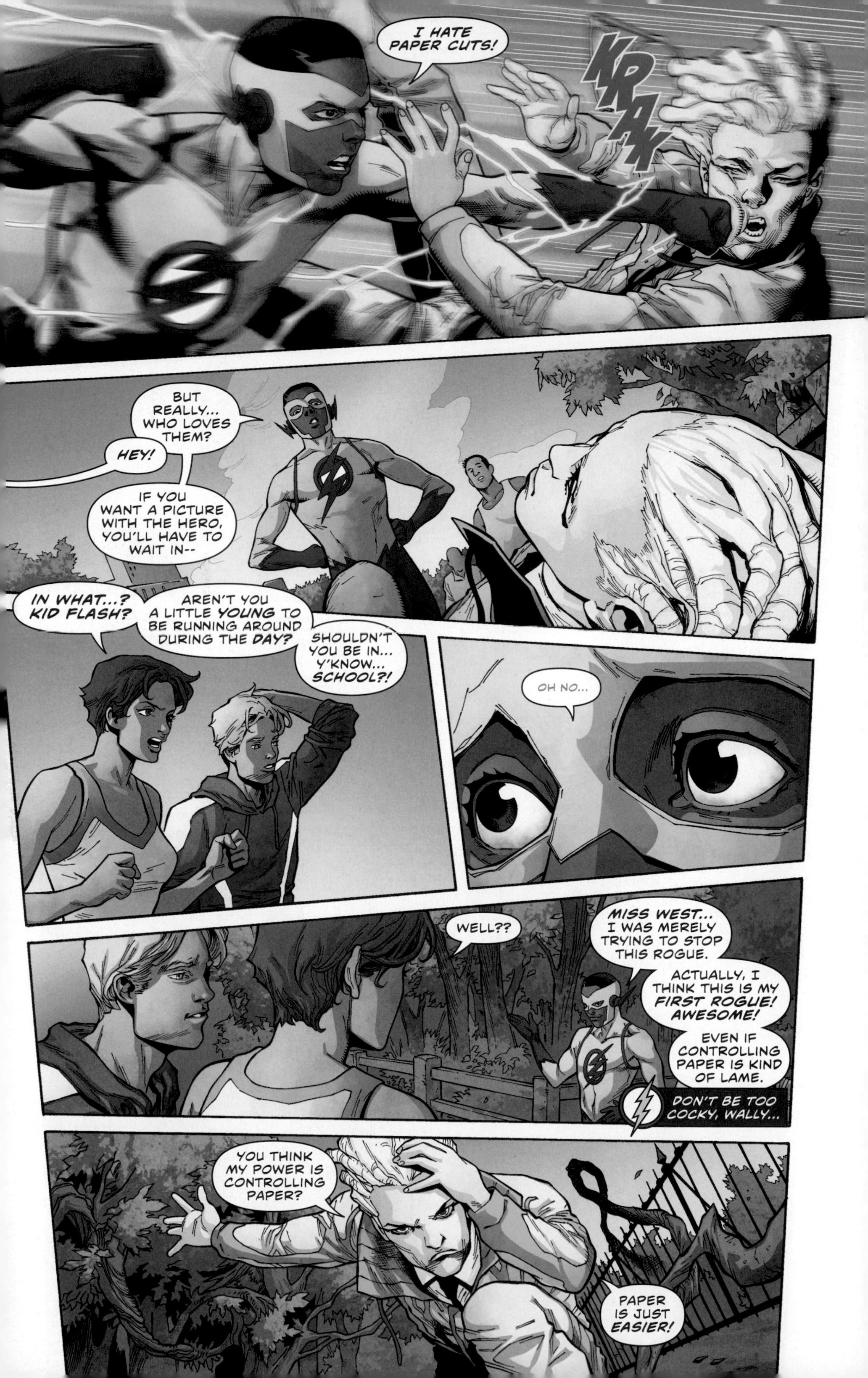
I HATE PAPER CUTS!
KRAK
BUT REALLY... WHO LOVES THEM?
HEY!
IF YOU WANT A PICTURE WITH THE HERO, YOU'LL HAVE TO WAIT IN--
IN WHAT...? KID FLASH?
AREN'T YOU A LITTLE YOUNG TO BE RUNNING AROUND DURING THE DAY?
SHOULDN'T YOU BE IN... Y'KNOW... SCHOOL?!
OH NO...
WELL??
MISS WEST... I WAS MERELY TRYING TO STOP THIS ROGUE.
ACTUALLY, I THINK THIS IS MY FIRST ROGUE! AWESOME!
EVEN IF CONTROLLING PAPER IS KIND OF LAME.
DON'T BE TOO COCKY, WALLY...
YOU THINK MY POWER IS CONTROLLING PAPER?
PAPER IS JUST EASIER!

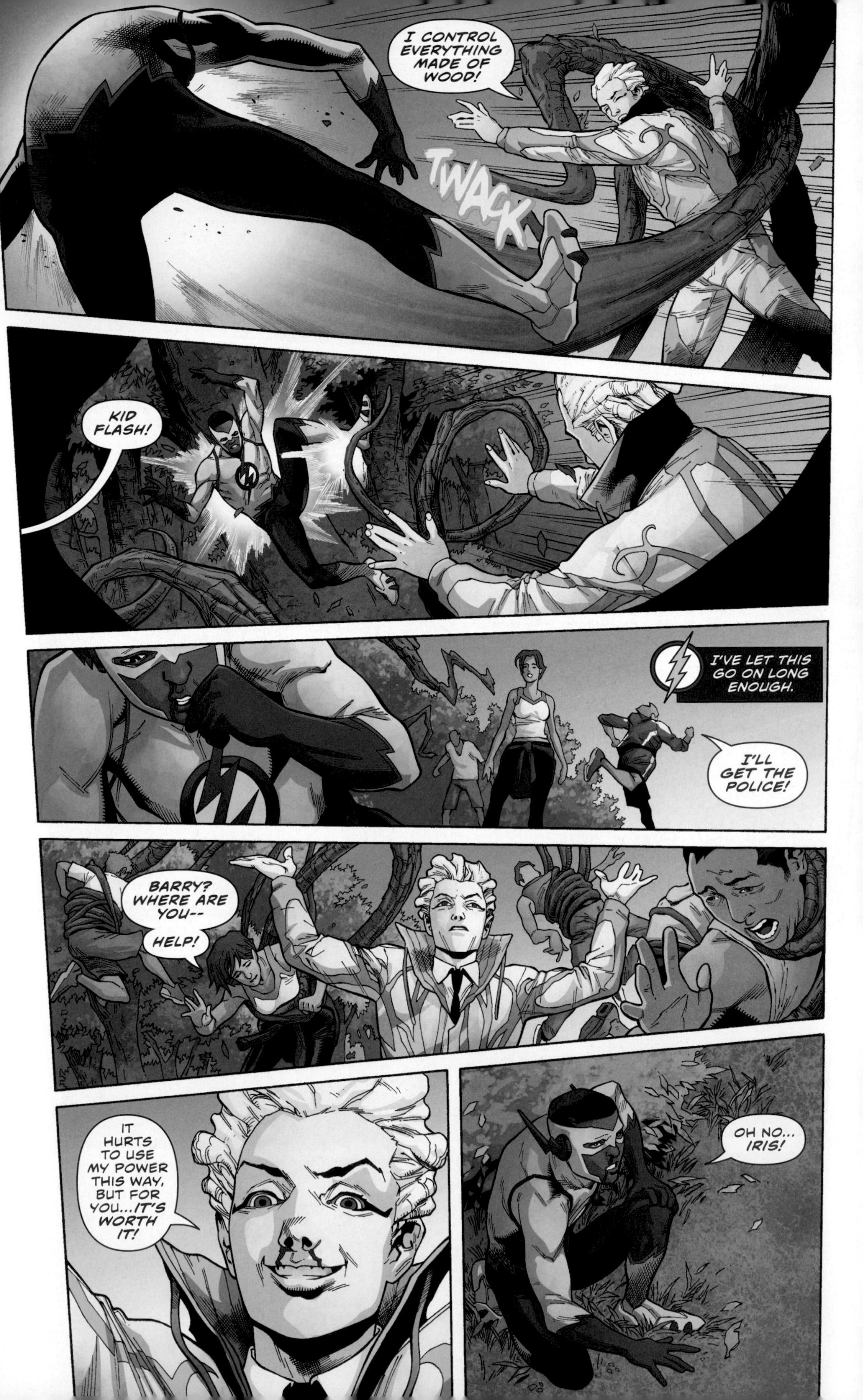
I CONTROL EVERYTHING MADE OF WOOD!
TWACK
KID FLASH!
I'VE LET THIS GO ON LONG ENOUGH.
I'LL GET THE POLICE!
BARRY? WHERE ARE YOU--
HELP!
IT HURTS TO USE MY POWER THIS WAY, BUT FOR YOU...IT'S WORTH IT!
OH NO... IRIS!

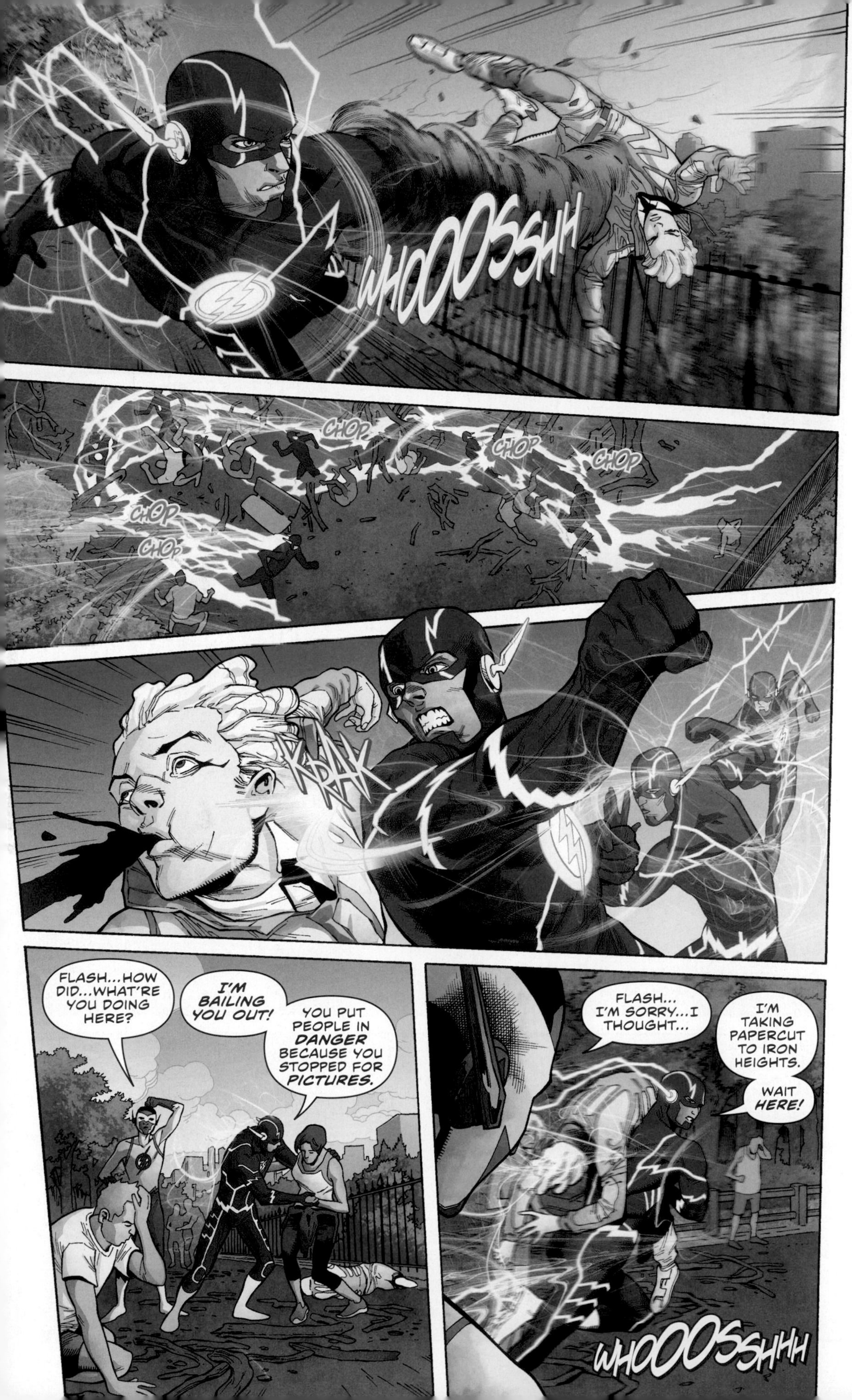
WHOOOOSSHH
CHOP
CHOP
CHOP
CHOP
CHOP
KRAK
FLASH...HOW DID...WHAT'RE YOU DOING HERE?
I'M BAILING YOU OUT!
YOU PUT PEOPLE IN DANGER BECAUSE YOU STOPPED FOR PICTURES.
FLASH... I'M SORRY...I THOUGHT...
I'M TAKING PAPERCUT TO IRON HEIGHTS.
WAIT HERE!
WHOOOOSSHHH

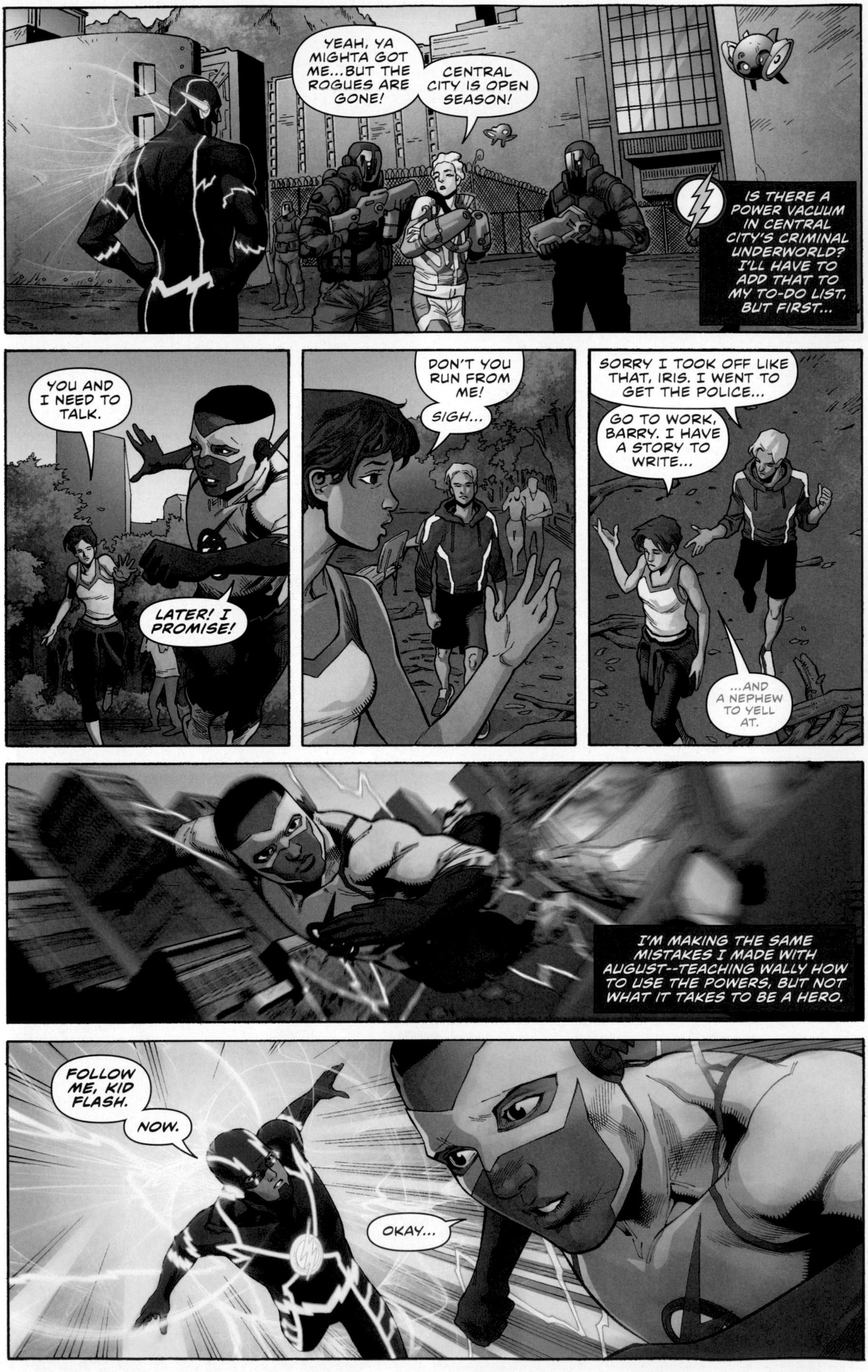
YEAH, YA MIGHTA GOT ME...BUT THE ROGUES ARE GONE!
CENTRAL CITY IS OPEN SEASON!
IS THERE A POWER VACUUM IN CENTRAL CITY'S CRIMINAL UNDERWORLD? I'LL HAVE TO ADD THAT TO MY TO-DO LIST, BUT FIRST...
YOU AND I NEED TO TALK.
LATER! I PROMISE!
DON'T YOU RUN FROM ME!
SIGH...
SORRY I TOOK OFF LIKE THAT, IRIS. I WENT TO GET THE POLICE...
GO TO WORK, BARRY. I HAVE A STORY TO WRITE...
...AND A NEPHEW TO YELL AT.
I'M MAKING THE SAME MISTAKES I MADE WITH AUGUST--TEACHING WALLY HOW TO USE THE POWERS, BUT NOT WHAT IT TAKES TO BE A HERO.
FOLLOW ME, KID FLASH.
NOW.
OKAY...

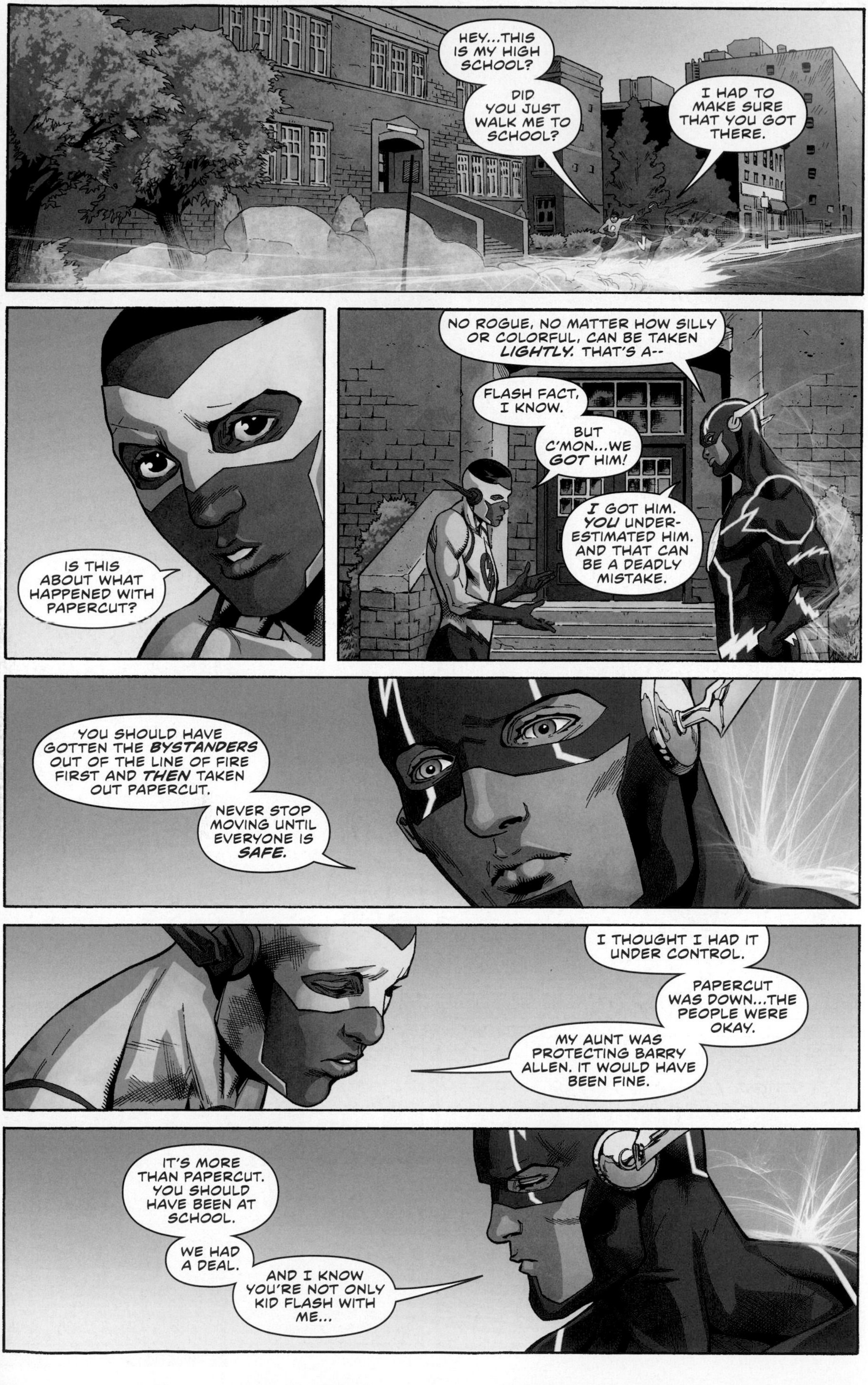
HEY...THIS IS MY HIGH SCHOOL?
DID YOU JUST WALK ME TO SCHOOL?
I HAD TO MAKE SURE THAT YOU GOT THERE.
IS THIS ABOUT WHAT HAPPENED WITH PAPERCUT?
NO ROGUE, NO MATTER HOW SILLY OR COLORFUL, CAN BE TAKEN LIGHTLY. THAT'S A--
FLASH FACT, I KNOW.
BUT C'MON...WE GOT HIM!
I GOT HIM. YOU UNDER-ESTIMATED HIM. AND THAT CAN BE A DEADLY MISTAKE.
YOU SHOULD HAVE GOTTEN THE BYSTANDERS OUT OF THE LINE OF FIRE FIRST AND THEN TAKEN OUT PAPERCUT.
NEVER STOP MOVING UNTIL EVERYONE IS SAFE.
I THOUGHT I HAD IT UNDER CONTROL.
PAPERCUT WAS DOWN...THE PEOPLE WERE OKAY.
MY AUNT WAS PROTECTING BARRY ALLEN. IT WOULD HAVE BEEN FINE.
IT'S MORE THAN PAPERCUT. YOU SHOULD HAVE BEEN AT SCHOOL.
WE HAD A DEAL.
AND I KNOW YOU'RE NOT ONLY KID FLASH WITH ME...

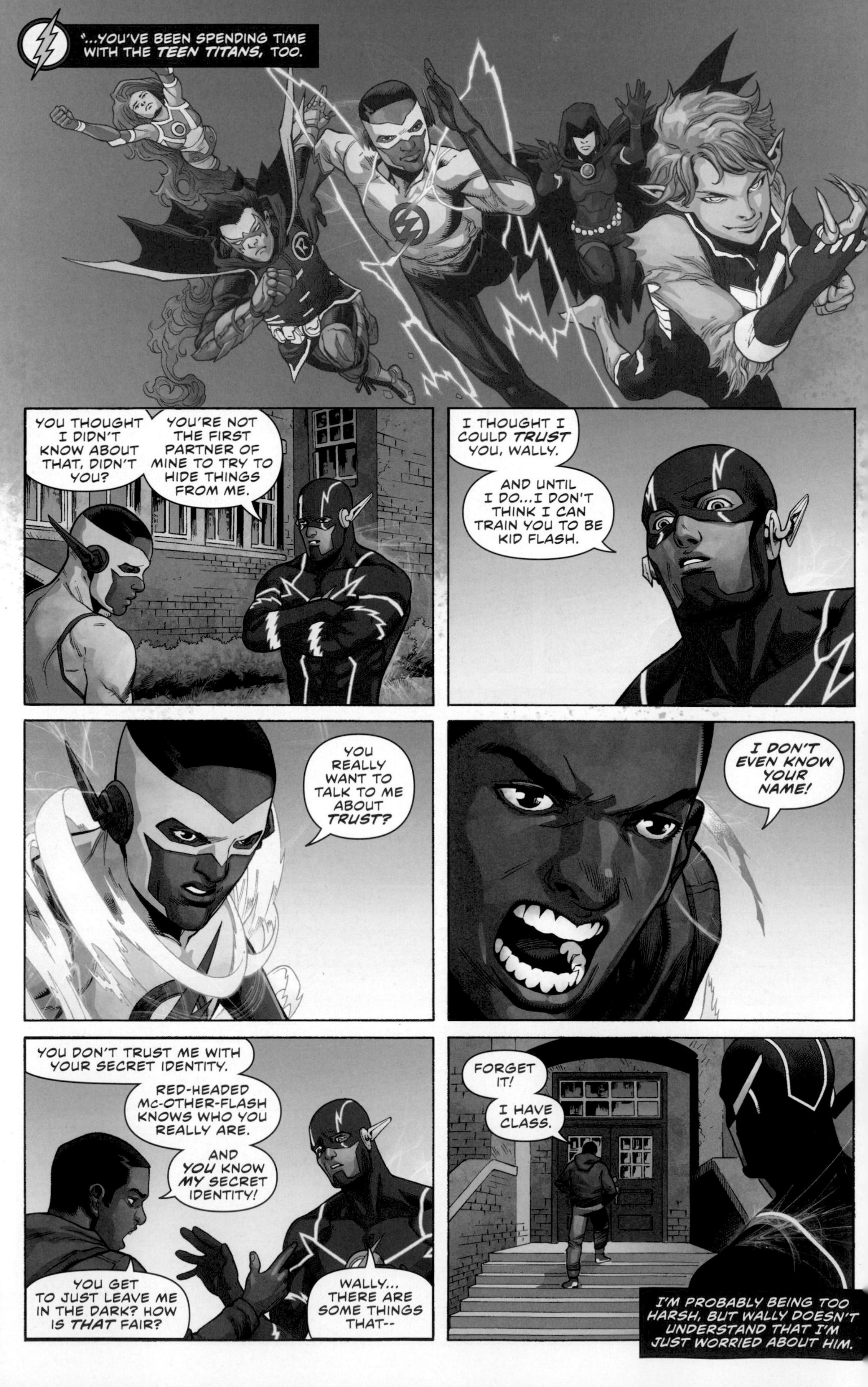
"...YOU'VE BEEN SPENDING TIME WITH THE *TEEN TITANS,* TOO.
YOU THOUGHT I DIDN'T KNOW ABOUT THAT, DIDN'T YOU?
YOU'RE NOT THE FIRST PARTNER OF MINE TO TRY TO HIDE THINGS FROM ME.
I THOUGHT I COULD *TRUST* YOU, WALLY.
AND UNTIL I DO...I DON'T THINK I CAN TRAIN YOU TO BE KID FLASH.
YOU REALLY WANT TO TALK TO ME ABOUT *TRUST?*
I DON'T EVEN KNOW YOUR NAME!
YOU DON'T TRUST ME WITH YOUR SECRET IDENTITY.
RED-HEADED Mc-OTHER-FLASH KNOWS WHO YOU REALLY ARE.
AND *YOU* KNOW *MY* SECRET IDENTITY!
YOU GET TO JUST LEAVE ME IN THE DARK? HOW IS *THAT* FAIR?
WALLY... THERE ARE SOME THINGS THAT--
FORGET IT!
I HAVE CLASS.
I'M PROBABLY BEING TOO HARSH, BUT WALLY DOESN'T UNDERSTAND THAT I'M JUST WORRIED ABOUT HIM.

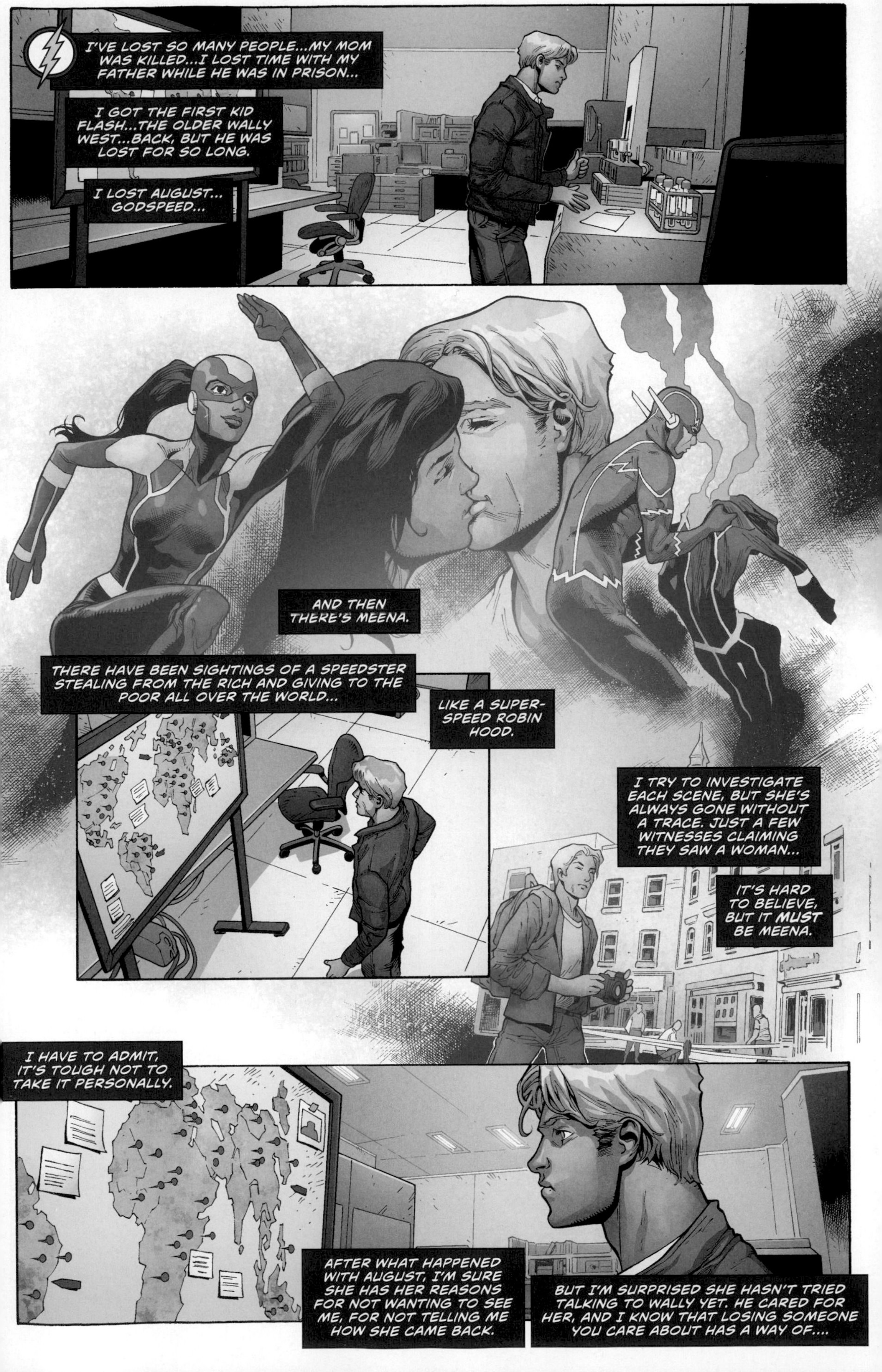
I'VE LOST SO MANY PEOPLE...MY MOM WAS KILLED...I LOST TIME WITH MY FATHER WHILE HE WAS IN PRISON...
I GOT THE FIRST KID FLASH...THE OLDER WALLY WEST...BACK, BUT HE WAS LOST FOR SO LONG.
I LOST AUGUST... GODSPEED...
AND THEN THERE'S MEENA.
THERE HAVE BEEN SIGHTINGS OF A SPEEDSTER STEALING FROM THE RICH AND GIVING TO THE POOR ALL OVER THE WORLD...
LIKE A SUPER-SPEED ROBIN HOOD.
I TRY TO INVESTIGATE EACH SCENE, BUT SHE'S ALWAYS GONE WITHOUT A TRACE. JUST A FEW WITNESSES CLAIMING THEY SAW A WOMAN...
IT'S HARD TO BELIEVE, BUT IT **MUST** BE MEENA.
I HAVE TO ADMIT, IT'S TOUGH NOT TO TAKE IT PERSONALLY.
AFTER WHAT HAPPENED WITH AUGUST, I'M SURE SHE HAS HER REASONS FOR NOT WANTING TO SEE ME, FOR NOT TELLING ME HOW SHE CAME BACK.
BUT I'M SURPRISED SHE HASN'T TRIED TALKING TO WALLY YET. HE CARED FOR HER, AND I KNOW THAT LOSING SOMEONE YOU CARE ABOUT HAS A WAY OF....

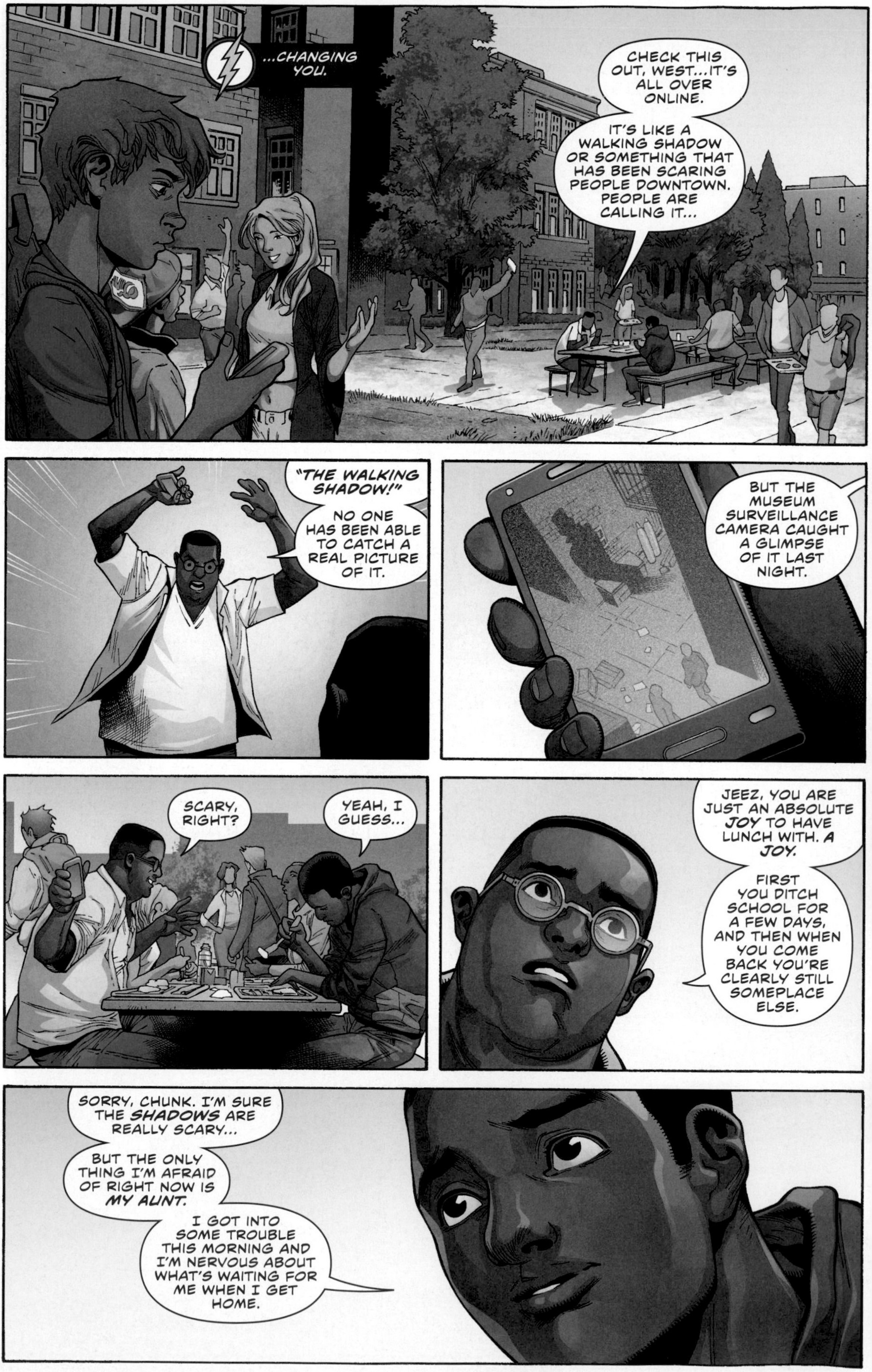
...CHANGING YOU.
CHECK THIS OUT, WEST...IT'S ALL OVER ONLINE.
IT'S LIKE A WALKING SHADOW OR SOMETHING THAT HAS BEEN SCARING PEOPLE DOWNTOWN. PEOPLE ARE CALLING IT...
"THE WALKING SHADOW!"
NO ONE HAS BEEN ABLE TO CATCH A REAL PICTURE OF IT.
BUT THE MUSEUM SURVEILLANCE CAMERA CAUGHT A GLIMPSE OF IT LAST NIGHT.
SCARY, RIGHT?
YEAH, I GUESS...
JEEZ, YOU ARE JUST AN ABSOLUTE JOY TO HAVE LUNCH WITH. A JOY.
FIRST YOU DITCH SCHOOL FOR A FEW DAYS, AND THEN WHEN YOU COME BACK YOU'RE CLEARLY STILL SOMEPLACE ELSE.
SORRY, CHUNK. I'M SURE THE SHADOWS ARE REALLY SCARY...
BUT THE ONLY THING I'M AFRAID OF RIGHT NOW IS MY AUNT.
I GOT INTO SOME TROUBLE THIS MORNING AND I'M NERVOUS ABOUT WHAT'S WAITING FOR ME WHEN I GET HOME.

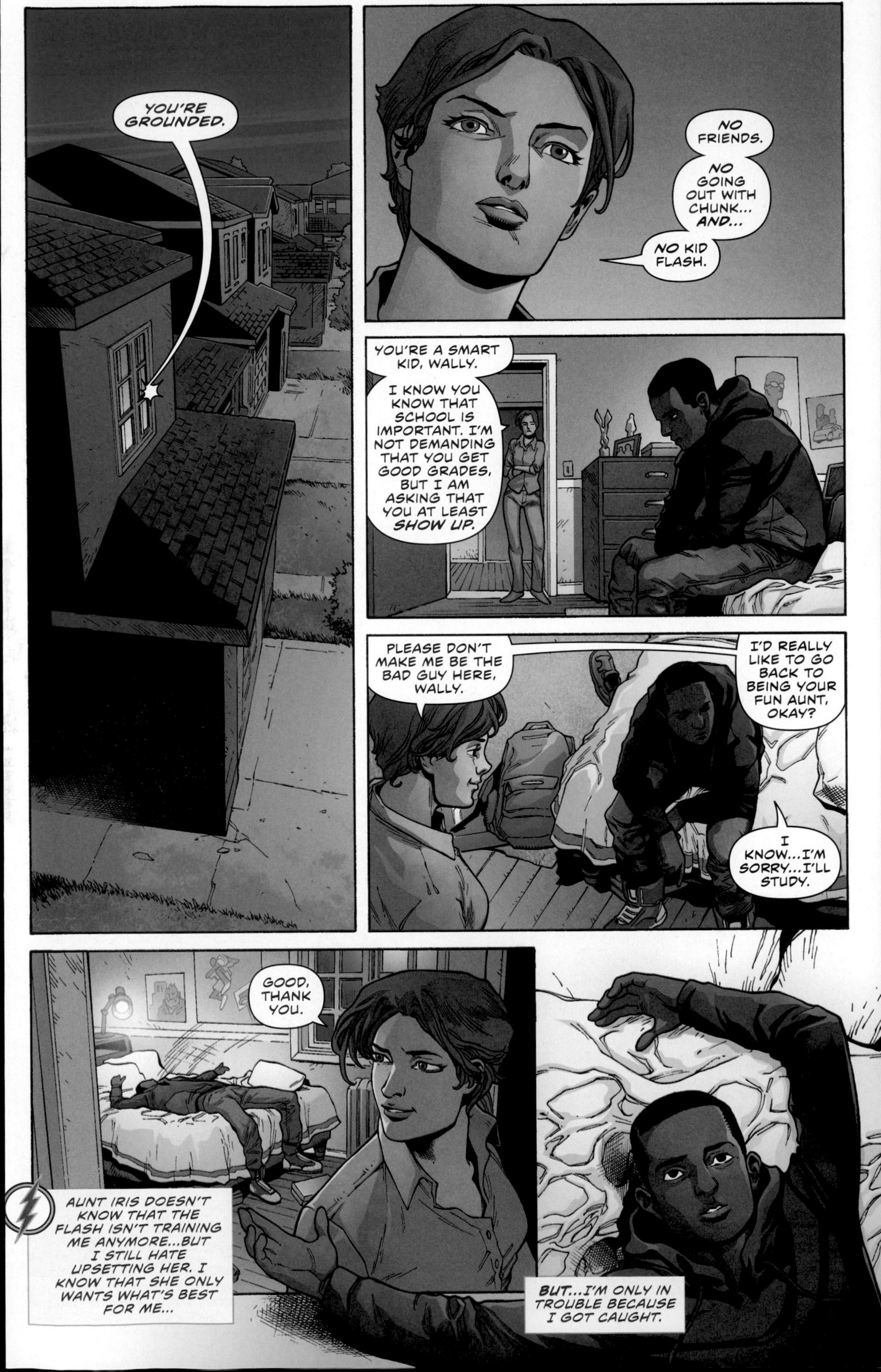
YOU'RE GROUNDED.
NO FRIENDS.
NO GOING OUT WITH CHUNK... AND...
NO KID FLASH.
YOU'RE A SMART KID, WALLY.
I KNOW YOU KNOW THAT SCHOOL IS IMPORTANT. I'M NOT DEMANDING THAT YOU GET GOOD GRADES, BUT I AM ASKING THAT YOU AT LEAST SHOW UP.
PLEASE DON'T MAKE ME BE THE BAD GUY HERE, WALLY.
I'D REALLY LIKE TO GO BACK TO BEING YOUR FUN AUNT, OKAY?
I KNOW...I'M SORRY...I'LL STUDY.
GOOD, THANK YOU.
AUNT IRIS DOESN'T KNOW THAT THE FLASH ISN'T TRAINING ME ANYMORE...BUT I STILL HATE UPSETTING HER. I KNOW THAT SHE ONLY WANTS WHAT'S BEST FOR ME...
BUT...I'M ONLY IN TROUBLE BECAUSE I GOT CAUGHT.

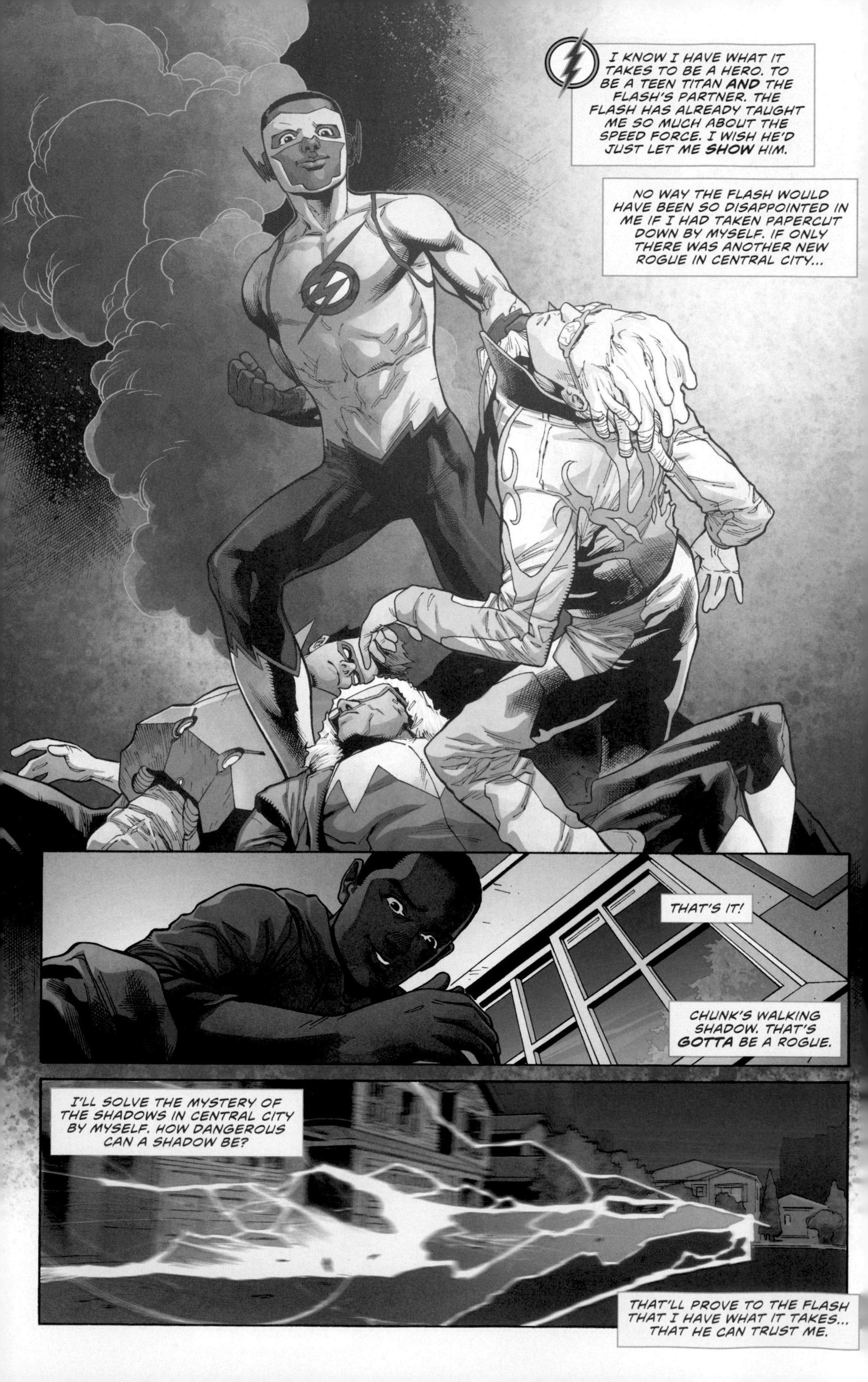
I KNOW I HAVE WHAT IT TAKES TO BE A HERO. TO BE A TEEN TITAN AND THE FLASH'S PARTNER. THE FLASH HAS ALREADY TAUGHT ME SO MUCH ABOUT THE SPEED FORCE. I WISH HE'D JUST LET ME SHOW HIM.
NO WAY THE FLASH WOULD HAVE BEEN SO DISAPPOINTED IN ME IF I HAD TAKEN PAPERCUT DOWN BY MYSELF. IF ONLY THERE WAS ANOTHER NEW ROGUE IN CENTRAL CITY...
THAT'S IT!
CHUNK'S WALKING SHADOW. THAT'S GOTTA BE A ROGUE.
I'LL SOLVE THE MYSTERY OF THE SHADOWS IN CENTRAL CITY BY MYSELF. HOW DANGEROUS CAN A SHADOW BE?
THAT'LL PROVE TO THE FLASH THAT I HAVE WHAT IT TAKES... THAT HE CAN TRUST ME.

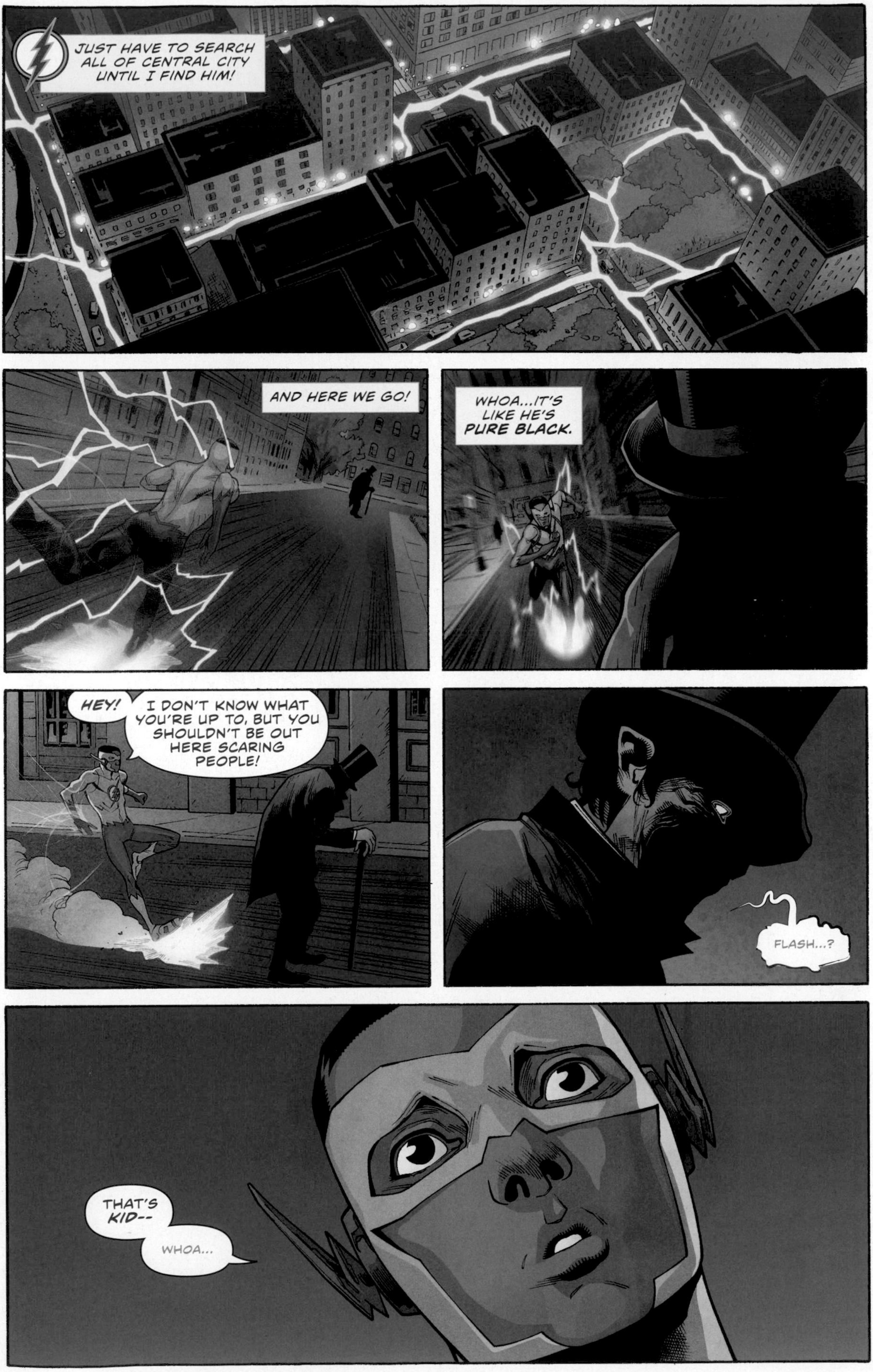

JUST HAVE TO SEARCH ALL OF CENTRAL CITY UNTIL I FIND HIM!
AND HERE WE GO!
WHOA...IT'S LIKE HE'S PURE BLACK.
HEY!
I DON'T KNOW WHAT YOU'RE UP TO, BUT YOU SHOULDN'T BE OUT HERE SCARING PEOPLE!
FLASH...?
THAT'S KID--
WHOA...

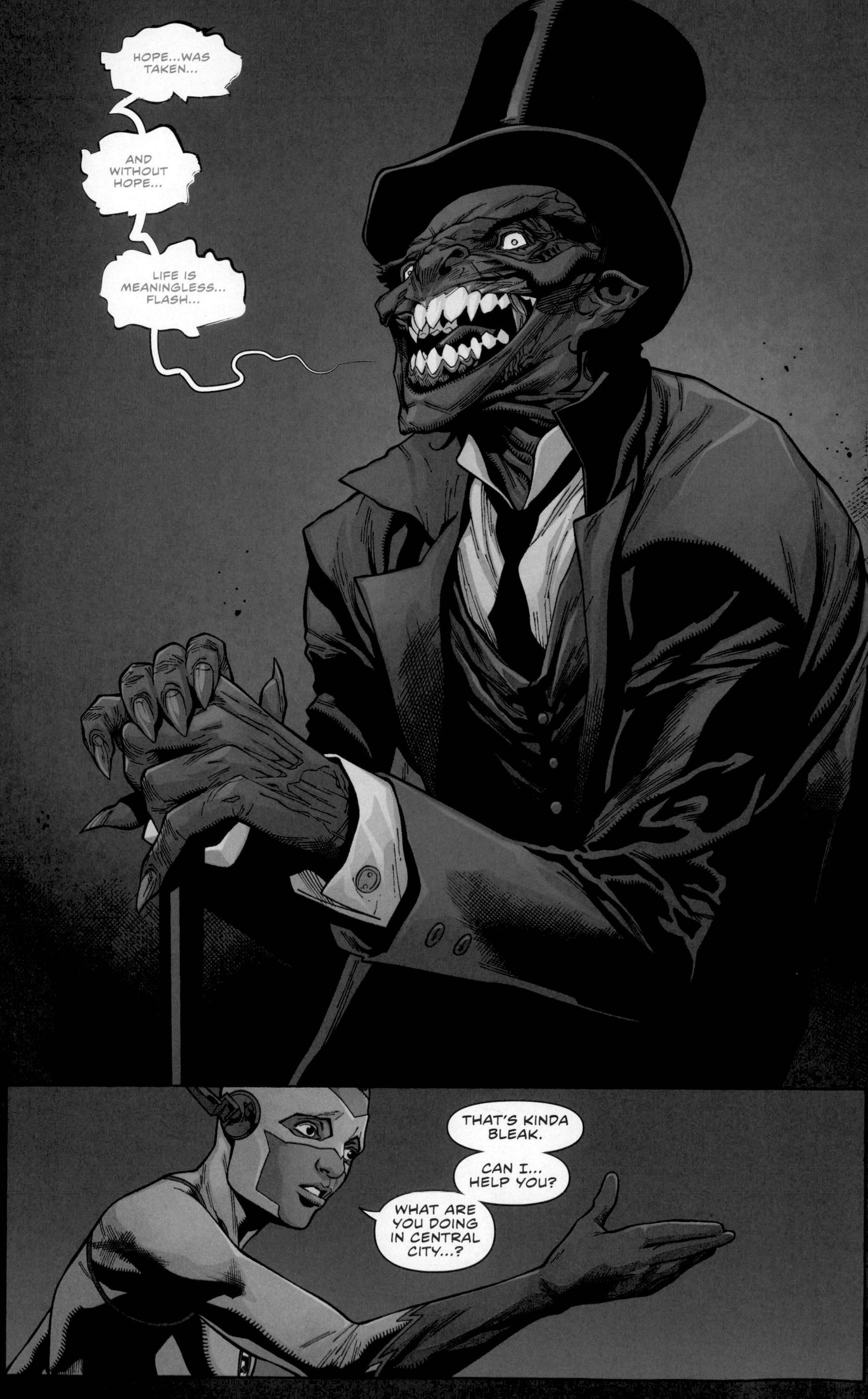
HOPE...WAS TAKEN...
AND WITHOUT HOPE...
LIFE IS MEANINGLESS... FLASH...
THAT'S KINDA BLEAK.
CAN I... HELP YOU?
WHAT ARE YOU DOING IN CENTRAL CITY...?

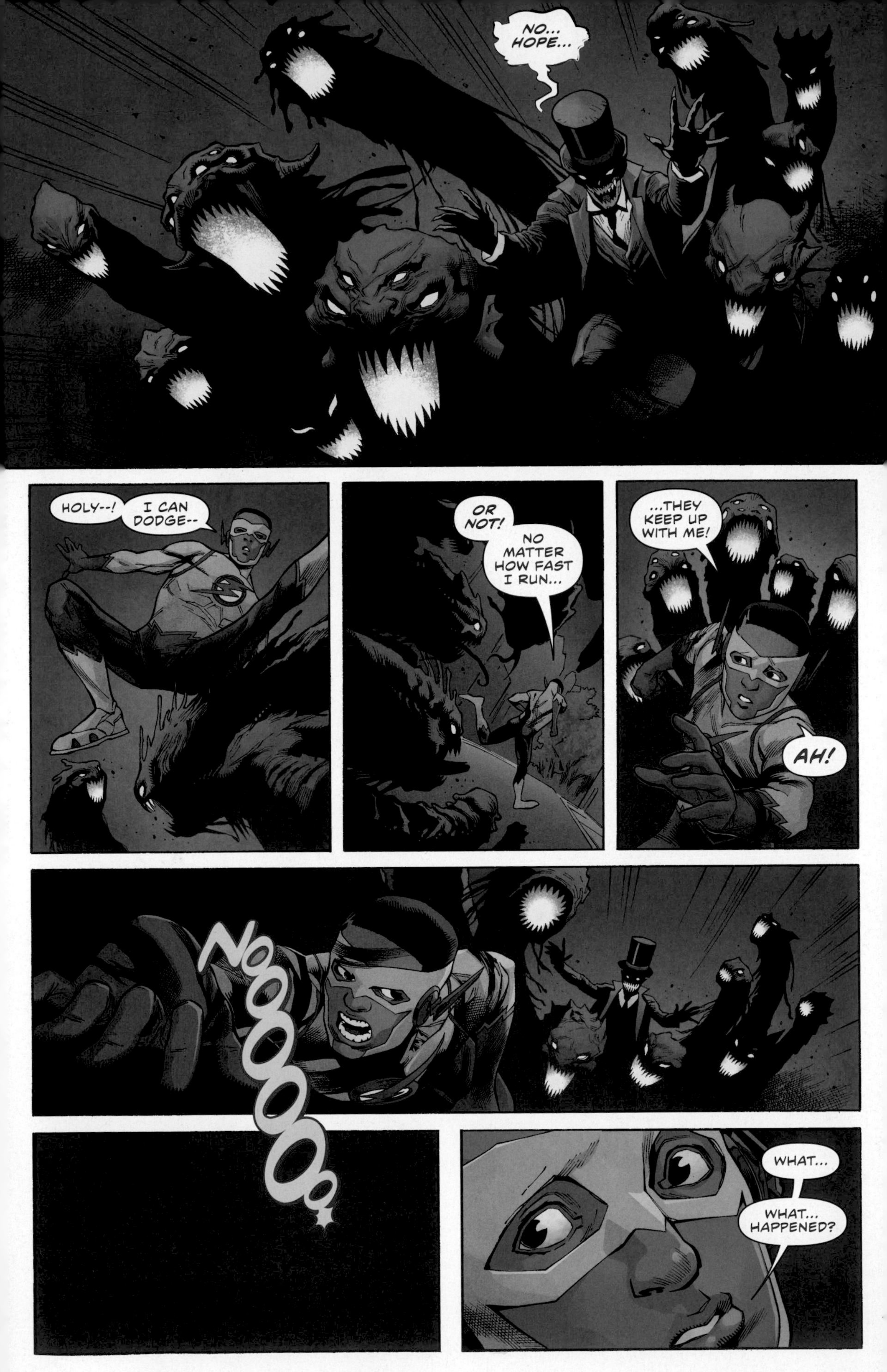
NO... HOPE...
HOLY--!
I CAN DODGE--
OR NOT!
NO MATTER HOW FAST I RUN...
...THEY KEEP UP WITH ME!
AH!
NOOOOOOO
WHAT...
WHAT... HAPPENED?

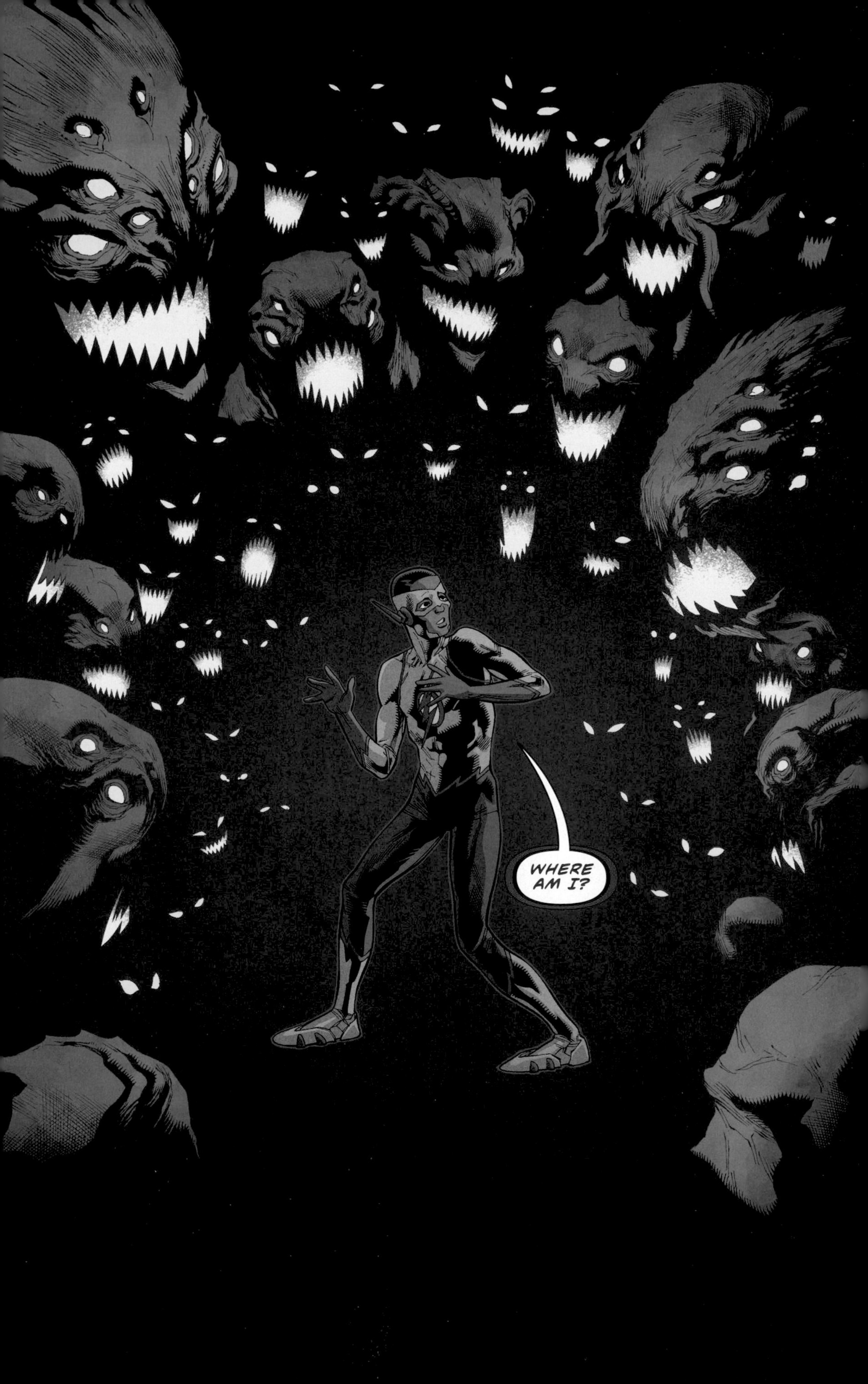
WHERE AM I?

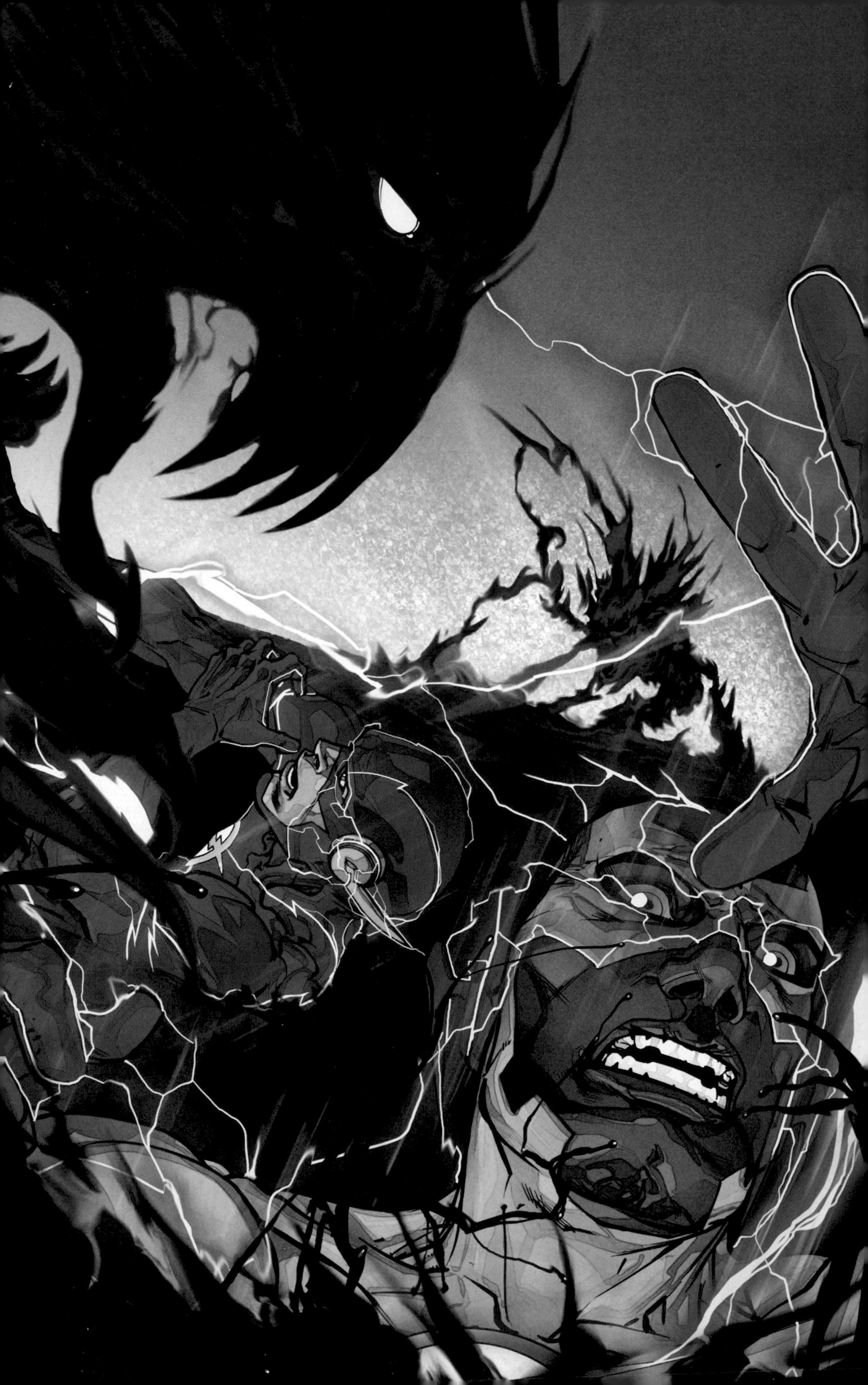

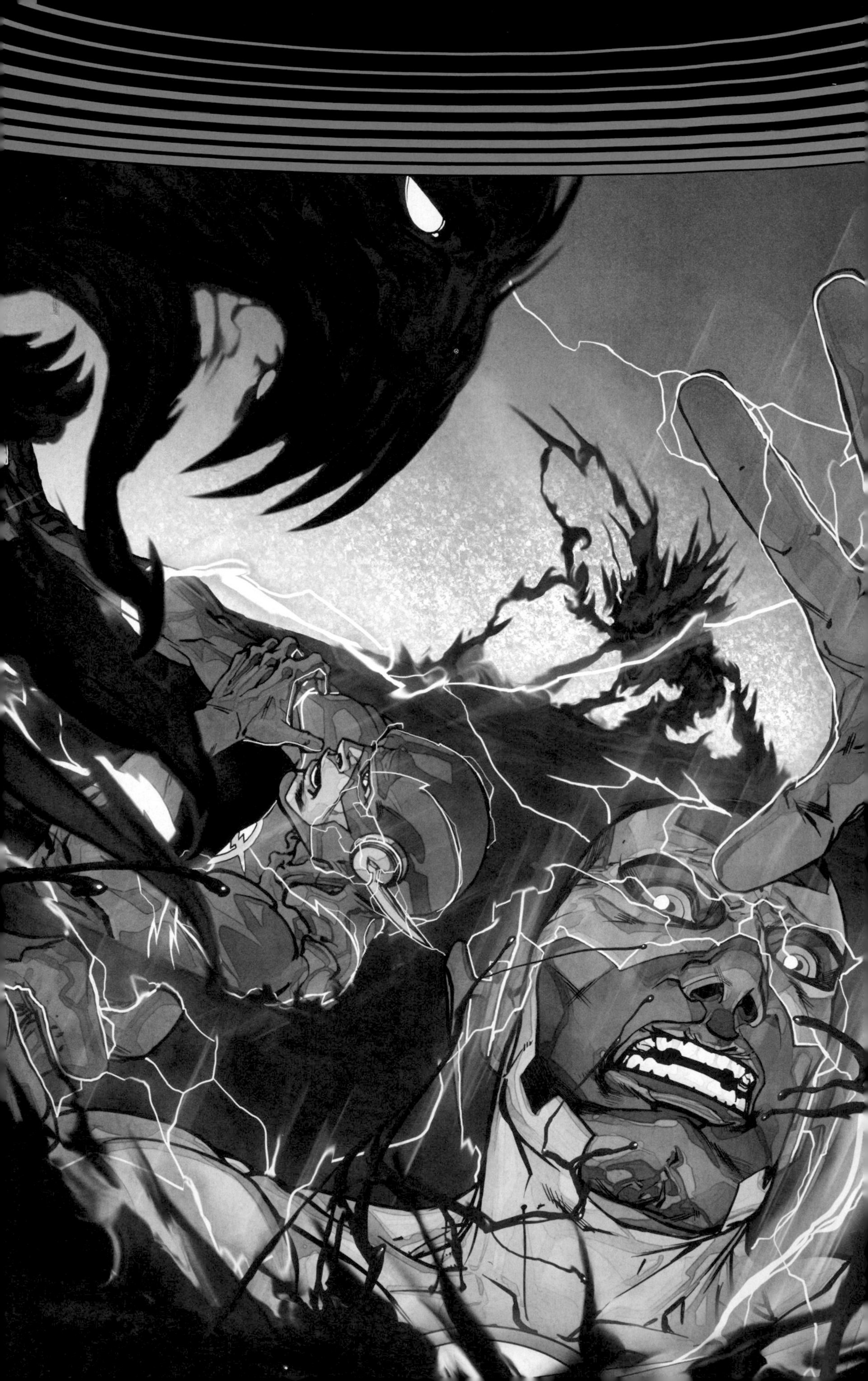

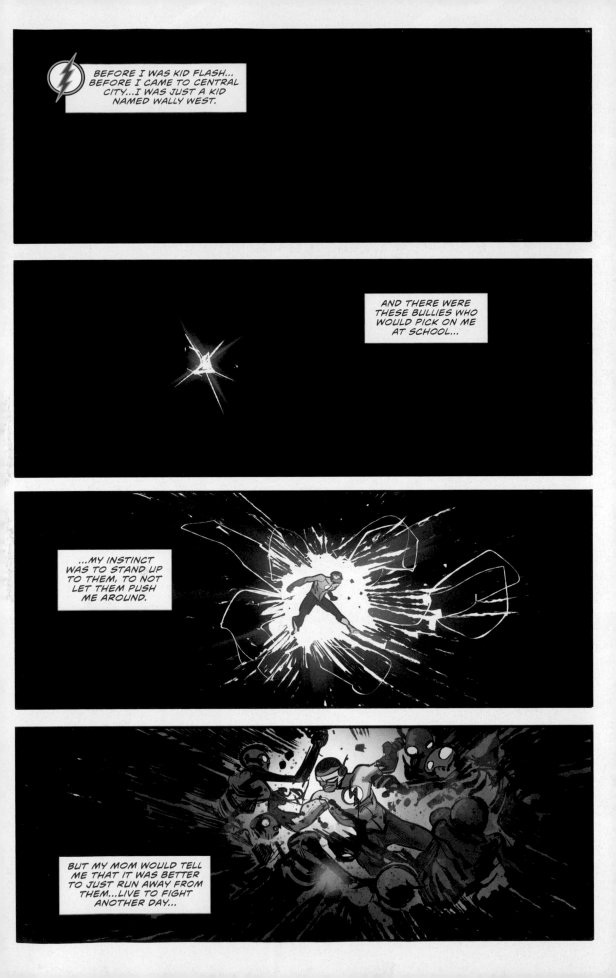

BEFORE I WAS KID FLASH... BEFORE I CAME TO CENTRAL CITY...I WAS JUST A KID NAMED WALLY WEST.

AND THERE WERE THESE BULLIES WHO WOULD PICK ON ME AT SCHOOL...

...MY INSTINCT WAS TO STAND UP TO THEM, TO NOT LET THEM PUSH ME AROUND.

BUT MY MOM WOULD TELL ME THAT IT WAS BETTER TO JUST RUN AWAY FROM THEM...LIVE TO FIGHT ANOTHER DAY...

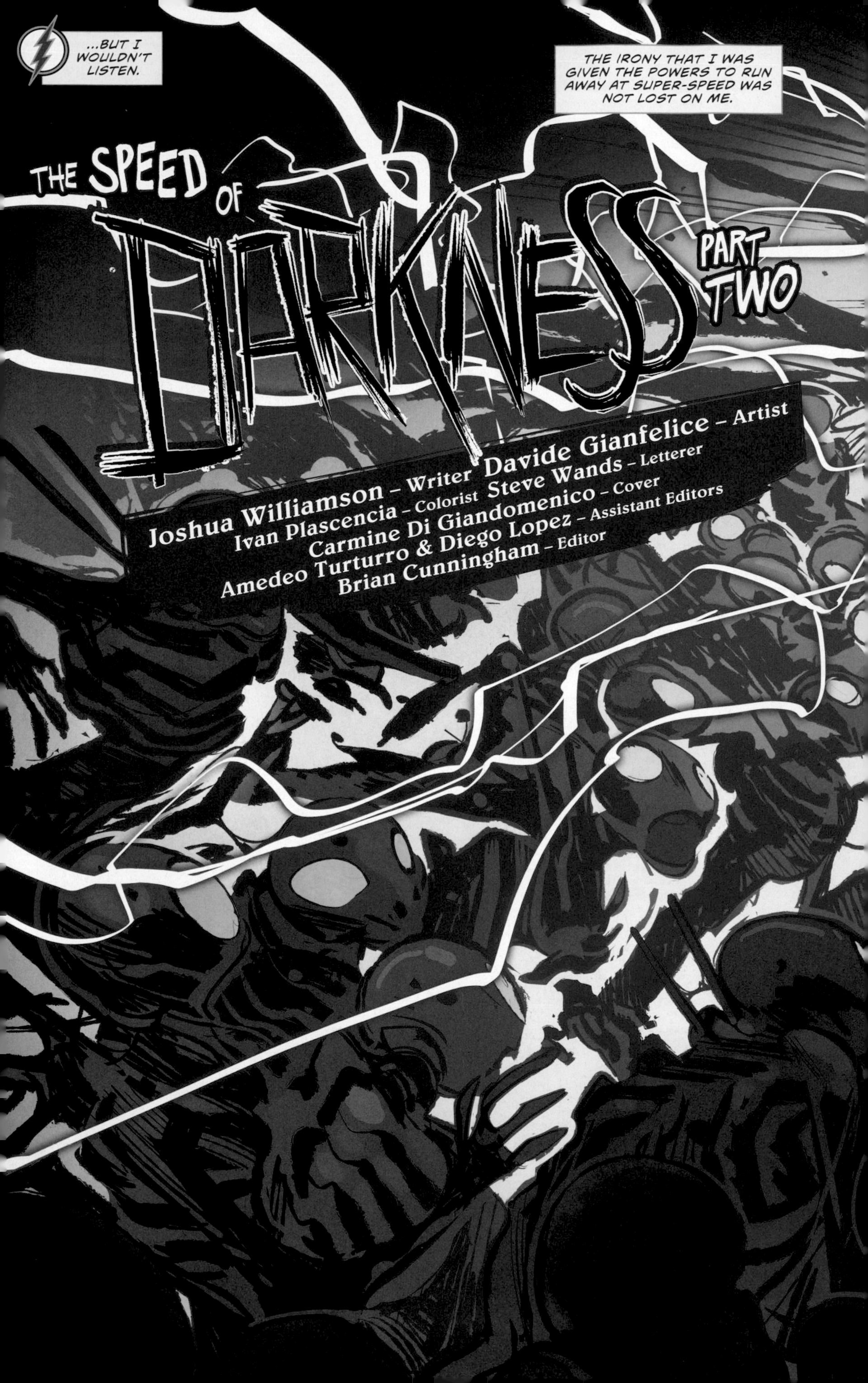
...BUT I WOULDN'T LISTEN.
THE IRONY THAT I WAS GIVEN THE POWERS TO RUN AWAY AT SUPER-SPEED WAS NOT LOST ON ME.
THE SPEED OF DARKNESS PART TWO
Joshua Williamson – Writer Davide Gianfelice – Artist
Ivan Plascencia – Colorist Steve Wands – Letterer
Carmine Di Giandomenico – Cover
Amedeo Turturro & Diego Lopez – Assistant Editors
Brian Cunningham – Editor

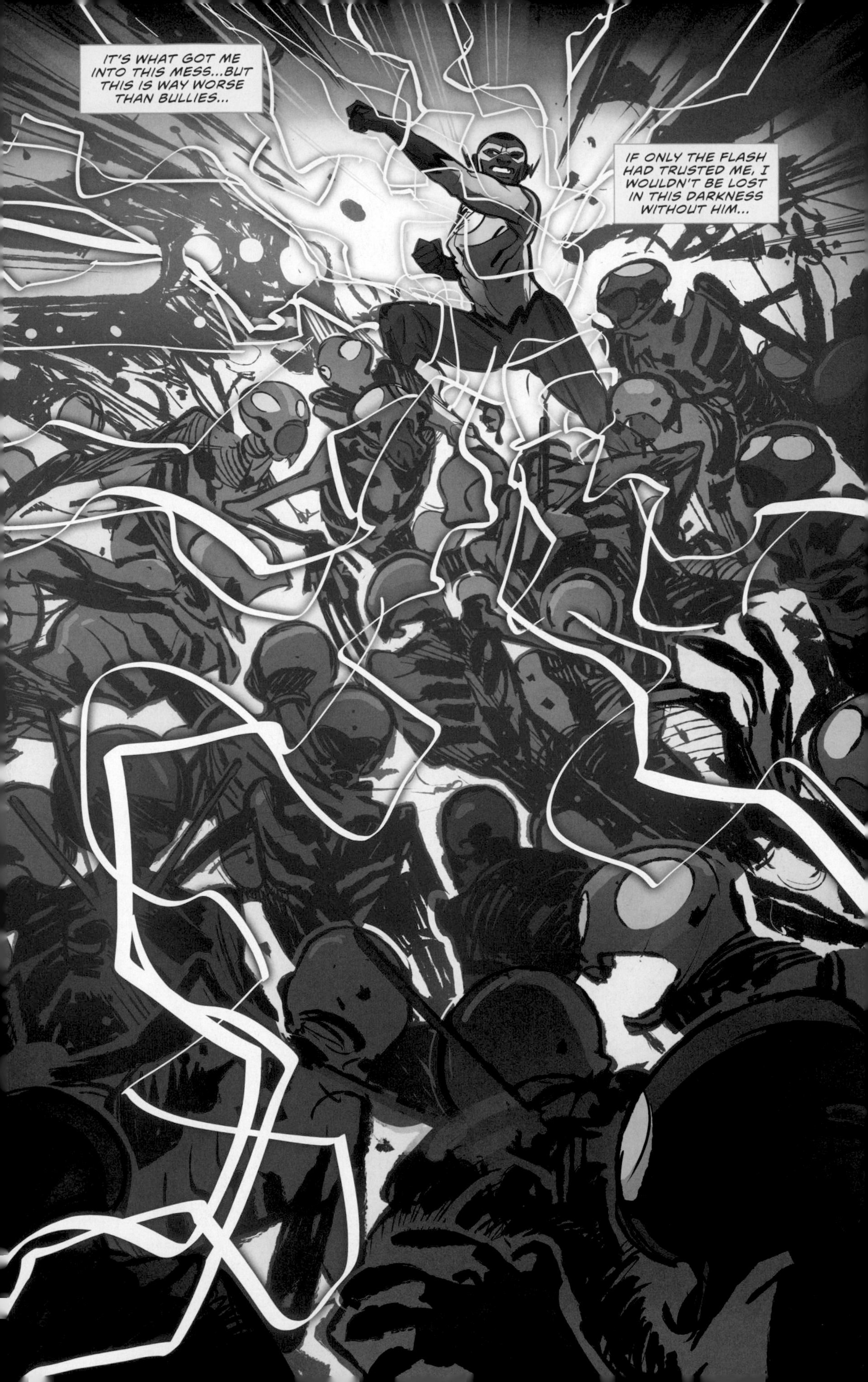
IT'S WHAT GOT ME INTO THIS MESS...BUT THIS IS WAY WORSE THAN BULLIES...
IF ONLY THE FLASH HAD TRUSTED ME, I WOULDN'T BE LOST IN THIS DARKNESS WITHOUT HIM...

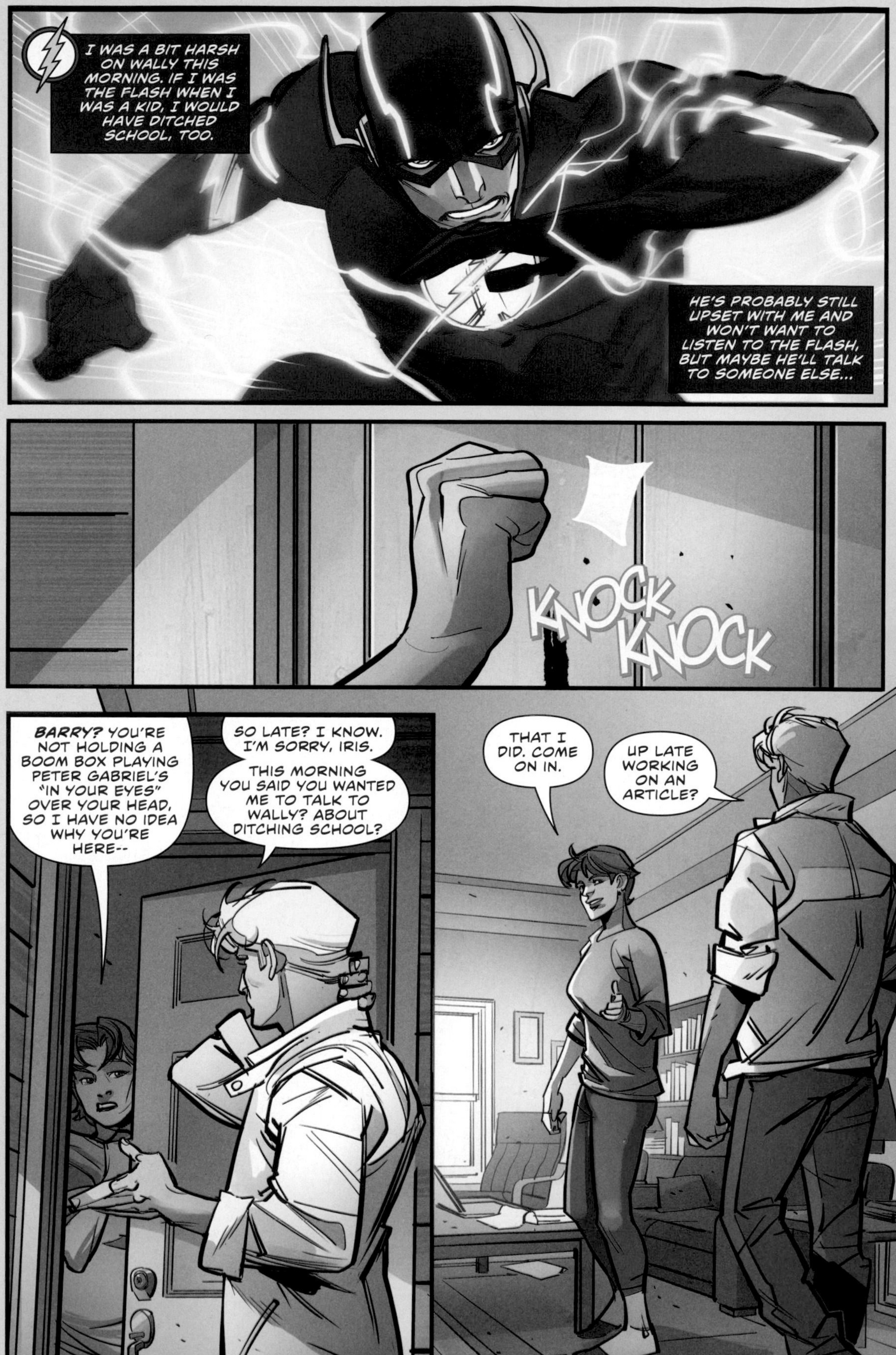
I WAS A BIT HARSH ON WALLY THIS MORNING. IF I WAS THE FLASH WHEN I WAS A KID, I WOULD HAVE DITCHED SCHOOL, TOO.
HE'S PROBABLY STILL UPSET WITH ME AND WON'T WANT TO LISTEN TO THE FLASH, BUT MAYBE HE'LL TALK TO SOMEONE ELSE...
KNOCK KNOCK
BARRY? YOU'RE NOT HOLDING A BOOM BOX PLAYING PETER GABRIEL'S "IN YOUR EYES" OVER YOUR HEAD, SO I HAVE NO IDEA WHY YOU'RE HERE--
SO LATE? I KNOW. I'M SORRY, IRIS.
THIS MORNING YOU SAID YOU WANTED ME TO TALK TO WALLY? ABOUT DITCHING SCHOOL?
THAT I DID. COME ON IN.
UP LATE WORKING ON AN ARTICLE?

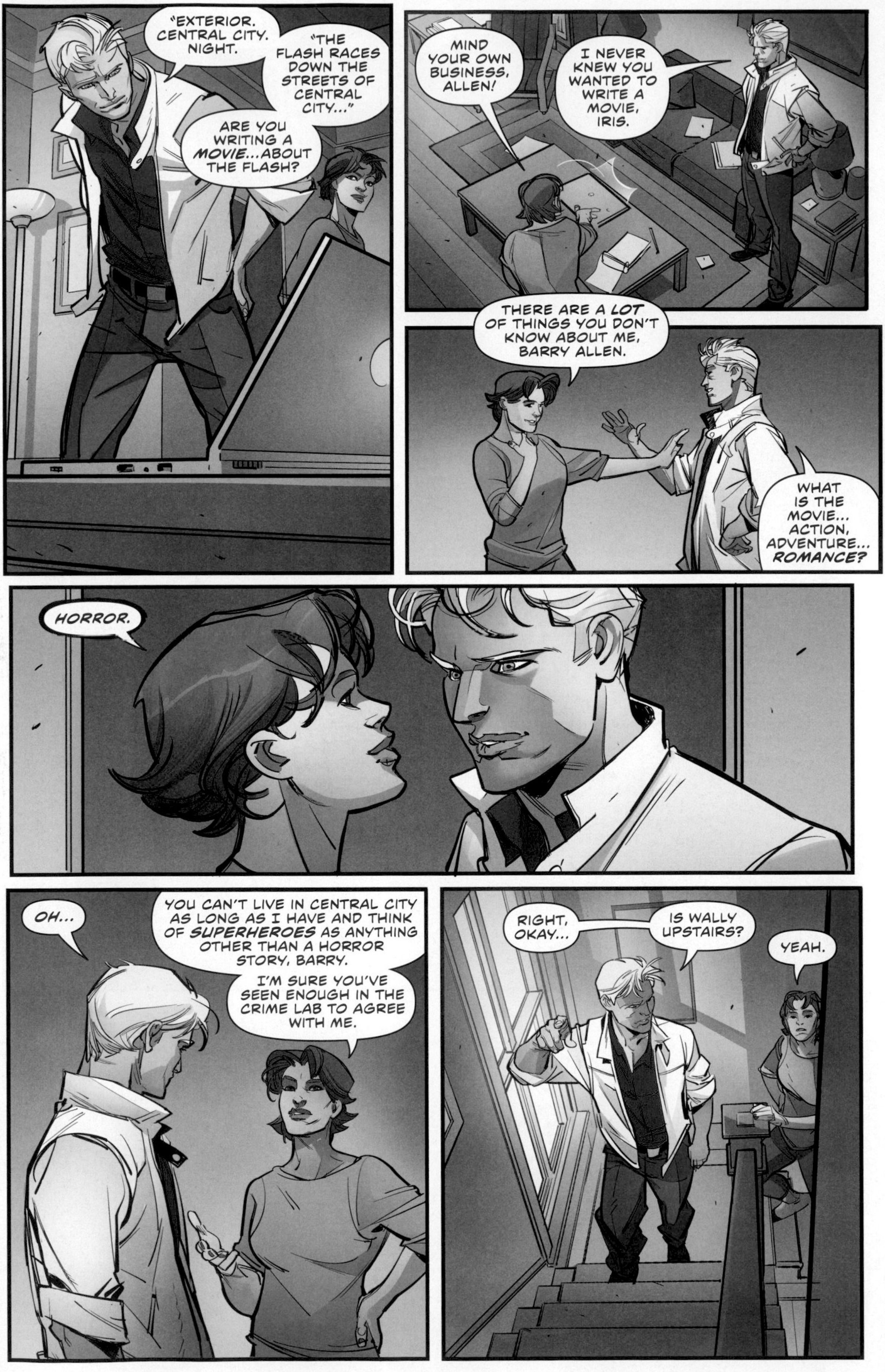
"EXTERIOR. CENTRAL CITY. NIGHT.
"THE FLASH RACES DOWN THE STREETS OF CENTRAL CITY..."
ARE YOU WRITING A MOVIE...ABOUT THE FLASH?
MIND YOUR OWN BUSINESS, ALLEN!
I NEVER KNEW YOU WANTED TO WRITE A MOVIE, IRIS.
THERE ARE A LOT OF THINGS YOU DON'T KNOW ABOUT ME, BARRY ALLEN.
WHAT IS THE MOVIE... ACTION, ADVENTURE... ROMANCE?
HORROR.
OH...
YOU CAN'T LIVE IN CENTRAL CITY AS LONG AS I HAVE AND THINK OF SUPERHEROES AS ANYTHING OTHER THAN A HORROR STORY, BARRY.
I'M SURE YOU'VE SEEN ENOUGH IN THE CRIME LAB TO AGREE WITH ME.
RIGHT, OKAY...
IS WALLY UPSTAIRS?
YEAH.

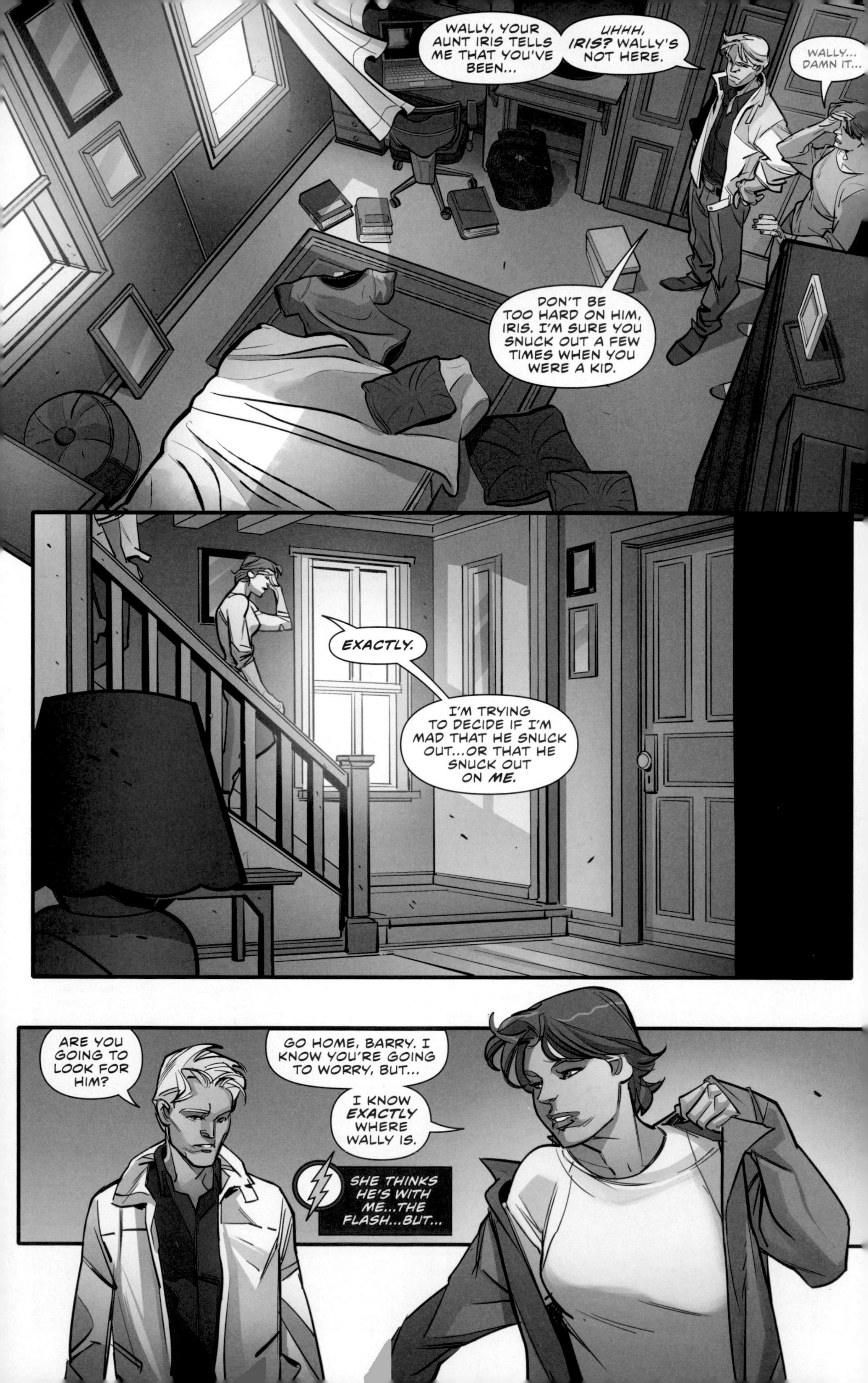
WALLY, YOUR AUNT IRIS TELLS ME THAT YOU'VE BEEN...
UHHH, IRIS? WALLY'S NOT HERE.
WALLY... DAMN IT...
DON'T BE TOO HARD ON HIM, IRIS. I'M SURE YOU SNUCK OUT A FEW TIMES WHEN YOU WERE A KID.
EXACTLY.
I'M TRYING TO DECIDE IF I'M MAD THAT HE SNUCK OUT...OR THAT HE SNUCK OUT ON ME.
ARE YOU GOING TO LOOK FOR HIM?
GO HOME, BARRY. I KNOW YOU'RE GOING TO WORRY, BUT...
I KNOW EXACTLY WHERE WALLY IS.
SHE THINKS HE'S WITH ME...THE FLASH...BUT...

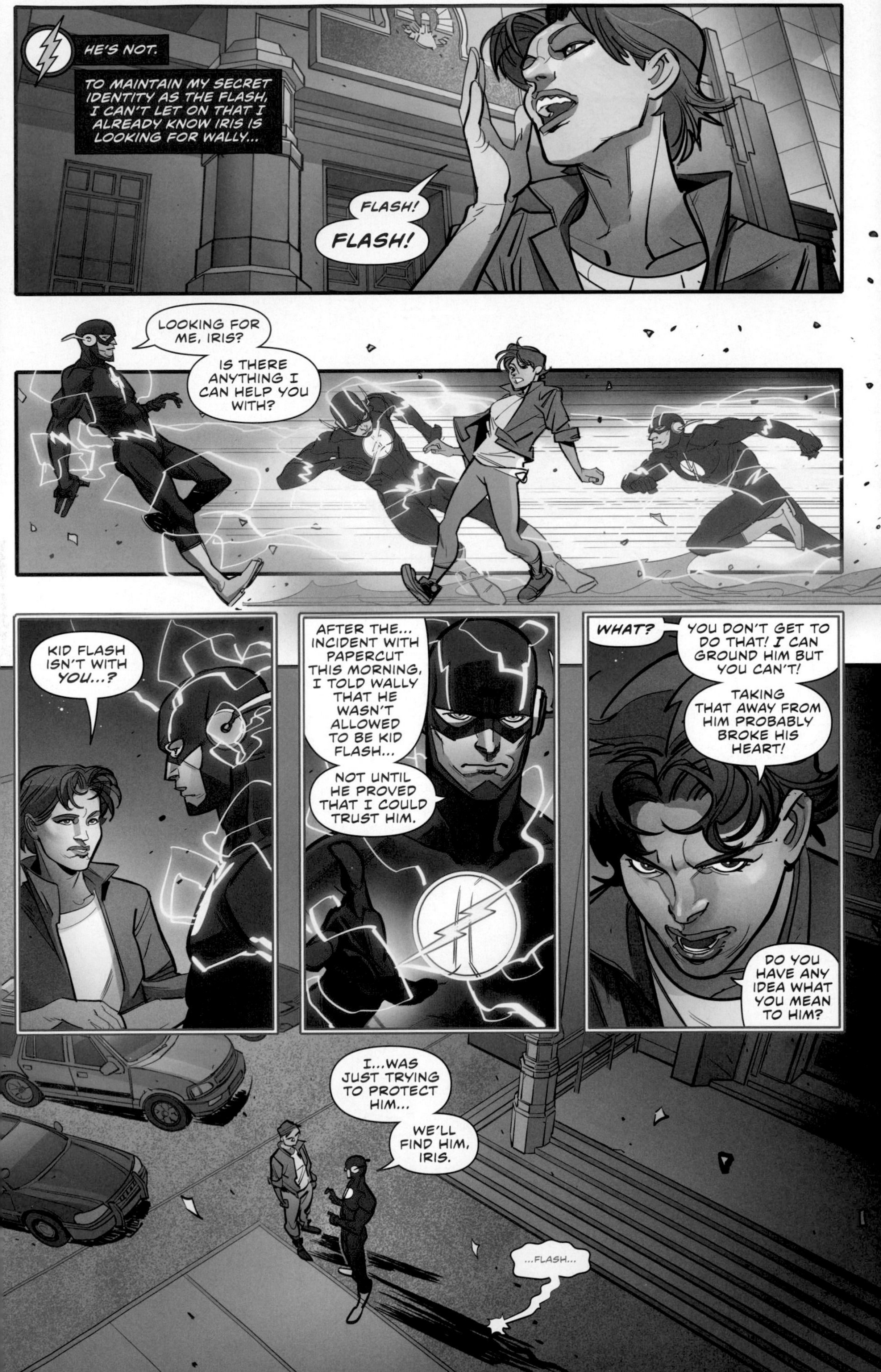
HE'S NOT.
TO MAINTAIN MY SECRET IDENTITY AS THE FLASH, I CAN'T LET ON THAT I ALREADY KNOW IRIS IS LOOKING FOR WALLY...
FLASH!
FLASH!
LOOKING FOR ME, IRIS?
IS THERE ANYTHING I CAN HELP YOU WITH?
KID FLASH ISN'T WITH YOU...?
AFTER THE... INCIDENT WITH PAPERCUT THIS MORNING, I TOLD WALLY THAT HE WASN'T ALLOWED TO BE KID FLASH...
NOT UNTIL HE PROVED THAT I COULD TRUST HIM.
WHAT?
YOU DON'T GET TO DO THAT! I CAN GROUND HIM BUT YOU CAN'T!
TAKING THAT AWAY FROM HIM PROBABLY BROKE HIS HEART!
DO YOU HAVE ANY IDEA WHAT YOU MEAN TO HIM?
I...WAS JUST TRYING TO PROTECT HIM...
WE'LL FIND HIM, IRIS.
...FLASH...

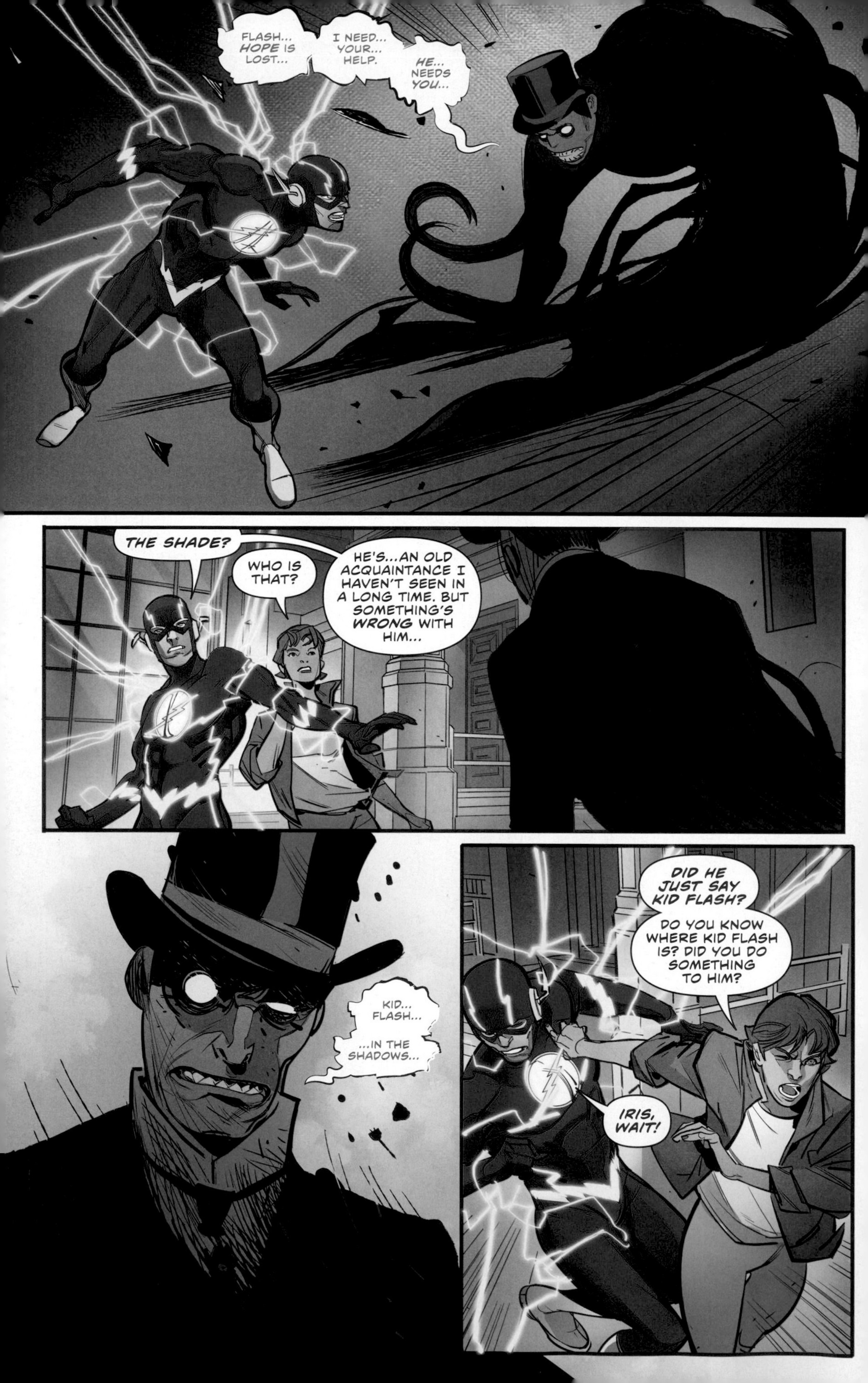
FLASH... HOPE IS LOST...
I NEED... YOUR... HELP.
HE... NEEDS YOU...
THE SHADE?
WHO IS THAT?
HE'S...AN OLD ACQUAINTANCE I HAVEN'T SEEN IN A LONG TIME. BUT SOMETHING'S WRONG WITH HIM...
KID... FLASH...
...IN THE SHADOWS...
DID HE JUST SAY KID FLASH?
DO YOU KNOW WHERE KID FLASH IS? DID YOU DO SOMETHING TO HIM?
IRIS, WAIT!

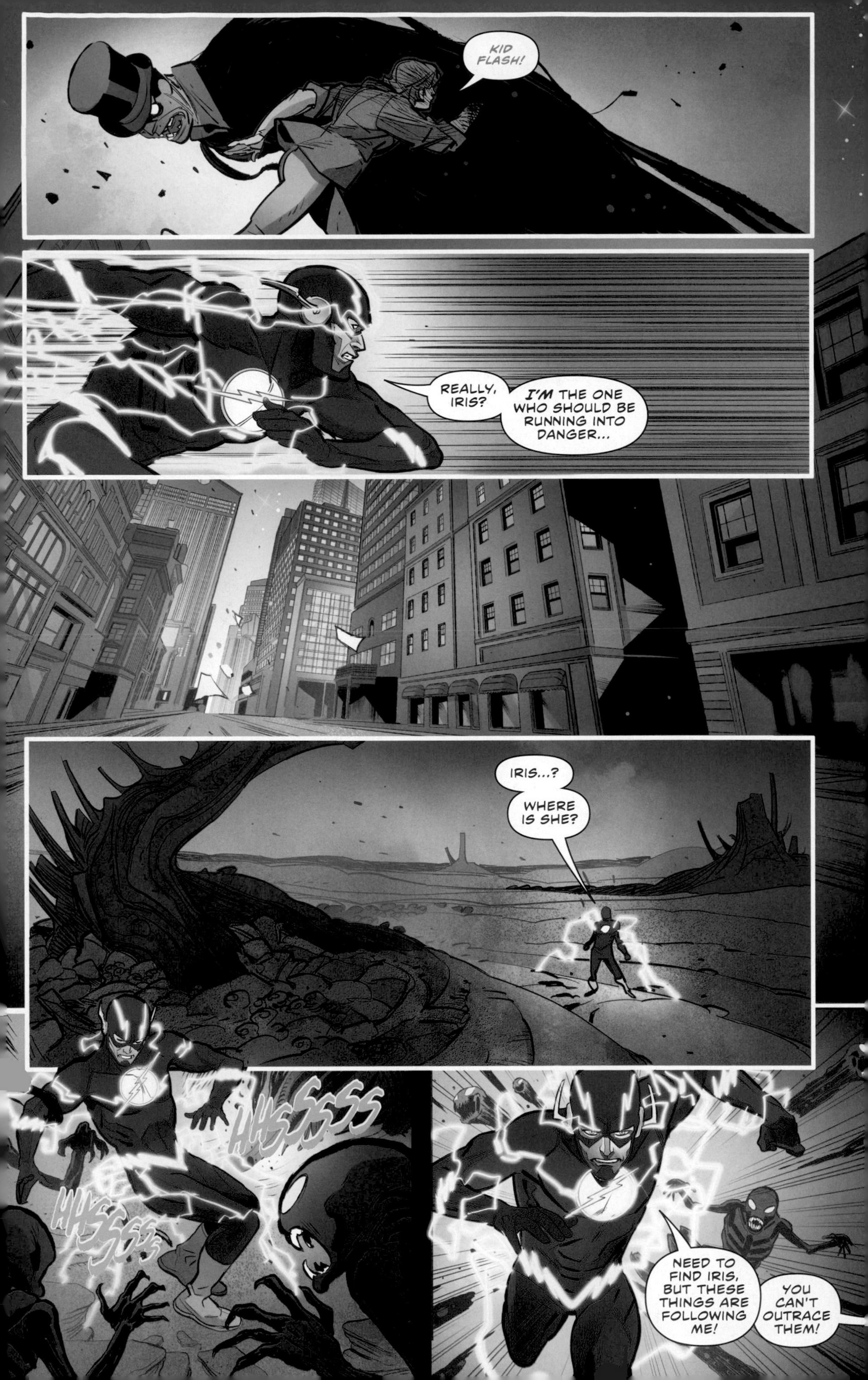
KID FLASH!
REALLY, IRIS?
I'M THE ONE WHO SHOULD BE RUNNING INTO DANGER...
IRIS...?
WHERE IS SHE?
HHSSSSS
HHSSSSS
NEED TO FIND IRIS, BUT THESE THINGS ARE FOLLOWING ME!
YOU CAN'T OUTRACE THEM!

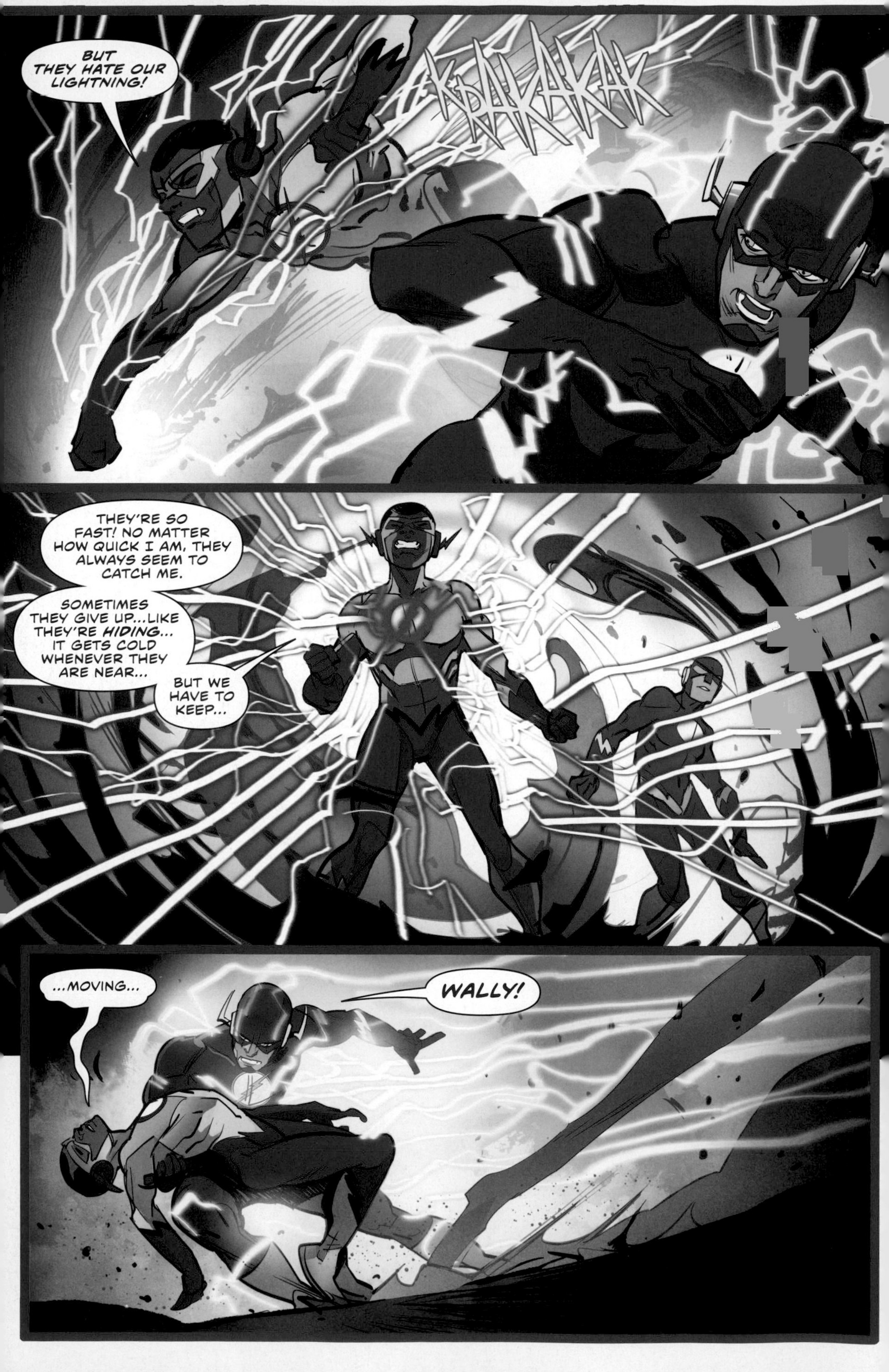
BUT THEY HATE OUR LIGHTNING!
KRAKAKAKAK
THEY'RE SO FAST! NO MATTER HOW QUICK I AM, THEY ALWAYS SEEM TO CATCH ME.
SOMETIMES THEY GIVE UP...LIKE THEY'RE HIDING... IT GETS COLD WHENEVER THEY ARE NEAR...
BUT WE HAVE TO KEEP...
...MOVING...
WALLY!

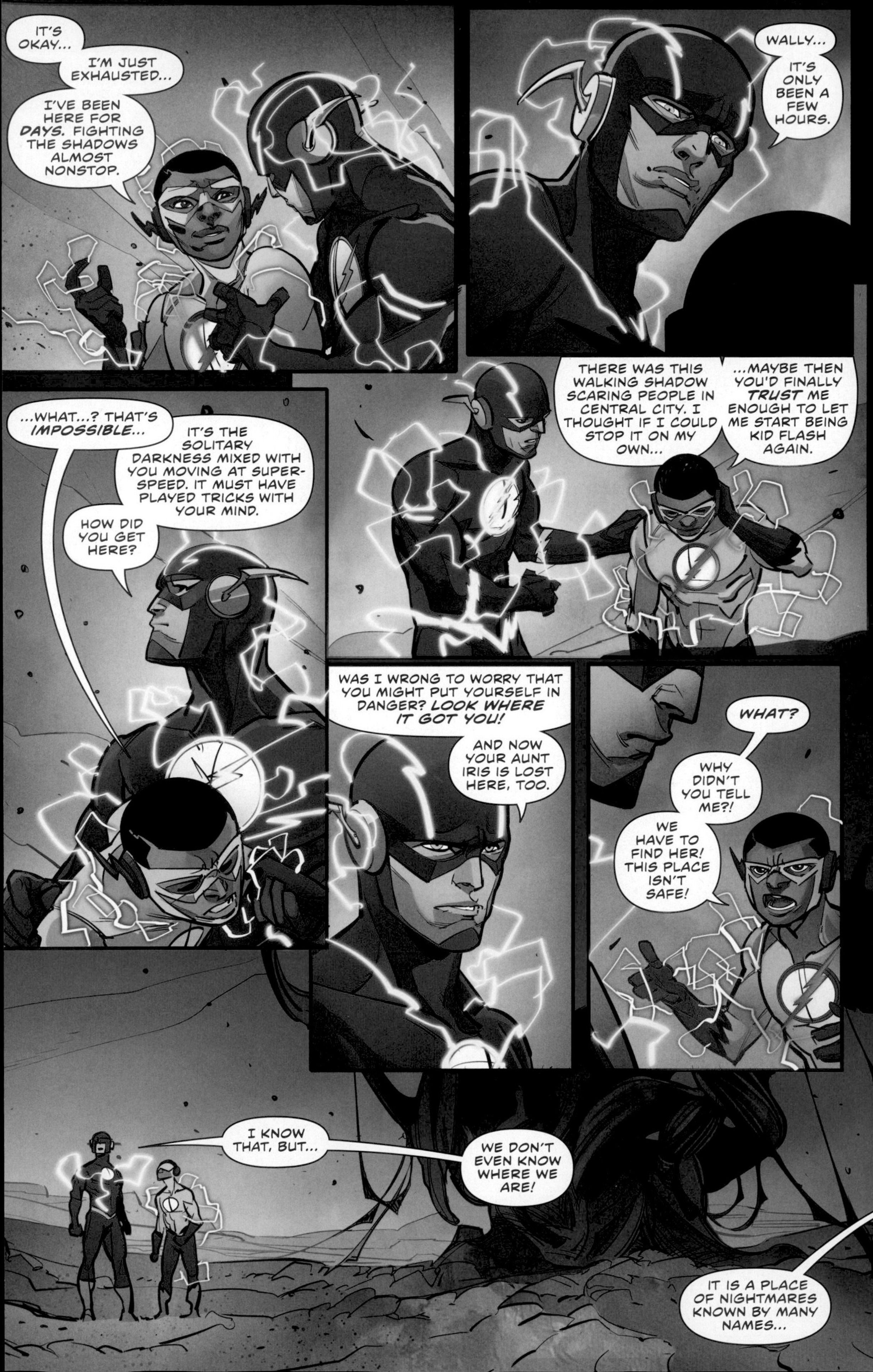
IT'S OKAY...
I'M JUST EXHAUSTED...
I'VE BEEN HERE FOR DAYS. FIGHTING THE SHADOWS ALMOST NONSTOP.
WALLY...
IT'S ONLY BEEN A FEW HOURS.
...WHAT...? THAT'S IMPOSSIBLE...
IT'S THE SOLITARY DARKNESS MIXED WITH YOU MOVING AT SUPER-SPEED. IT MUST HAVE PLAYED TRICKS WITH YOUR MIND.
HOW DID YOU GET HERE?
THERE WAS THIS WALKING SHADOW SCARING PEOPLE IN CENTRAL CITY. I THOUGHT IF I COULD STOP IT ON MY OWN...
...MAYBE THEN YOU'D FINALLY TRUST ME ENOUGH TO LET ME START BEING KID FLASH AGAIN.
WAS I WRONG TO WORRY THAT YOU MIGHT PUT YOURSELF IN DANGER? LOOK WHERE IT GOT YOU!
AND NOW YOUR AUNT IRIS IS LOST HERE, TOO.
WHAT?
WHY DIDN'T YOU TELL ME?!
WE HAVE TO FIND HER! THIS PLACE ISN'T SAFE!
I KNOW THAT, BUT...
WE DON'T EVEN KNOW WHERE WE ARE!
IT IS A PLACE OF NIGHTMARES KNOWN BY MANY NAMES...

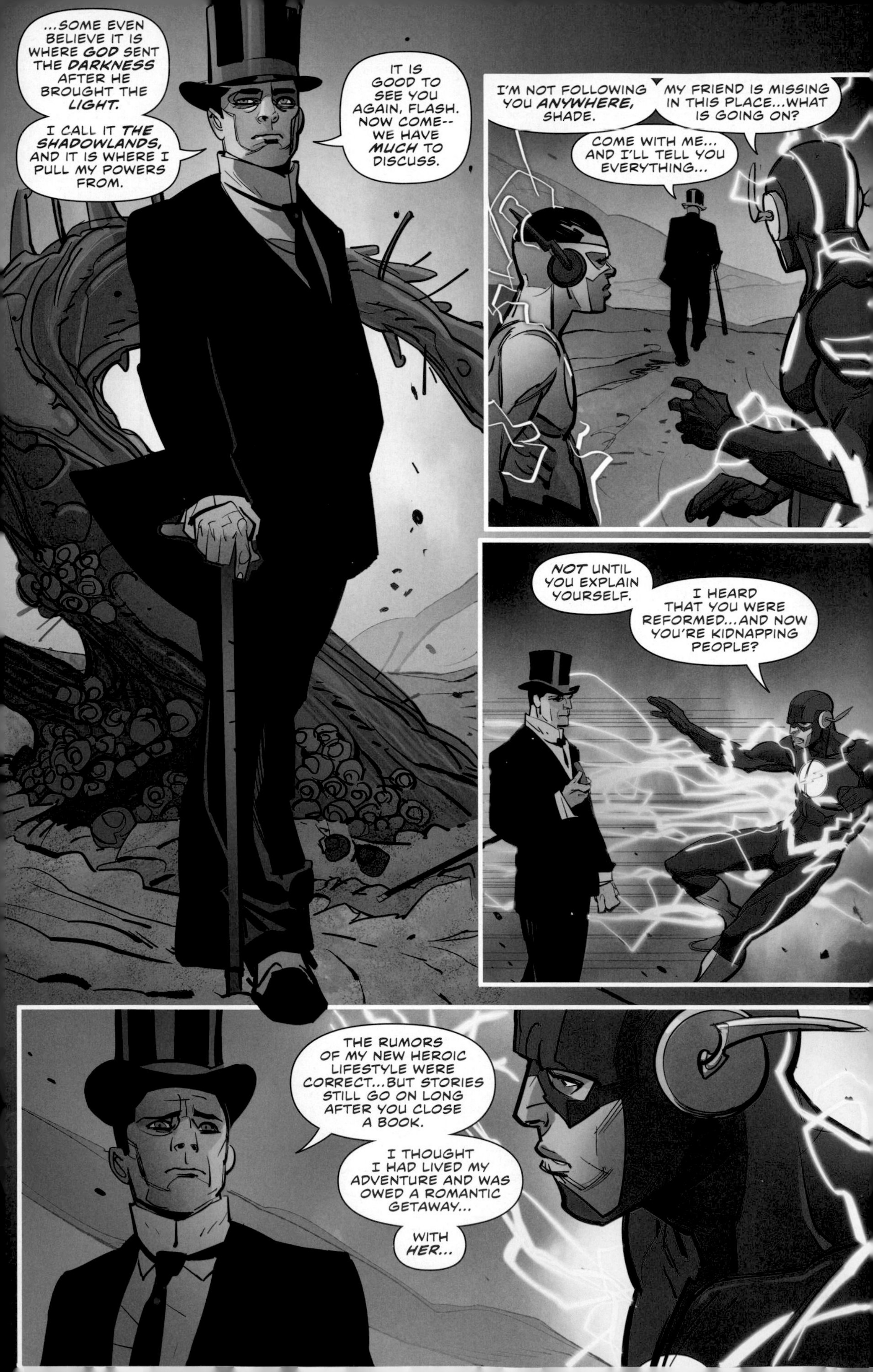
...SOME EVEN BELIEVE IT IS WHERE GOD SENT THE DARKNESS AFTER HE BROUGHT THE LIGHT.
I CALL IT THE SHADOWLANDS, AND IT IS WHERE I PULL MY POWERS FROM.
IT IS GOOD TO SEE YOU AGAIN, FLASH. NOW COME-- WE HAVE MUCH TO DISCUSS.
I'M NOT FOLLOWING YOU ANYWHERE, SHADE.
MY FRIEND IS MISSING IN THIS PLACE...WHAT IS GOING ON?
COME WITH ME... AND I'LL TELL YOU EVERYTHING...
NOT UNTIL YOU EXPLAIN YOURSELF.
I HEARD THAT YOU WERE REFORMED...AND NOW YOU'RE KIDNAPPING PEOPLE?
THE RUMORS OF MY NEW HEROIC LIFESTYLE WERE CORRECT...BUT STORIES STILL GO ON LONG AFTER YOU CLOSE A BOOK.
I THOUGHT I HAD LIVED MY ADVENTURE AND WAS OWED A ROMANTIC GETAWAY...
WITH HER...

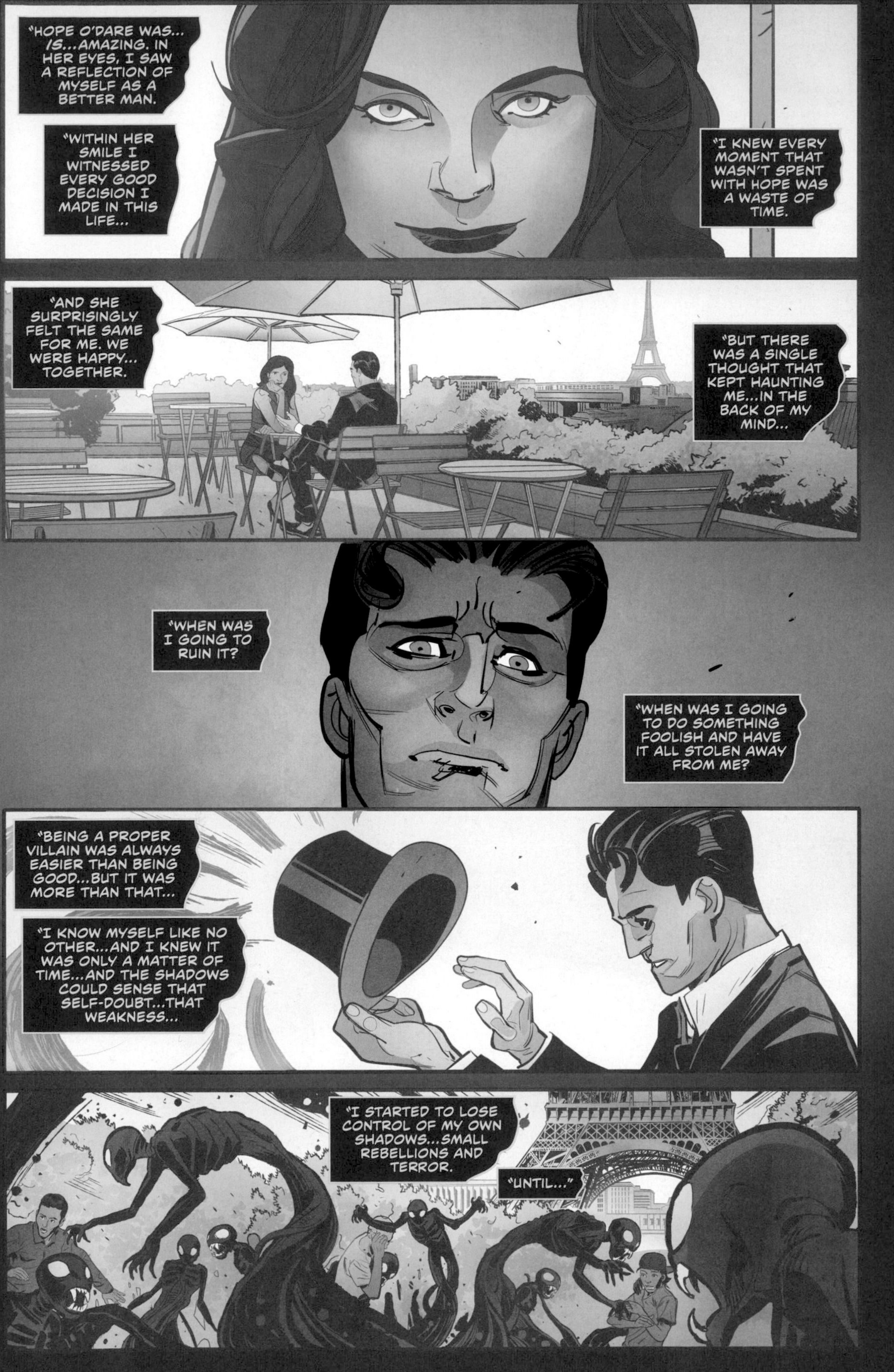
"HOPE O'DARE WAS... IS...AMAZING. IN HER EYES, I SAW A REFLECTION OF MYSELF AS A BETTER MAN.
"WITHIN HER SMILE I WITNESSED EVERY GOOD DECISION I MADE IN THIS LIFE...
"I KNEW EVERY MOMENT THAT WASN'T SPENT WITH HOPE WAS A WASTE OF TIME.
"AND SHE SURPRISINGLY FELT THE SAME FOR ME. WE WERE HAPPY... TOGETHER.
"BUT THERE WAS A SINGLE THOUGHT THAT KEPT HAUNTING ME...IN THE BACK OF MY MIND...
"WHEN WAS I GOING TO RUIN IT?
"WHEN WAS I GOING TO DO SOMETHING FOOLISH AND HAVE IT ALL STOLEN AWAY FROM ME?
"BEING A PROPER VILLAIN WAS ALWAYS EASIER THAN BEING GOOD...BUT IT WAS MORE THAN THAT...
"I KNOW MYSELF LIKE NO OTHER...AND I KNEW IT WAS ONLY A MATTER OF TIME...AND THE SHADOWS COULD SENSE THAT SELF-DOUBT...THAT WEAKNESS...
"I STARTED TO LOSE CONTROL OF MY OWN SHADOWS...SMALL REBELLIONS AND TERROR.
"UNTIL..."

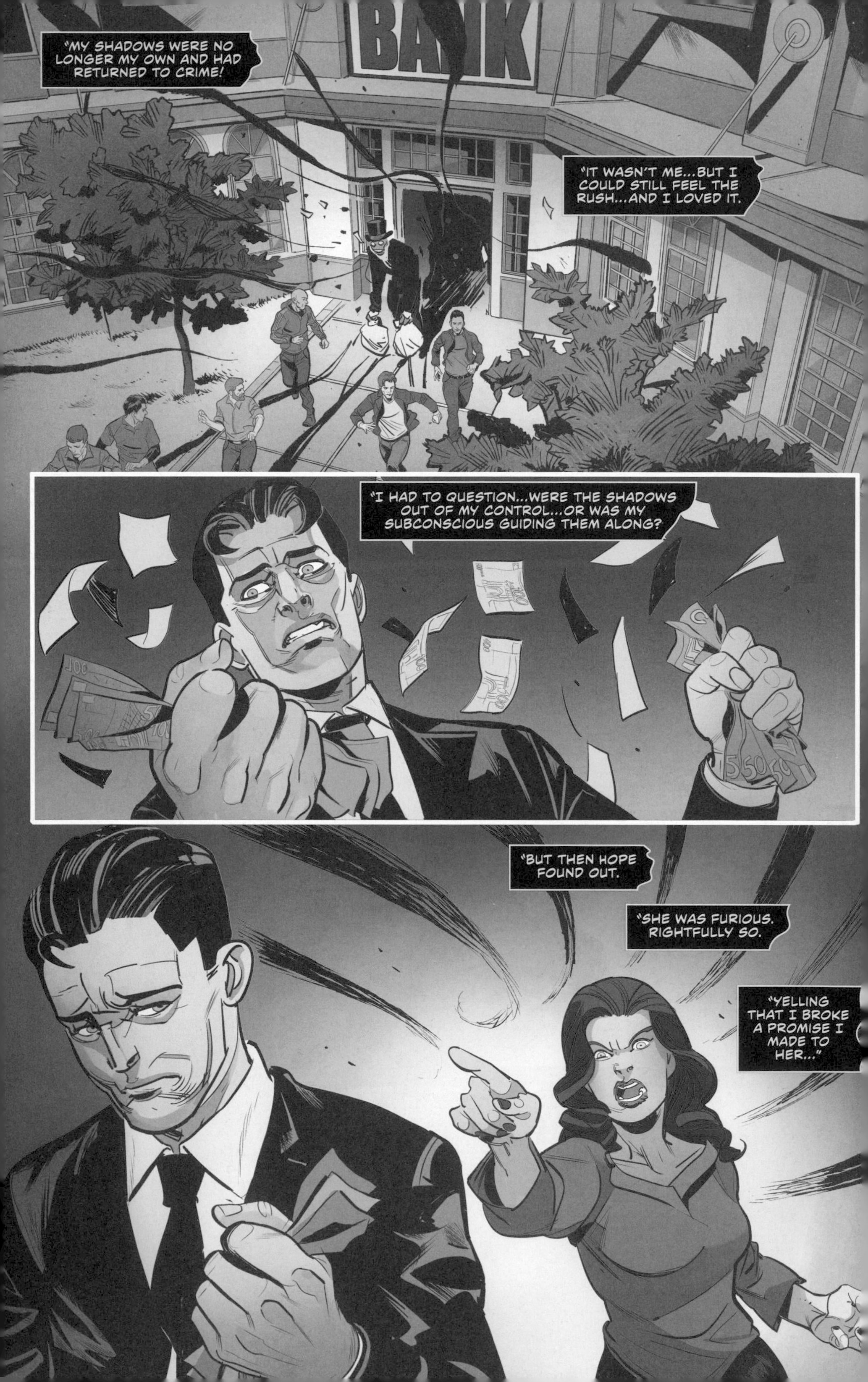

BANK
"MY SHADOWS WERE NO LONGER MY OWN AND HAD RETURNED TO CRIME!
"IT WASN'T ME...BUT I COULD STILL FEEL THE RUSH...AND I LOVED IT.
"I HAD TO QUESTION...WERE THE SHADOWS OUT OF MY CONTROL...OR WAS MY SUBCONSCIOUS GUIDING THEM ALONG?
"BUT THEN HOPE FOUND OUT.
"SHE WAS FURIOUS. RIGHTFULLY SO.
"YELLING THAT I BROKE A PROMISE I MADE TO HER..."

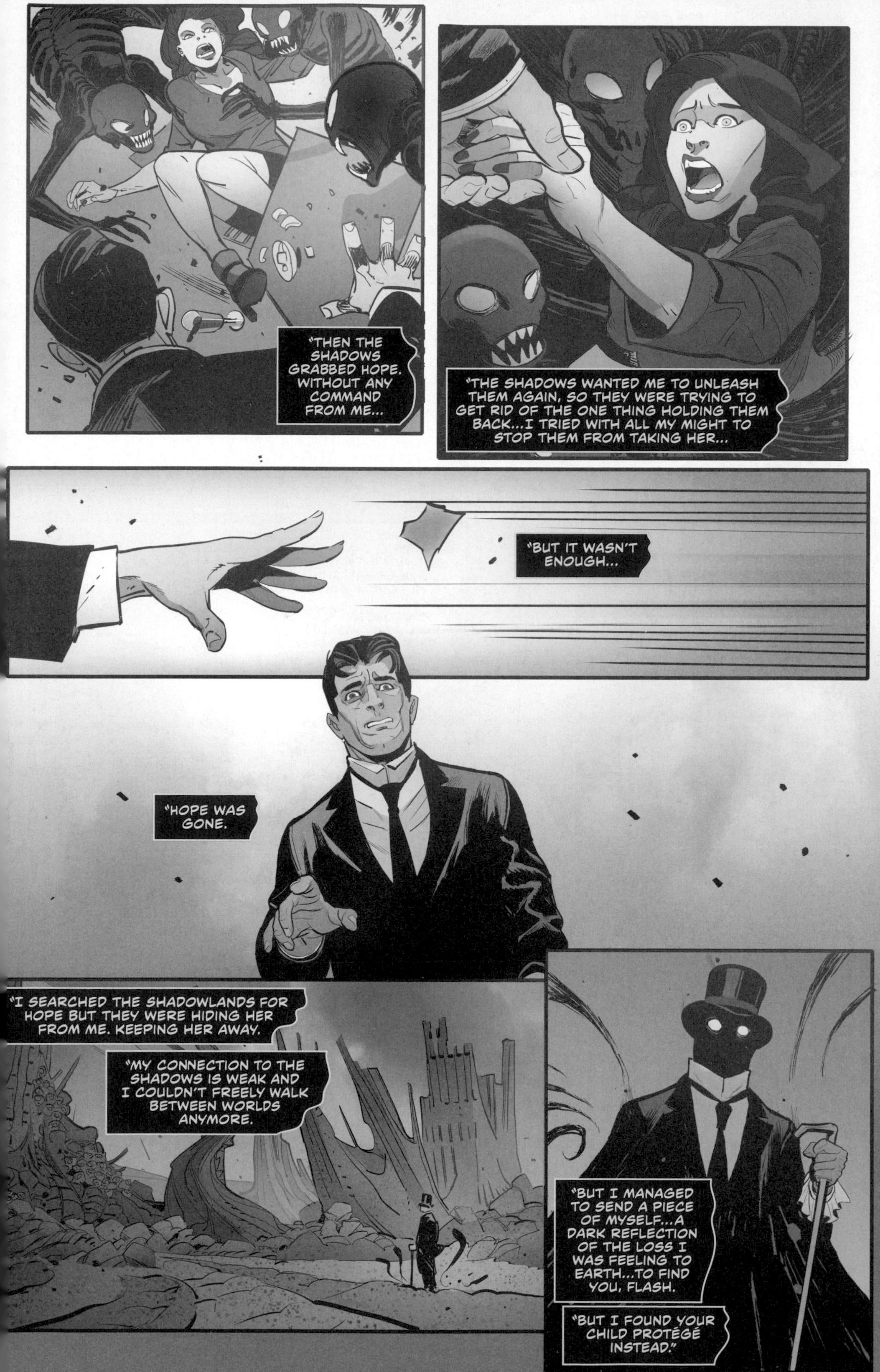
"THEN THE SHADOWS GRABBED HOPE. WITHOUT ANY COMMAND FROM ME...
"THE SHADOWS WANTED ME TO UNLEASH THEM AGAIN, SO THEY WERE TRYING TO GET RID OF THE ONE THING HOLDING THEM BACK...I TRIED WITH ALL MY MIGHT TO STOP THEM FROM TAKING HER...
"BUT IT WASN'T ENOUGH...
"HOPE WAS GONE.
"I SEARCHED THE SHADOWLANDS FOR HOPE BUT THEY WERE HIDING HER FROM ME. KEEPING HER AWAY.
"MY CONNECTION TO THE SHADOWS IS WEAK AND I COULDN'T FREELY WALK BETWEEN WORLDS ANYMORE.
"BUT I MANAGED TO SEND A PIECE OF MYSELF...A DARK REFLECTION OF THE LOSS I WAS FEELING TO EARTH...TO FIND YOU, FLASH.
"BUT I FOUND YOUR CHILD PROTÉGÉ INSTEAD."

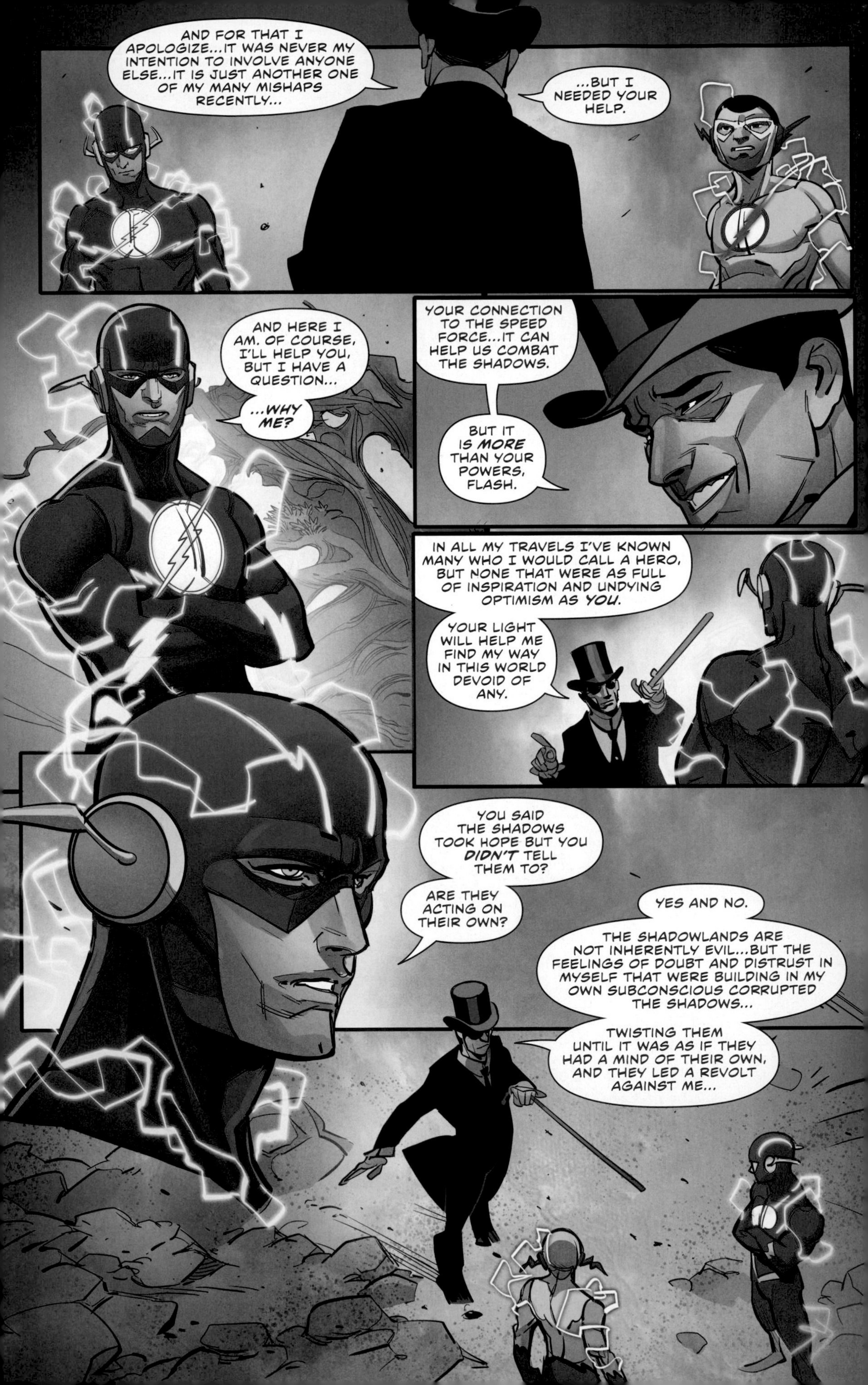

AND FOR THAT I APOLOGIZE...IT WAS NEVER MY INTENTION TO INVOLVE ANYONE ELSE...IT IS JUST ANOTHER ONE OF MY MANY MISHAPS RECENTLY...
...BUT I NEEDED YOUR HELP.
AND HERE I AM. OF COURSE, I'LL HELP YOU, BUT I HAVE A QUESTION...
...WHY ME?
YOUR CONNECTION TO THE SPEED FORCE...IT CAN HELP US COMBAT THE SHADOWS.
BUT IT IS MORE THAN YOUR POWERS, FLASH.
IN ALL MY TRAVELS I'VE KNOWN MANY WHO I WOULD CALL A HERO, BUT NONE THAT WERE AS FULL OF INSPIRATION AND UNDYING OPTIMISM AS YOU.
YOUR LIGHT WILL HELP ME FIND MY WAY IN THIS WORLD DEVOID OF ANY.
YOU SAID THE SHADOWS TOOK HOPE BUT YOU DIDN'T TELL THEM TO?
ARE THEY ACTING ON THEIR OWN?
YES AND NO.
THE SHADOWLANDS ARE NOT INHERENTLY EVIL...BUT THE FEELINGS OF DOUBT AND DISTRUST IN MYSELF THAT WERE BUILDING IN MY OWN SUBCONSCIOUS CORRUPTED THE SHADOWS...
TWISTING THEM UNTIL IT WAS AS IF THEY HAD A MIND OF THEIR OWN, AND THEY LED A REVOLT AGAINST ME...

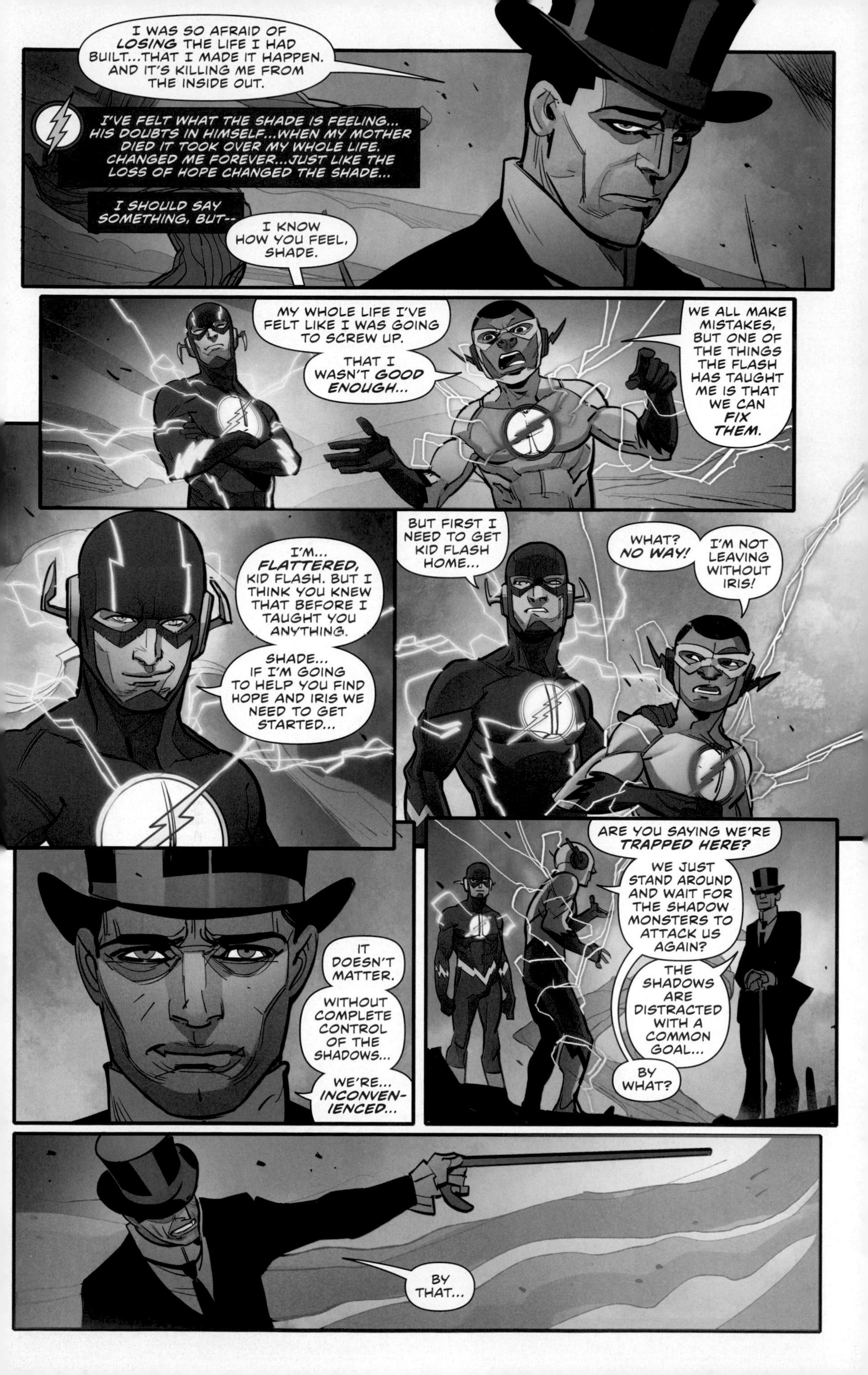
I WAS SO AFRAID OF LOSING THE LIFE I HAD BUILT...THAT I MADE IT HAPPEN. AND IT'S KILLING ME FROM THE INSIDE OUT.
I'VE FELT WHAT THE SHADE IS FEELING... HIS DOUBTS IN HIMSELF...WHEN MY MOTHER DIED IT TOOK OVER MY WHOLE LIFE. CHANGED ME FOREVER...JUST LIKE THE LOSS OF HOPE CHANGED THE SHADE...
I SHOULD SAY SOMETHING, BUT--
I KNOW HOW YOU FEEL, SHADE.
MY WHOLE LIFE I'VE FELT LIKE I WAS GOING TO SCREW UP.
THAT I WASN'T GOOD ENOUGH...
WE ALL MAKE MISTAKES, BUT ONE OF THE THINGS THE FLASH HAS TAUGHT ME IS THAT WE CAN FIX THEM.
I'M... FLATTERED, KID FLASH. BUT I THINK YOU KNEW THAT BEFORE I TAUGHT YOU ANYTHING.
SHADE... IF I'M GOING TO HELP YOU FIND HOPE AND IRIS WE NEED TO GET STARTED...
BUT FIRST I NEED TO GET KID FLASH HOME...
WHAT? NO WAY!
I'M NOT LEAVING WITHOUT IRIS!
IT DOESN'T MATTER.
WITHOUT COMPLETE CONTROL OF THE SHADOWS...
WE'RE... INCONVEN-IENCED...
ARE YOU SAYING WE'RE TRAPPED HERE?
WE JUST STAND AROUND AND WAIT FOR THE SHADOW MONSTERS TO ATTACK US AGAIN?
THE SHADOWS ARE DISTRACTED WITH A COMMON GOAL...
BY WHAT?
BY THAT...

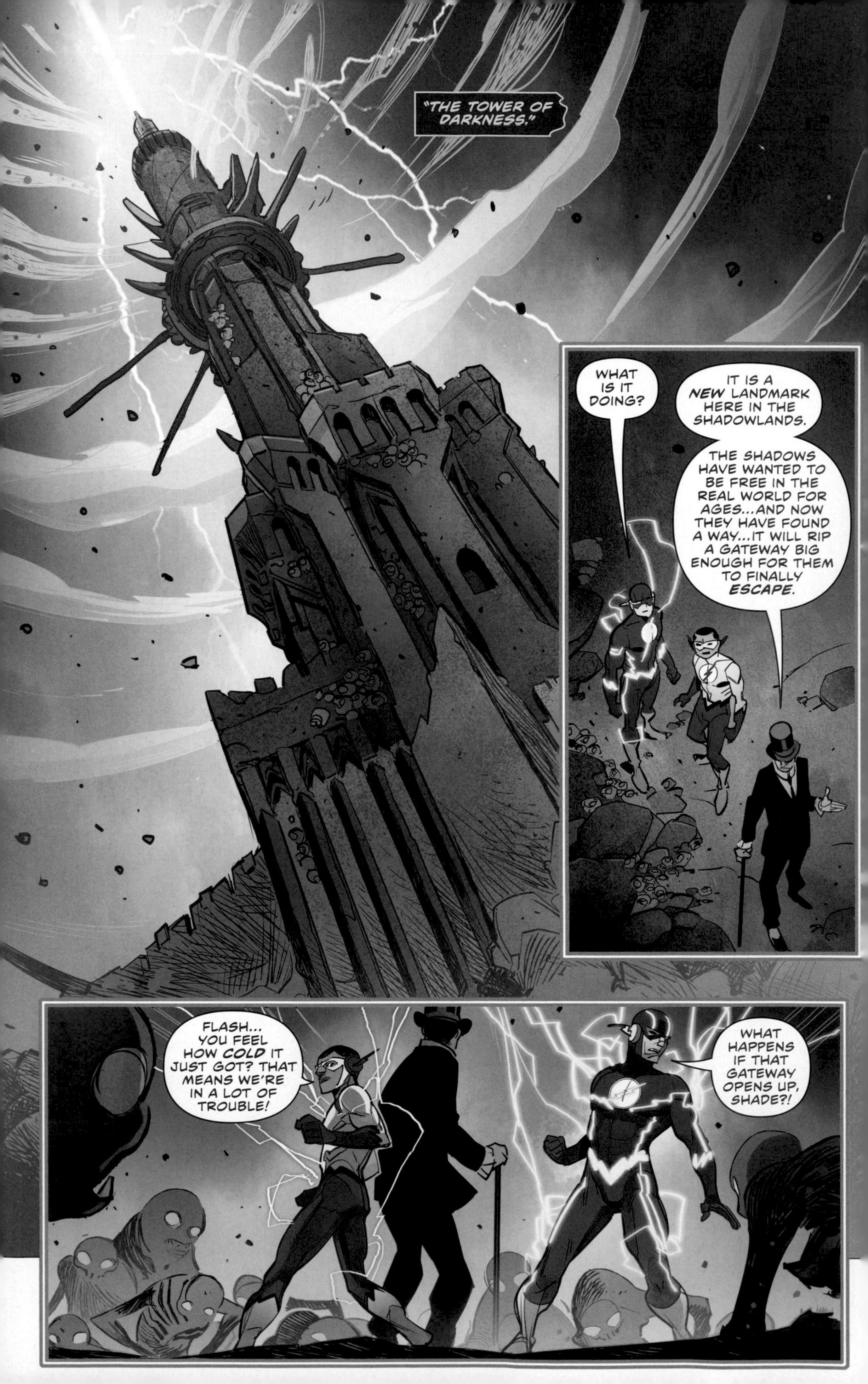
"THE TOWER OF DARKNESS."
WHAT IS IT DOING?
IT IS A NEW LANDMARK HERE IN THE SHADOWLANDS.
THE SHADOWS HAVE WANTED TO BE FREE IN THE REAL WORLD FOR AGES...AND NOW THEY HAVE FOUND A WAY...IT WILL RIP A GATEWAY BIG ENOUGH FOR THEM TO FINALLY ESCAPE.
FLASH... YOU FEEL HOW COLD IT JUST GOT? THAT MEANS WE'RE IN A LOT OF TROUBLE!
WHAT HAPPENS IF THAT GATEWAY OPENS UP, SHADE?!

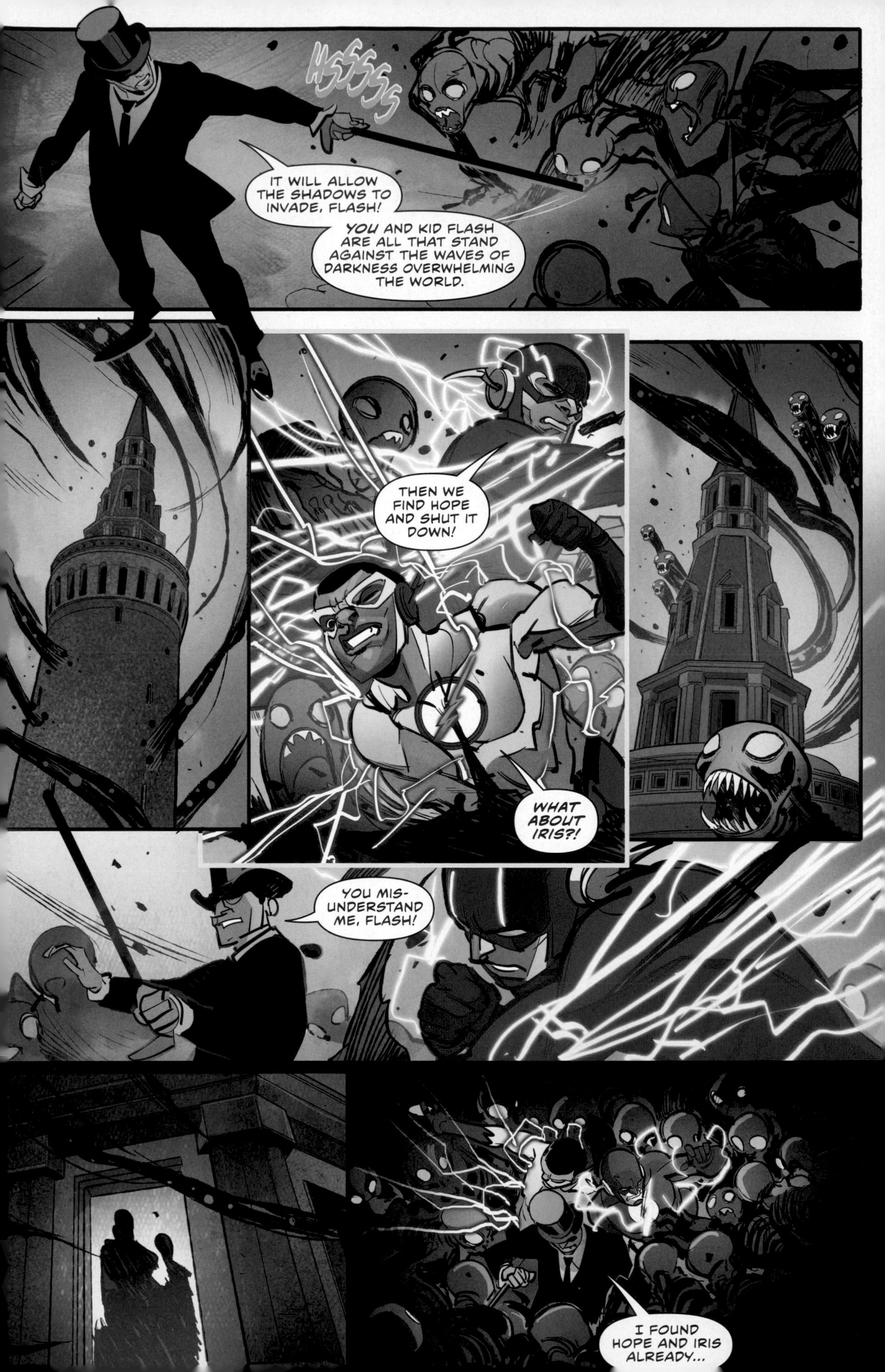
HSSSSS
IT WILL ALLOW THE SHADOWS TO INVADE, FLASH!
YOU AND KID FLASH ARE ALL THAT STAND AGAINST THE WAVES OF DARKNESS OVERWHELMING THE WORLD.
THEN WE FIND HOPE AND SHUT IT DOWN!
WHAT ABOUT IRIS?!
YOU MIS-UNDERSTAND ME, FLASH!
I FOUND HOPE AND IRIS ALREADY...

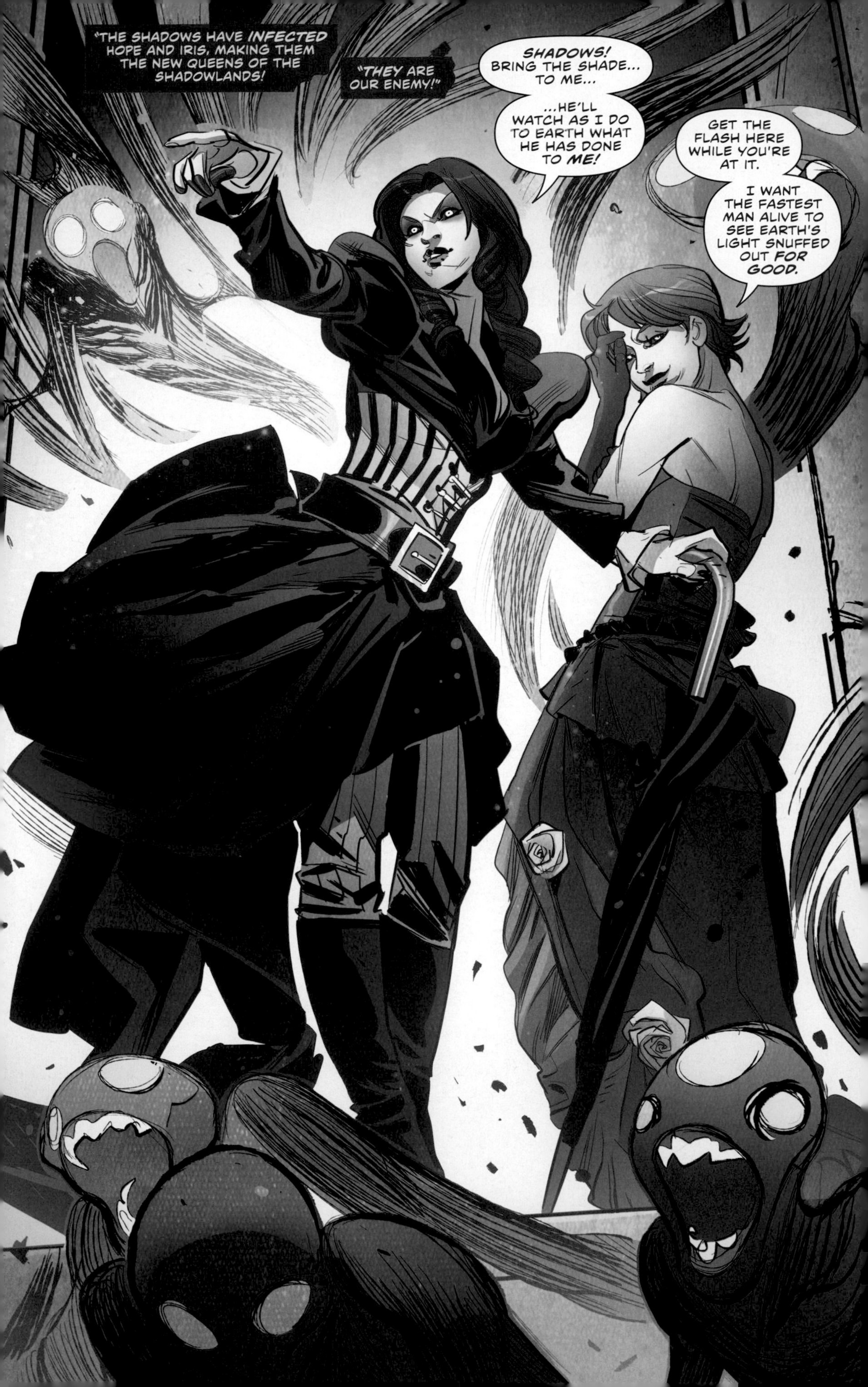
"THE SHADOWS HAVE INFECTED HOPE AND IRIS, MAKING THEM THE NEW QUEENS OF THE SHADOWLANDS!
"THEY ARE OUR ENEMY!"
SHADOWS! BRING THE SHADE... TO ME...
...HE'LL WATCH AS I DO TO EARTH WHAT HE HAS DONE TO ME!
GET THE FLASH HERE WHILE YOU'RE AT IT.
I WANT THE FASTEST MAN ALIVE TO SEE EARTH'S LIGHT SNUFFED OUT FOR GOOD.

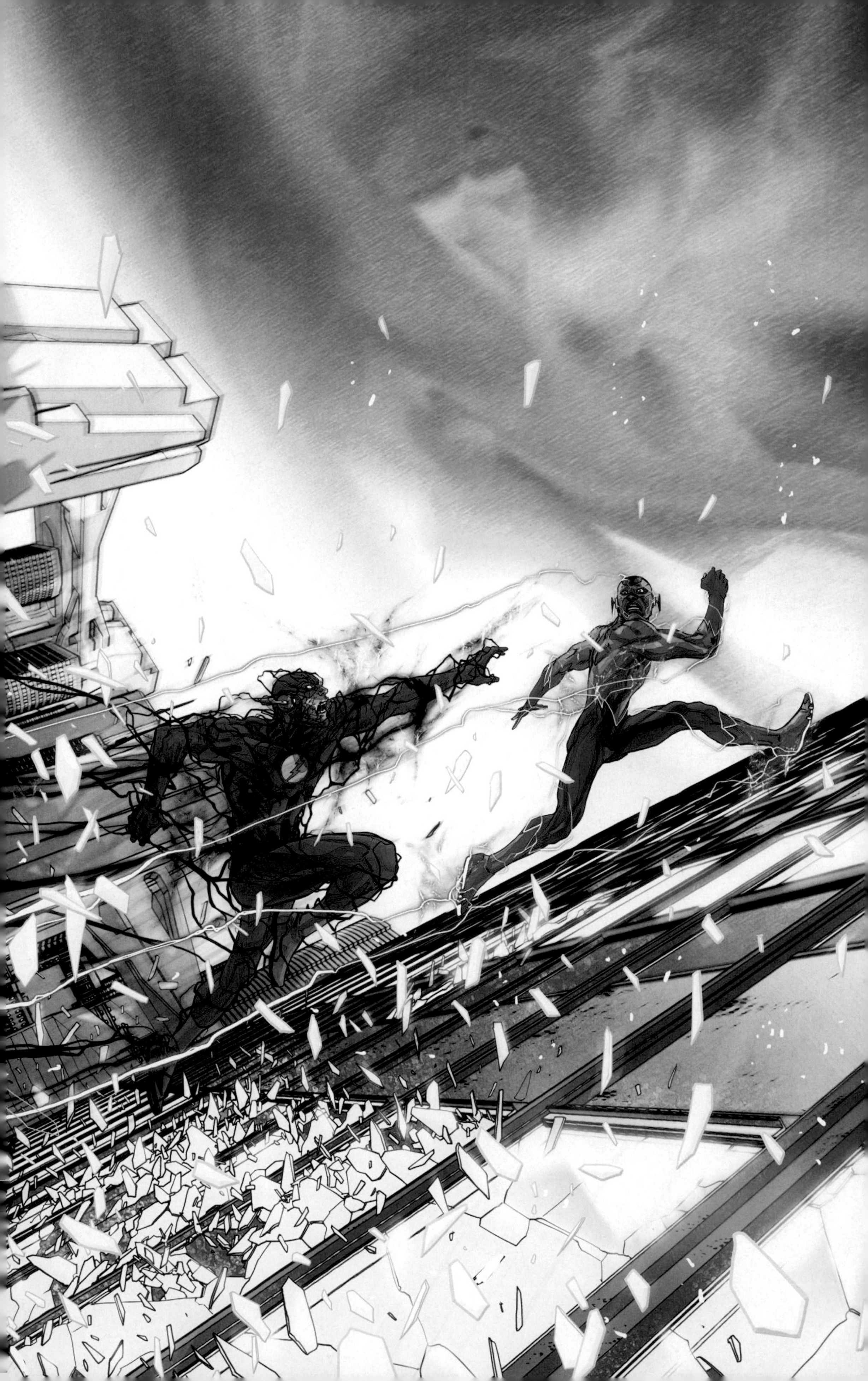

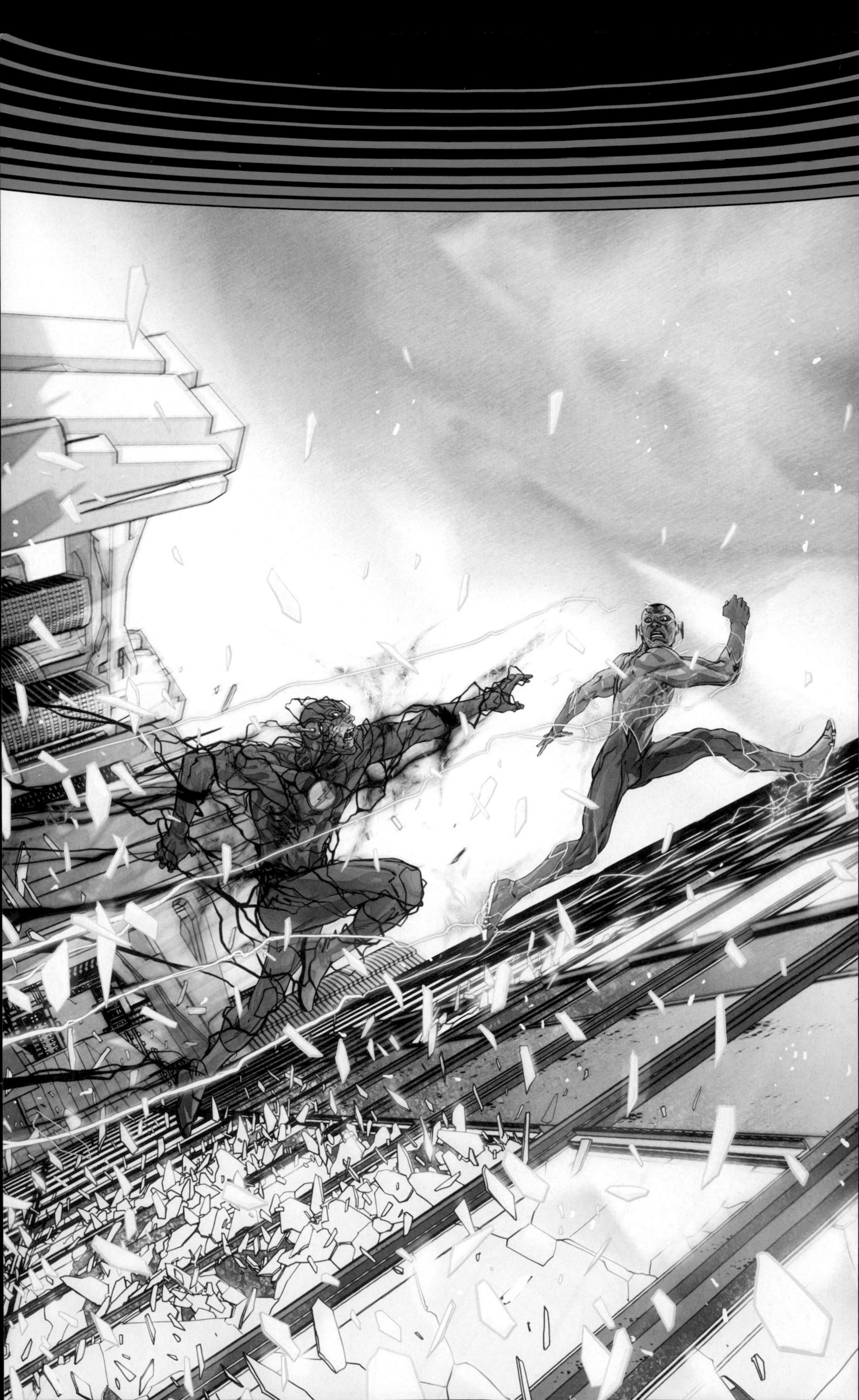

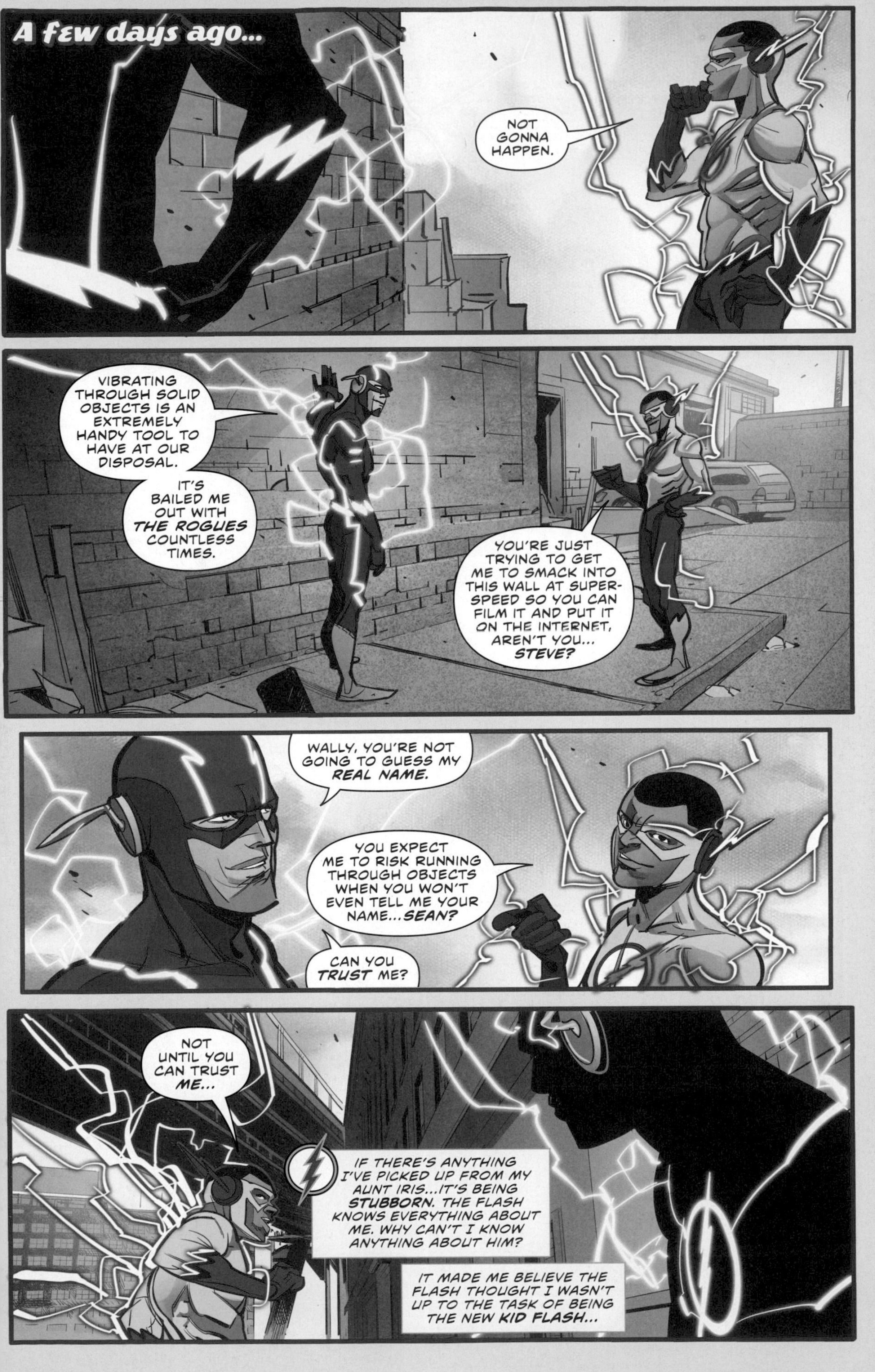
A few days ago...
NOT GONNA HAPPEN.
VIBRATING THROUGH SOLID OBJECTS IS AN EXTREMELY HANDY TOOL TO HAVE AT OUR DISPOSAL.
IT'S BAILED ME OUT WITH *THE ROGUES* COUNTLESS TIMES.
YOU'RE JUST TRYING TO GET ME TO SMACK INTO THIS WALL AT SUPER-SPEED SO YOU CAN FILM IT AND PUT IT ON THE INTERNET, AREN'T YOU... ***STEVE?***
WALLY, YOU'RE NOT GOING TO GUESS MY ***REAL NAME.***
YOU EXPECT ME TO RISK RUNNING THROUGH OBJECTS WHEN YOU WON'T EVEN TELL ME YOUR NAME... ***SEAN?***
CAN YOU ***TRUST*** ME?
NOT UNTIL YOU CAN TRUST ***ME...***
IF THERE'S ANYTHING I'VE PICKED UP FROM MY AUNT IRIS...IT'S BEING **STUBBORN**. THE FLASH KNOWS EVERYTHING ABOUT ME. WHY CAN'T I KNOW ANYTHING ABOUT HIM?
IT MADE ME BELIEVE THE FLASH THOUGHT I WASN'T UP TO THE TASK OF BEING THE NEW ***KID FLASH...***

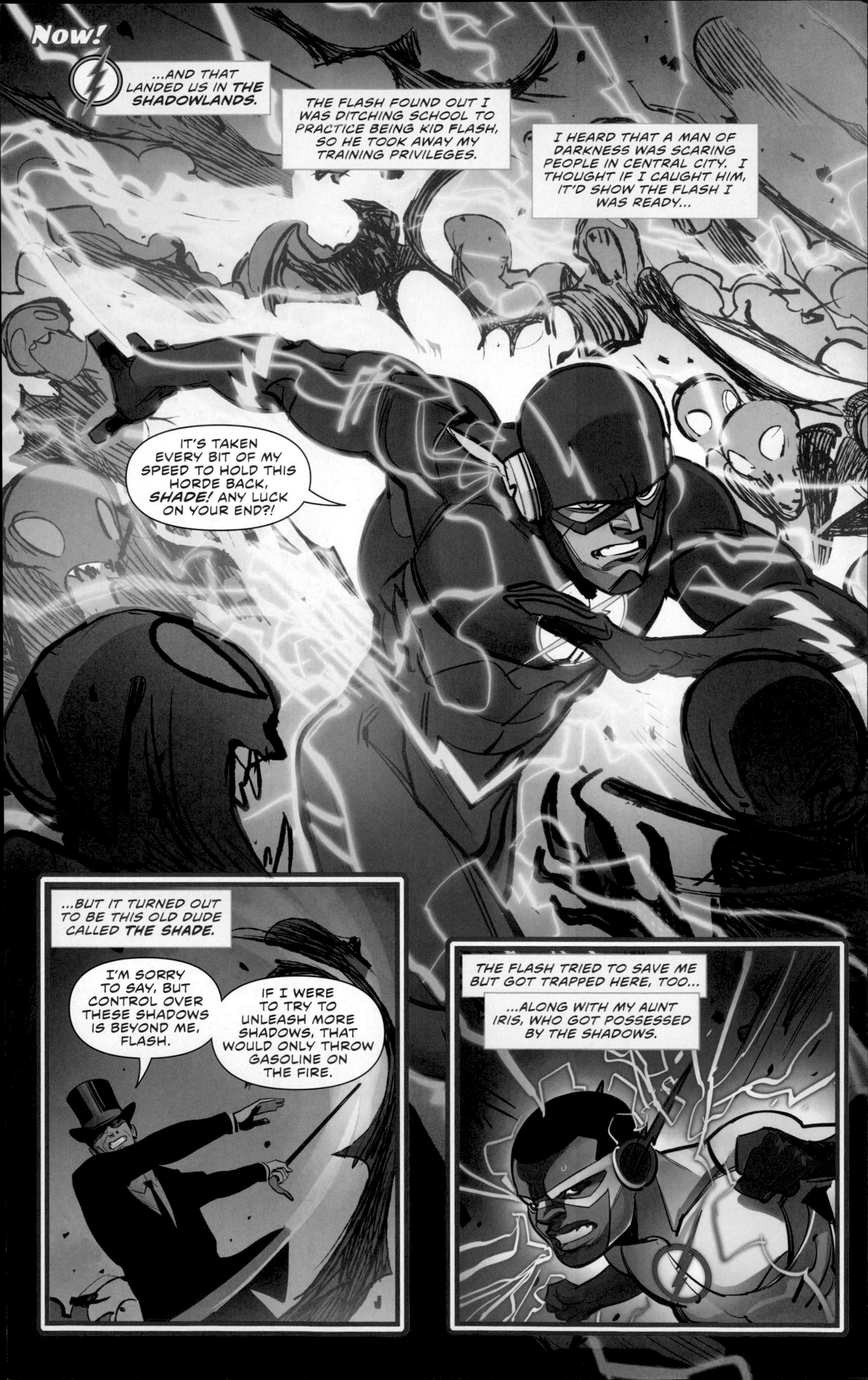
NOW!
...AND THAT LANDED US IN THE SHADOWLANDS.
THE FLASH FOUND OUT I WAS DITCHING SCHOOL TO PRACTICE BEING KID FLASH, SO HE TOOK AWAY MY TRAINING PRIVILEGES.
I HEARD THAT A MAN OF DARKNESS WAS SCARING PEOPLE IN CENTRAL CITY. I THOUGHT IF I CAUGHT HIM, IT'D SHOW THE FLASH I WAS READY...
IT'S TAKEN EVERY BIT OF MY SPEED TO HOLD THIS HORDE BACK, SHADE! ANY LUCK ON YOUR END?!
...BUT IT TURNED OUT TO BE THIS OLD DUDE CALLED THE SHADE.
I'M SORRY TO SAY, BUT CONTROL OVER THESE SHADOWS IS BEYOND ME, FLASH.
IF I WERE TO TRY TO UNLEASH MORE SHADOWS, THAT WOULD ONLY THROW GASOLINE ON THE FIRE.
THE FLASH TRIED TO SAVE ME BUT GOT TRAPPED HERE, TOO...
...ALONG WITH MY AUNT IRIS, WHO GOT POSSESSED BY THE SHADOWS.

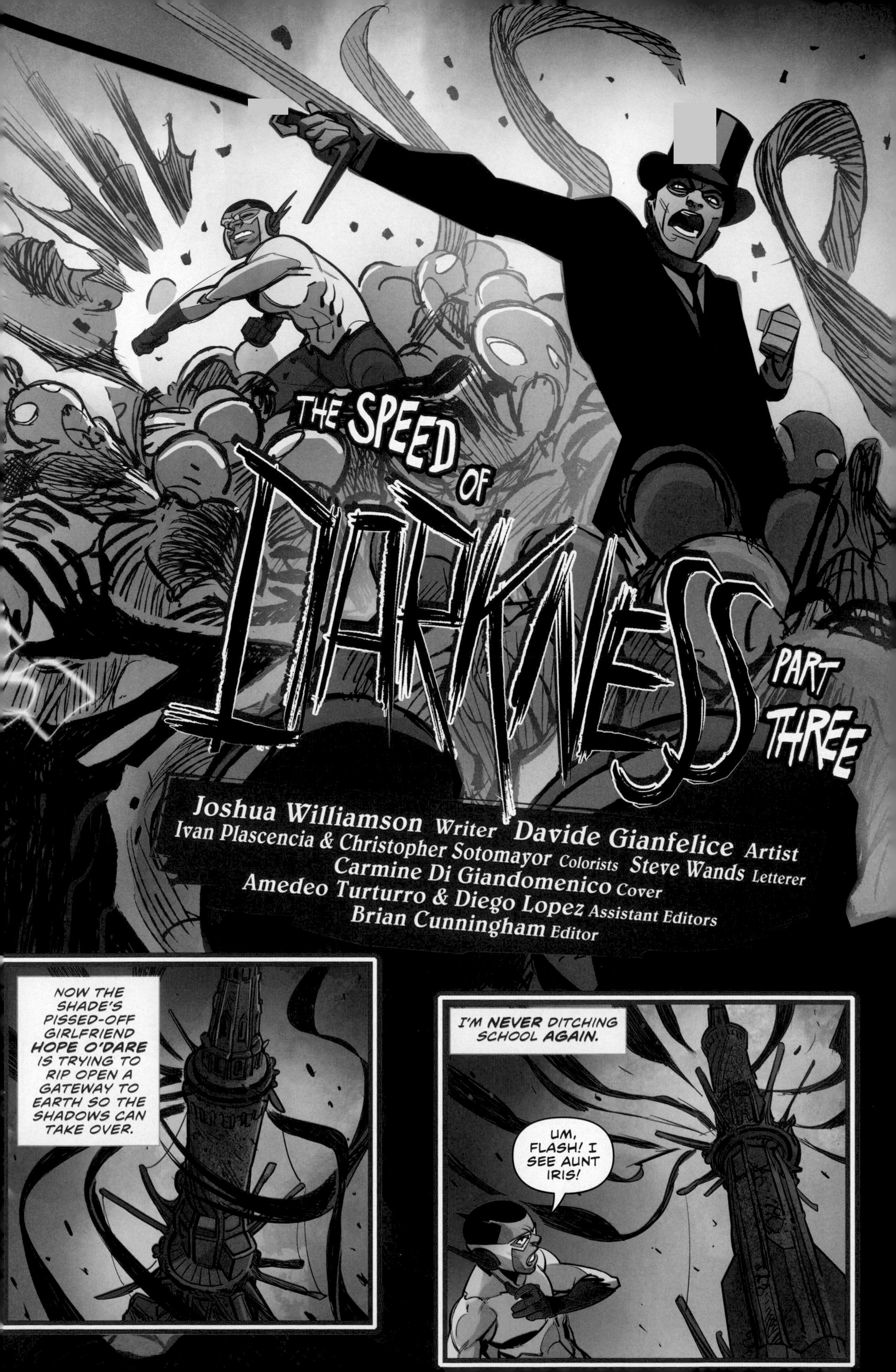
THE SPEED OF DARKNESS PART THREE
Joshua Williamson Writer Davide Gianfelice Artist
Ivan Plascencia & Christopher Sotomayor Colorists Steve Wands Letterer
Carmine Di Giandomenico Cover
Amedeo Turturro & Diego Lopez Assistant Editors
Brian Cunningham Editor
NOW THE SHADE'S PISSED-OFF GIRLFRIEND HOPE O'DARE IS TRYING TO RIP OPEN A GATEWAY TO EARTH SO THE SHADOWS CAN TAKE OVER.
I'M NEVER DITCHING SCHOOL AGAIN.
UM, FLASH! I SEE AUNT IRIS!

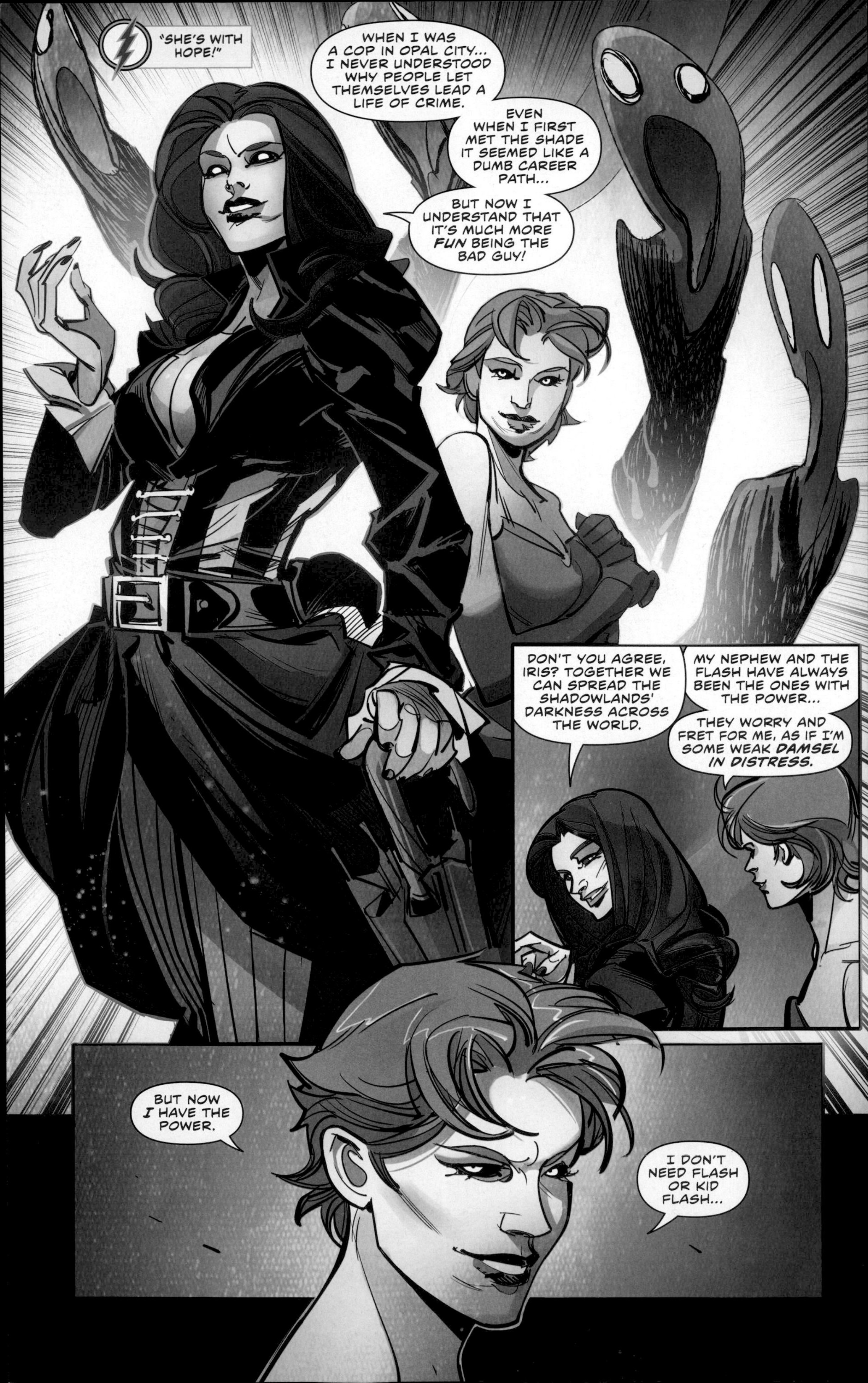
"SHE'S WITH HOPE!"
WHEN I WAS A COP IN OPAL CITY... I NEVER UNDERSTOOD WHY PEOPLE LET THEMSELVES LEAD A LIFE OF CRIME.
EVEN WHEN I FIRST MET THE SHADE IT SEEMED LIKE A DUMB CAREER PATH...
BUT NOW I UNDERSTAND THAT IT'S MUCH MORE FUN BEING THE BAD GUY!
DON'T YOU AGREE, IRIS? TOGETHER WE CAN SPREAD THE SHADOWLANDS' DARKNESS ACROSS THE WORLD.
MY NEPHEW AND THE FLASH HAVE ALWAYS BEEN THE ONES WITH THE POWER...
THEY WORRY AND FRET FOR ME, AS IF I'M SOME WEAK DAMSEL IN DISTRESS.
BUT NOW I HAVE THE POWER.
I DON'T NEED FLASH OR KID FLASH...

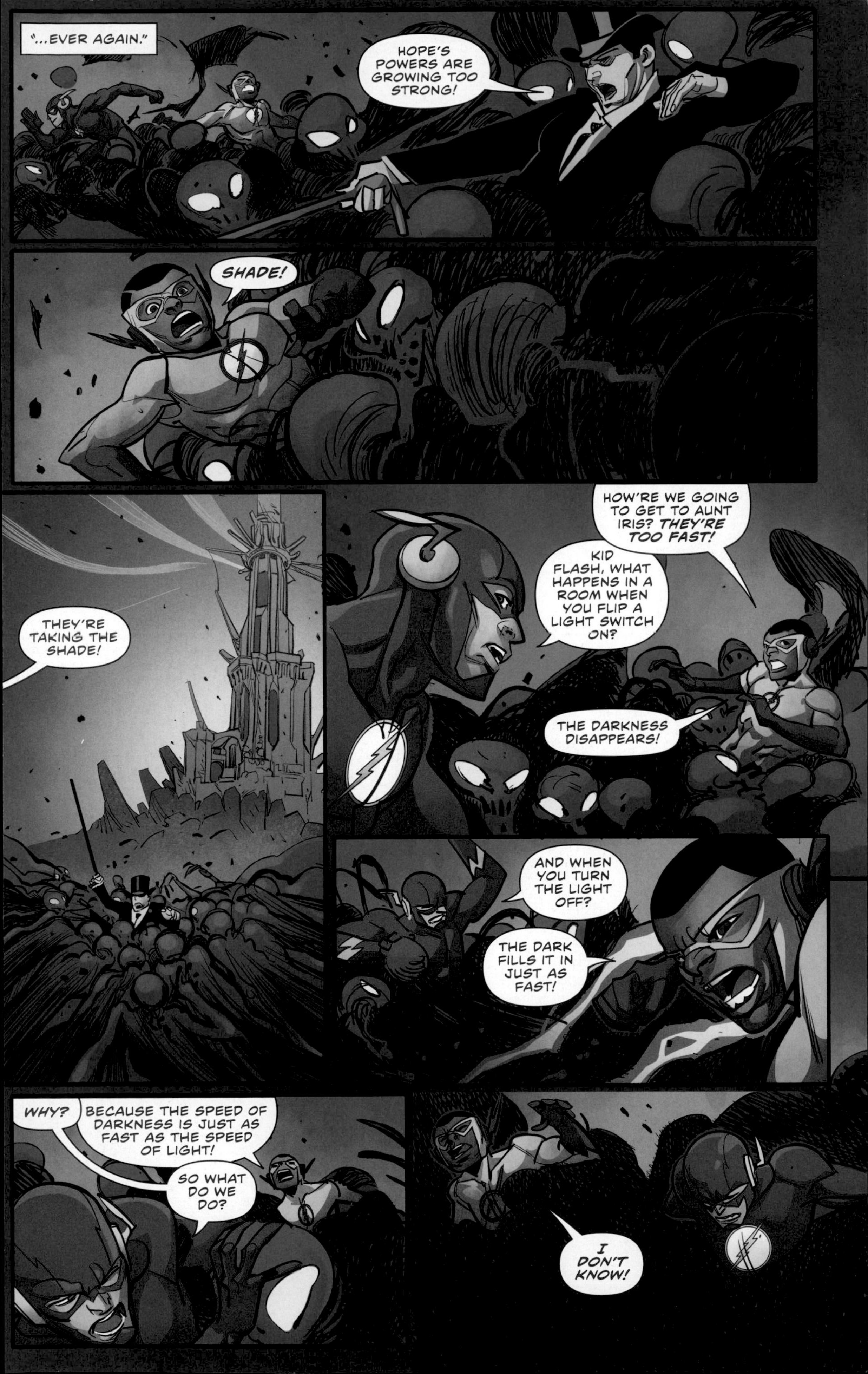
"...EVER AGAIN."
HOPE'S POWERS ARE GROWING TOO STRONG!
SHADE!
THEY'RE TAKING THE SHADE!
HOW'RE WE GOING TO GET TO AUNT IRIS? THEY'RE TOO FAST!
KID FLASH, WHAT HAPPENS IN A ROOM WHEN YOU FLIP A LIGHT SWITCH ON?
THE DARKNESS DISAPPEARS!
AND WHEN YOU TURN THE LIGHT OFF?
THE DARK FILLS IT IN JUST AS FAST!
WHY?
BECAUSE THE SPEED OF DARKNESS IS JUST AS FAST AS THE SPEED OF LIGHT!
SO WHAT DO WE DO?
I DON'T KNOW!

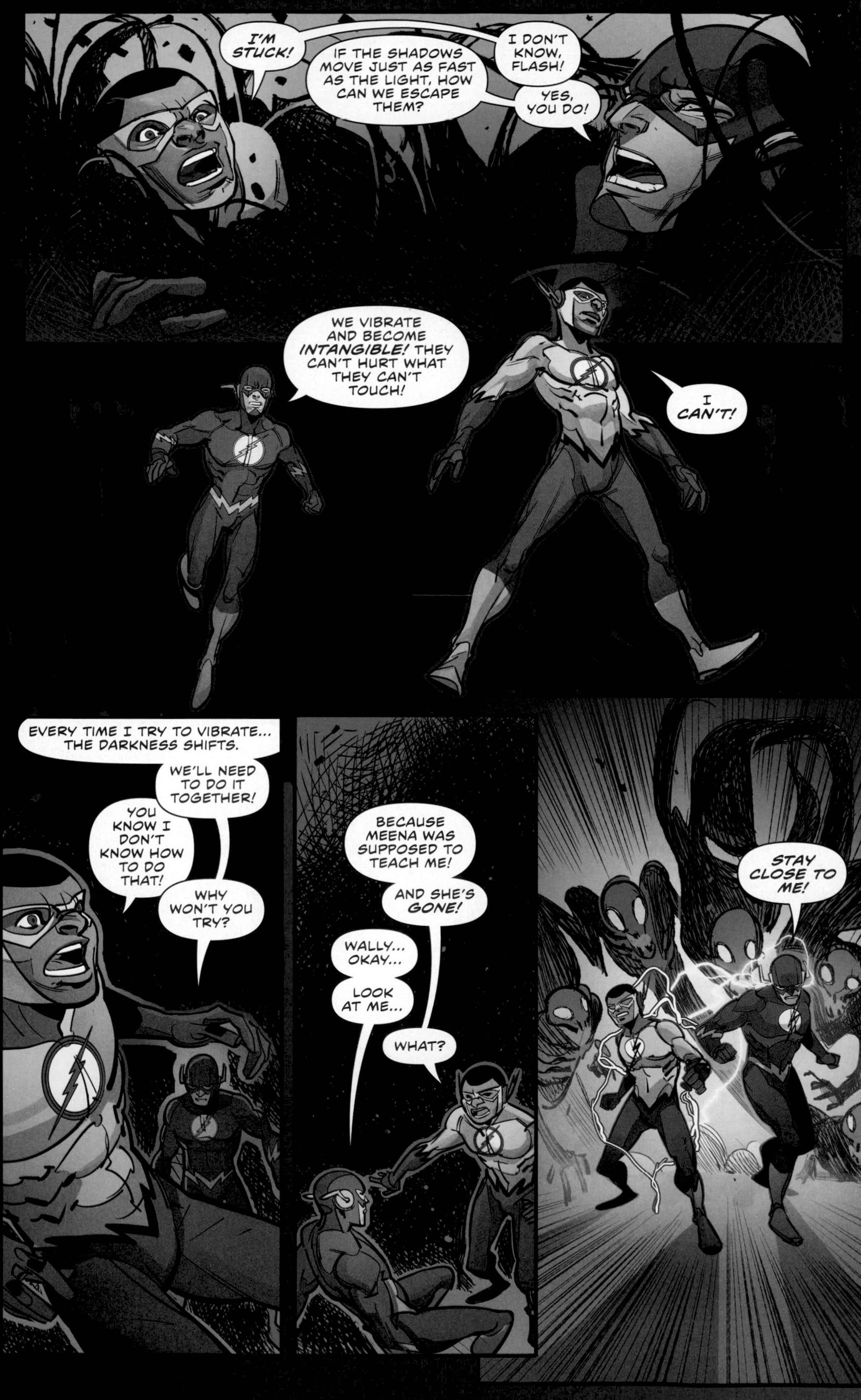
I'M STUCK!
IF THE SHADOWS MOVE JUST AS FAST AS THE LIGHT, HOW CAN WE ESCAPE THEM?
I DON'T KNOW, FLASH!
YES, YOU DO!
WE VIBRATE AND BECOME INTANGIBLE! THEY CAN'T HURT WHAT THEY CAN'T TOUCH!
I CAN'T!
EVERY TIME I TRY TO VIBRATE... THE DARKNESS SHIFTS.
WE'LL NEED TO DO IT TOGETHER!
YOU KNOW I DON'T KNOW HOW TO DO THAT!
WHY WON'T YOU TRY?
BECAUSE MEENA WAS SUPPOSED TO TEACH ME!
AND SHE'S GONE!
WALLY... OKAY...
LOOK AT ME...
WHAT?
STAY CLOSE TO ME!

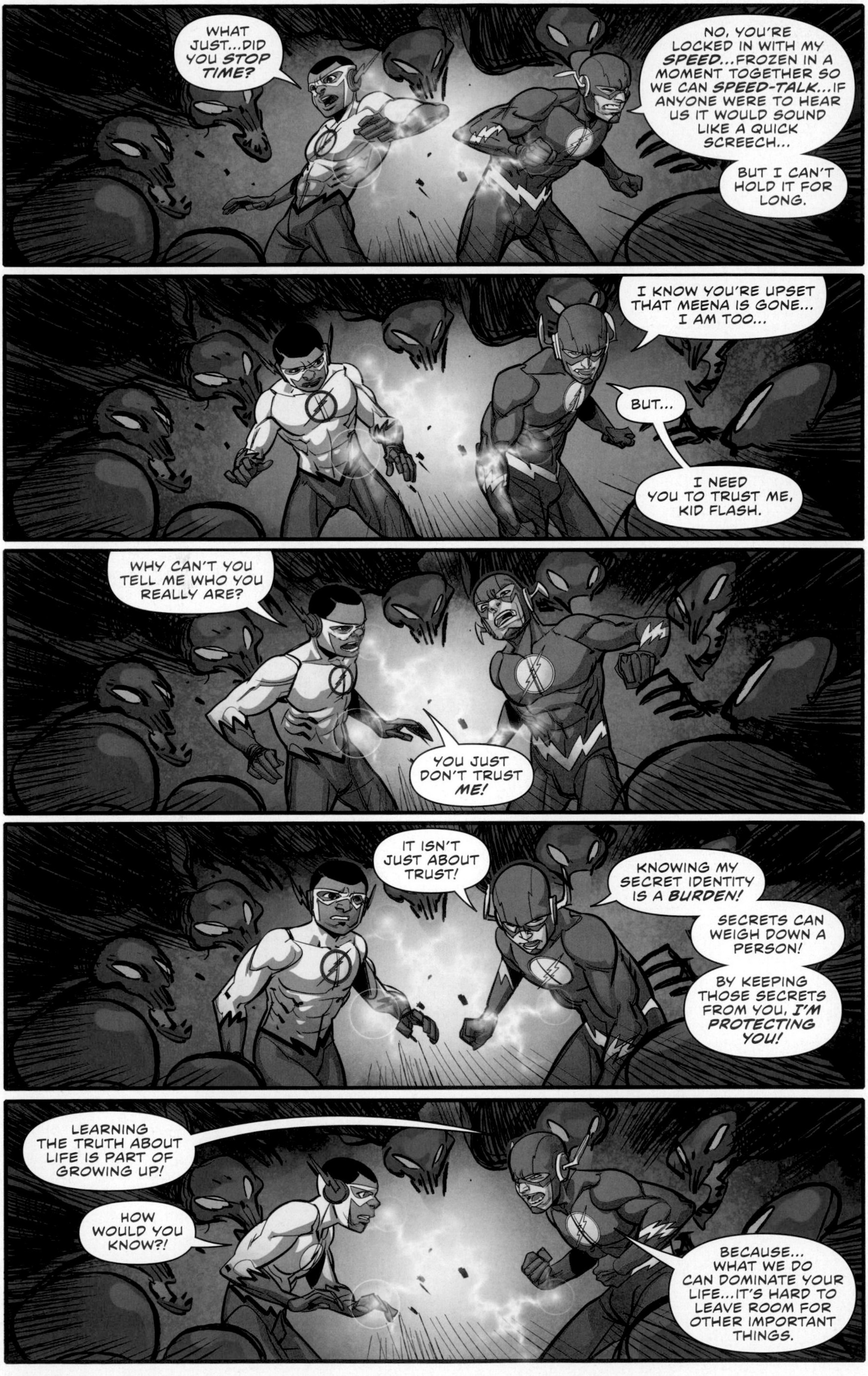
WHAT JUST...DID YOU STOP TIME?
NO, YOU'RE LOCKED IN WITH MY SPEED...FROZEN IN A MOMENT TOGETHER SO WE CAN SPEED-TALK...IF ANYONE WERE TO HEAR US IT WOULD SOUND LIKE A QUICK SCREECH...
BUT I CAN'T HOLD IT FOR LONG.
I KNOW YOU'RE UPSET THAT MEENA IS GONE... I AM TOO...
BUT...
I NEED YOU TO TRUST ME, KID FLASH.
WHY CAN'T YOU TELL ME WHO YOU REALLY ARE?
YOU JUST DON'T TRUST ME!
IT ISN'T JUST ABOUT TRUST!
KNOWING MY SECRET IDENTITY IS A BURDEN!
SECRETS CAN WEIGH DOWN A PERSON!
BY KEEPING THOSE SECRETS FROM YOU, I'M PROTECTING YOU!
LEARNING THE TRUTH ABOUT LIFE IS PART OF GROWING UP!
HOW WOULD YOU KNOW?!
BECAUSE... WHAT WE DO CAN DOMINATE YOUR LIFE...IT'S HARD TO LEAVE ROOM FOR OTHER IMPORTANT THINGS.

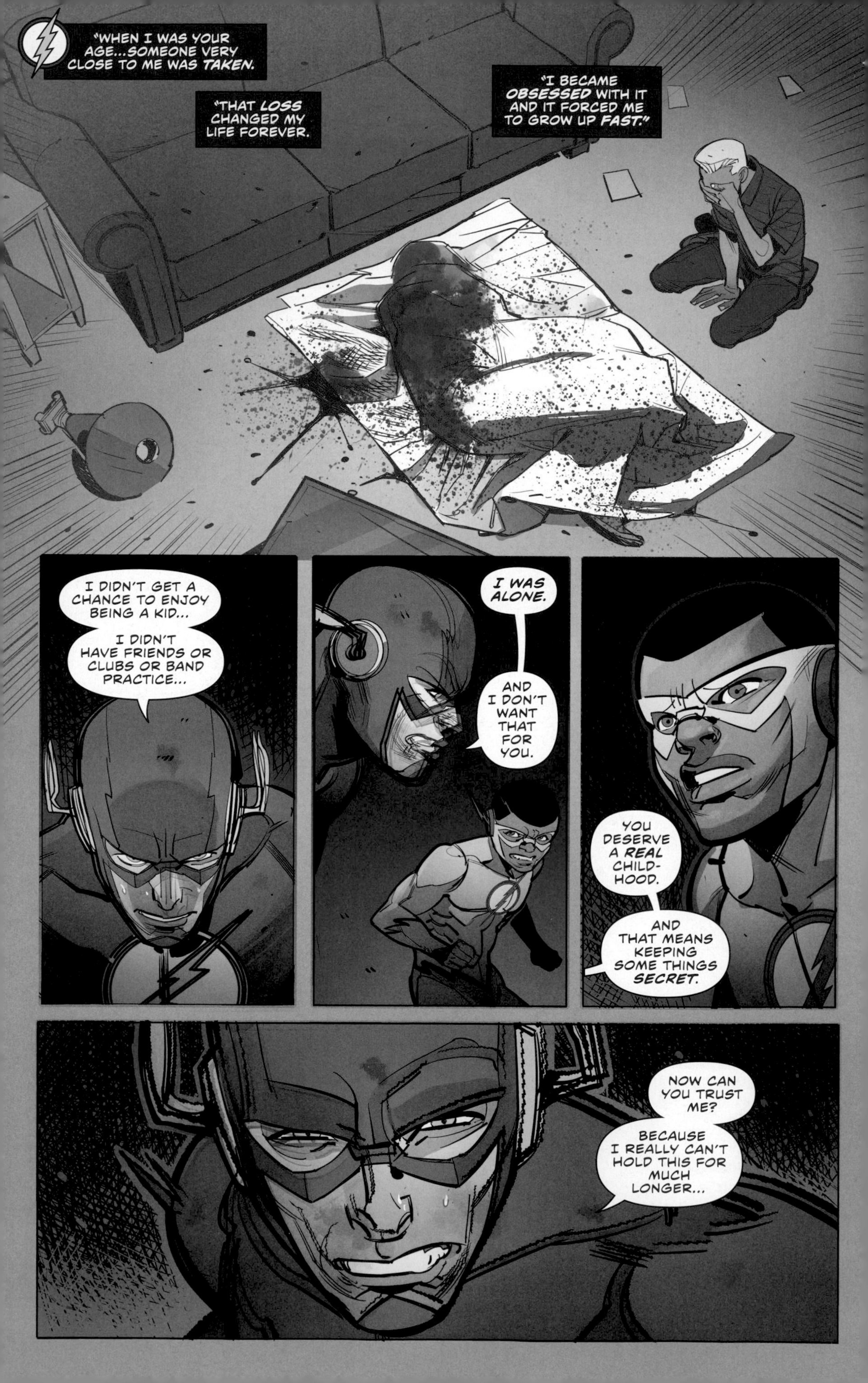
"WHEN I WAS YOUR AGE...SOMEONE VERY CLOSE TO ME WAS TAKEN.
"THAT LOSS CHANGED MY LIFE FOREVER.
"I BECAME OBSESSED WITH IT AND IT FORCED ME TO GROW UP FAST."
I DIDN'T GET A CHANCE TO ENJOY BEING A KID...
I DIDN'T HAVE FRIENDS OR CLUBS OR BAND PRACTICE...
I WAS ALONE.
AND I DON'T WANT THAT FOR YOU.
YOU DESERVE A REAL CHILD-HOOD.
AND THAT MEANS KEEPING SOME THINGS SECRET.
NOW CAN YOU TRUST ME?
BECAUSE I REALLY CAN'T HOLD THIS FOR MUCH LONGER...

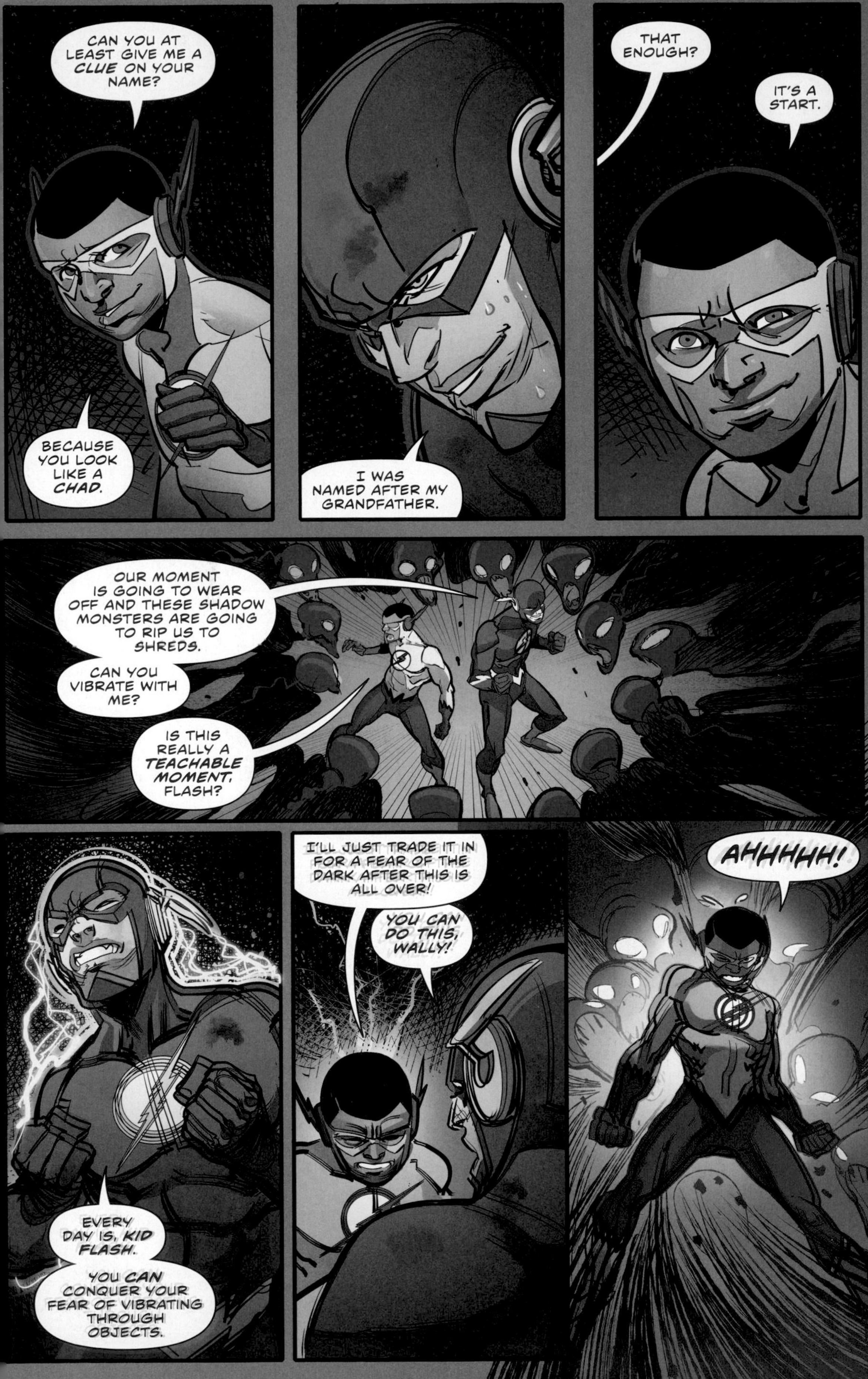
CAN YOU AT LEAST GIVE ME A CLUE ON YOUR NAME?
BECAUSE YOU LOOK LIKE A CHAD.
I WAS NAMED AFTER MY GRANDFATHER.
THAT ENOUGH?
IT'S A START.
OUR MOMENT IS GOING TO WEAR OFF AND THESE SHADOW MONSTERS ARE GOING TO RIP US TO SHREDS.
CAN YOU VIBRATE WITH ME?
IS THIS REALLY A TEACHABLE MOMENT, FLASH?
EVERY DAY IS, KID FLASH.
YOU CAN CONQUER YOUR FEAR OF VIBRATING THROUGH OBJECTS.
I'LL JUST TRADE IT IN FOR A FEAR OF THE DARK AFTER THIS IS ALL OVER!
YOU CAN DO THIS, WALLY!
AHHHHH!

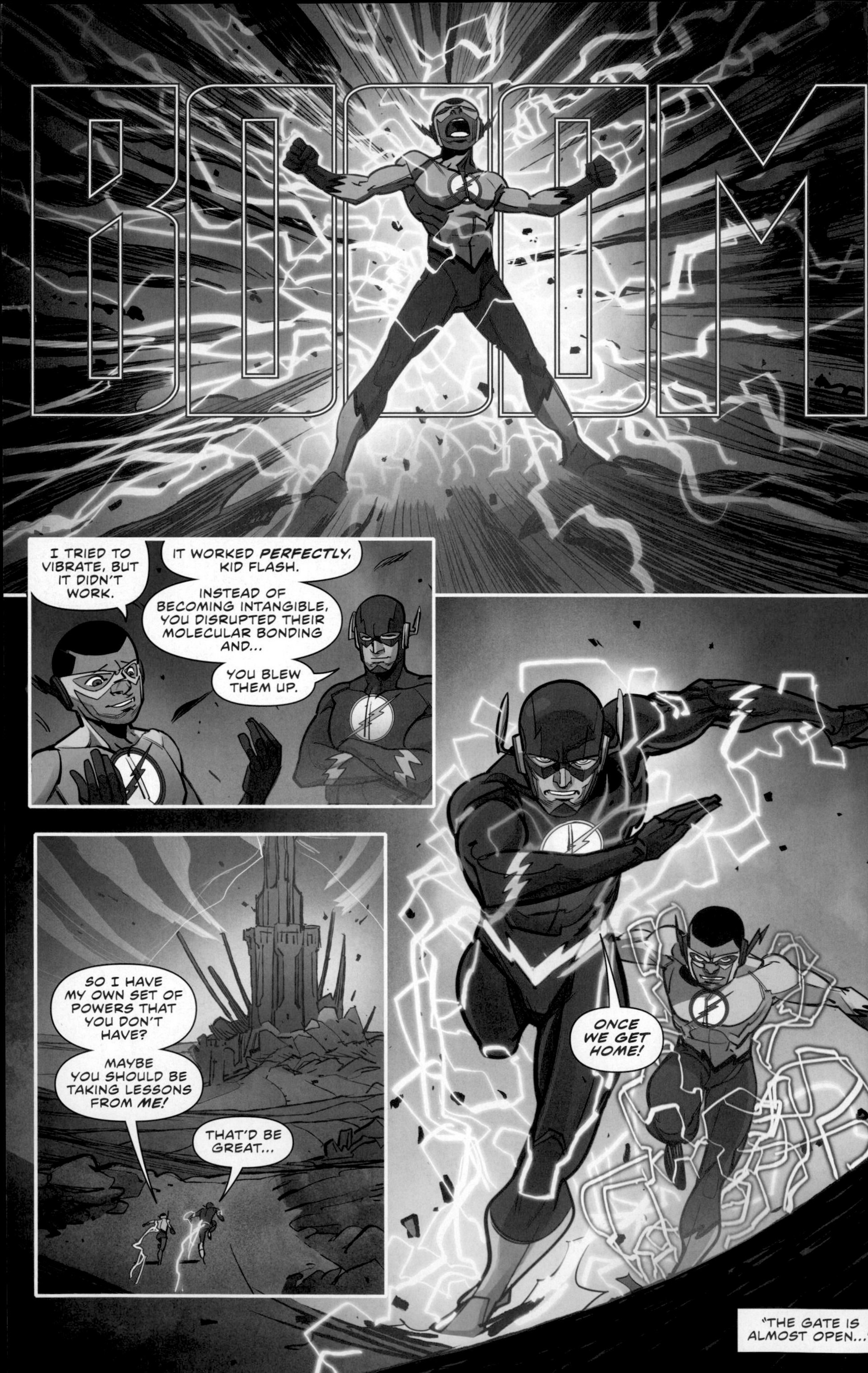
BOOOM
I TRIED TO VIBRATE, BUT IT DIDN'T WORK.
IT WORKED *PERFECTLY,* KID FLASH.
INSTEAD OF BECOMING INTANGIBLE, YOU DISRUPTED THEIR MOLECULAR BONDING AND...
YOU BLEW THEM UP.
SO I HAVE MY OWN SET OF POWERS THAT YOU DON'T HAVE?
MAYBE YOU SHOULD BE TAKING LESSONS FROM *ME!*
THAT'D BE GREAT...
ONCE WE GET HOME!
"THE GATE IS ALMOST OPEN...

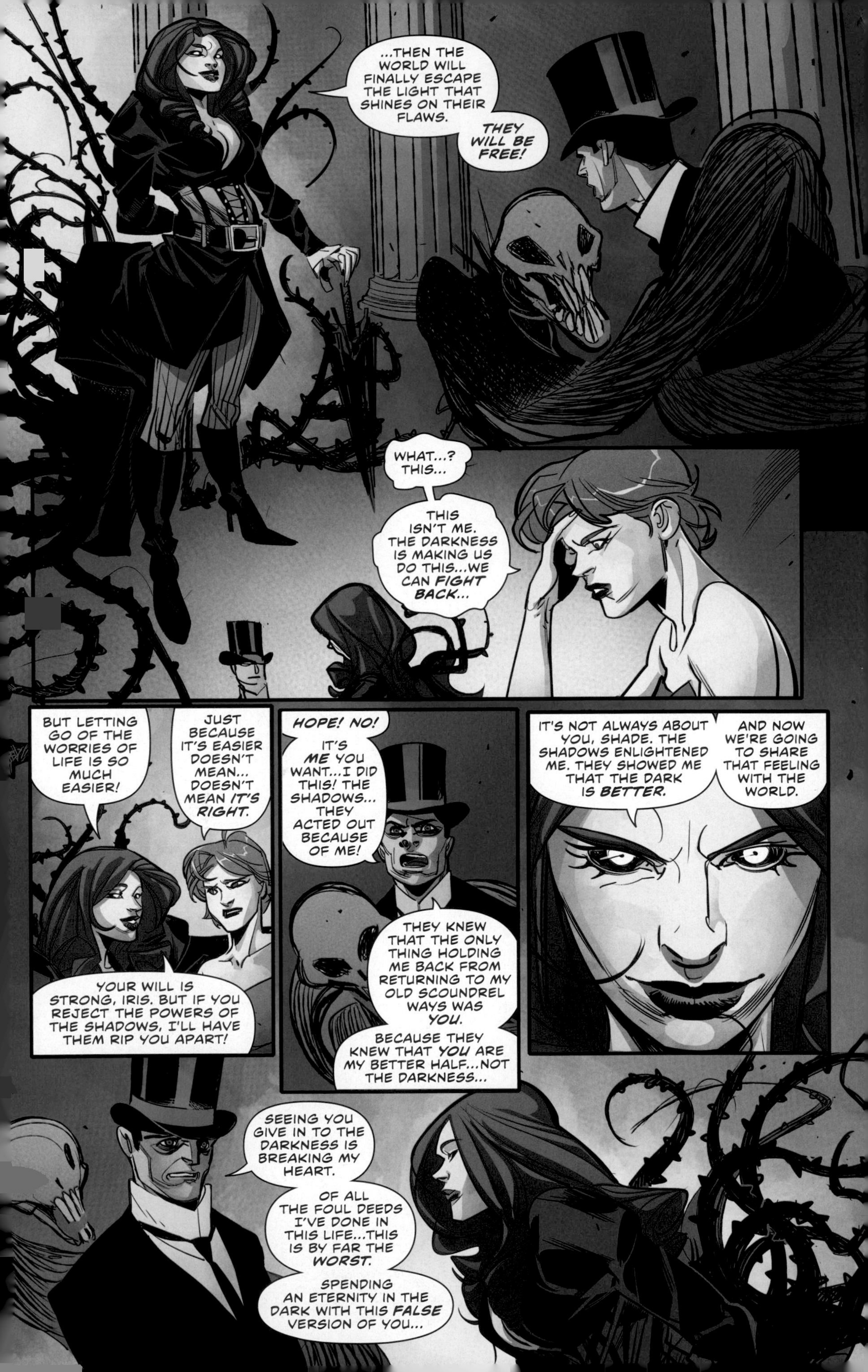
...THEN THE WORLD WILL FINALLY ESCAPE THE LIGHT THAT SHINES ON THEIR FLAWS.
THEY WILL BE FREE!
WHAT...? THIS...
THIS ISN'T ME. THE DARKNESS IS MAKING US DO THIS...WE CAN FIGHT BACK...
BUT LETTING GO OF THE WORRIES OF LIFE IS SO MUCH EASIER!
JUST BECAUSE IT'S EASIER DOESN'T MEAN... DOESN'T MEAN IT'S RIGHT.
YOUR WILL IS STRONG, IRIS. BUT IF YOU REJECT THE POWERS OF THE SHADOWS, I'LL HAVE THEM RIP YOU APART!
HOPE! NO!
IT'S ME YOU WANT...I DID THIS! THE SHADOWS... THEY ACTED OUT BECAUSE OF ME!
THEY KNEW THAT THE ONLY THING HOLDING ME BACK FROM RETURNING TO MY OLD SCOUNDREL WAYS WAS YOU.
BECAUSE THEY KNEW THAT YOU ARE MY BETTER HALF...NOT THE DARKNESS...
IT'S NOT ALWAYS ABOUT YOU, SHADE. THE SHADOWS ENLIGHTENED ME. THEY SHOWED ME THAT THE DARK IS BETTER.
AND NOW WE'RE GOING TO SHARE THAT FEELING WITH THE WORLD.
SEEING YOU GIVE IN TO THE DARKNESS IS BREAKING MY HEART.
OF ALL THE FOUL DEEDS I'VE DONE IN THIS LIFE...THIS IS BY FAR THE WORST.
SPENDING AN ETERNITY IN THE DARK WITH THIS FALSE VERSION OF YOU...

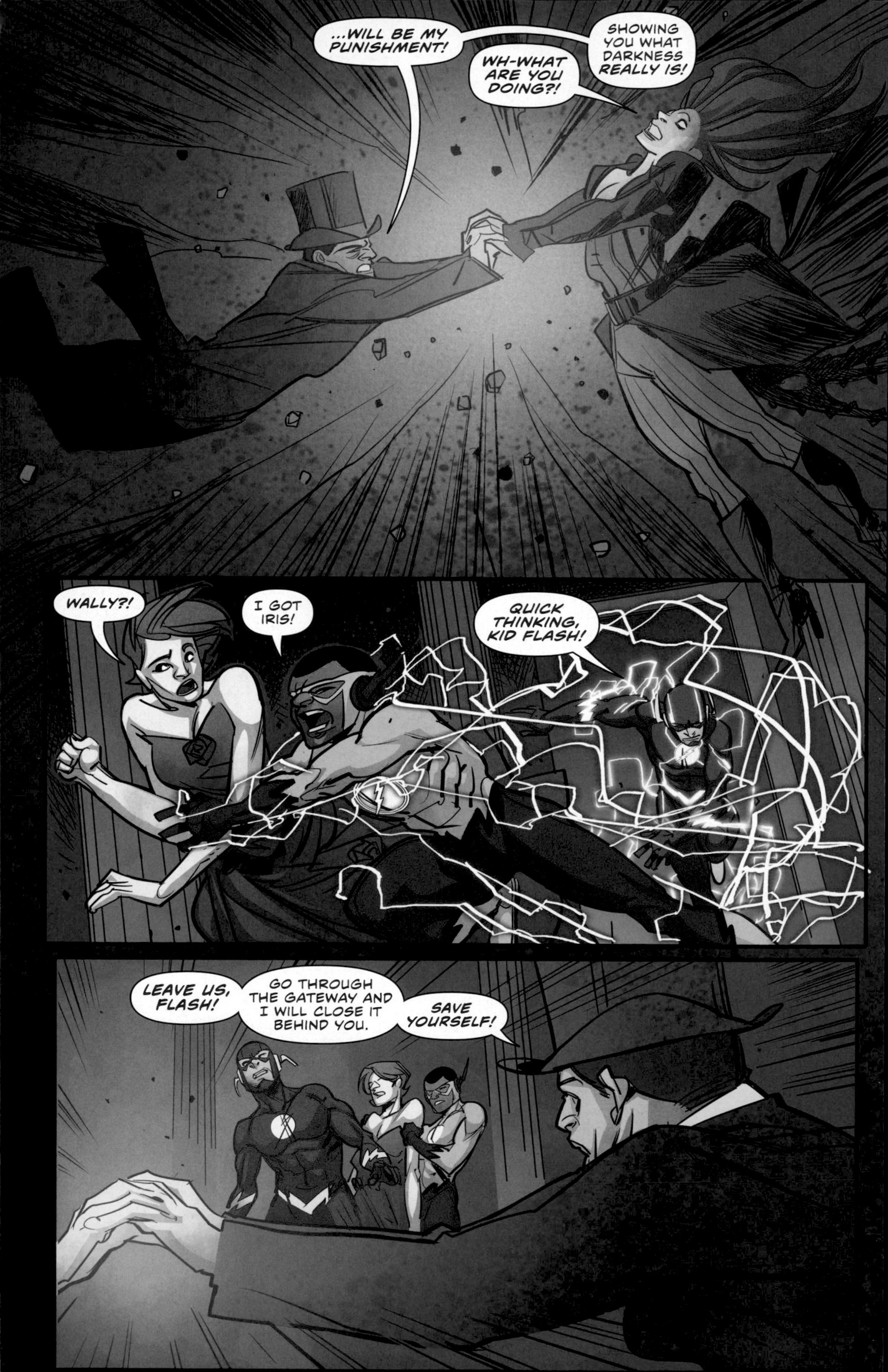
...WILL BE MY PUNISHMENT!
WH-WHAT ARE YOU DOING?!
SHOWING YOU WHAT DARKNESS REALLY IS!
WALLY?!
I GOT IRIS!
QUICK THINKING, KID FLASH!
LEAVE US, FLASH!
GO THROUGH THE GATEWAY AND I WILL CLOSE IT BEHIND YOU.
SAVE YOURSELF!

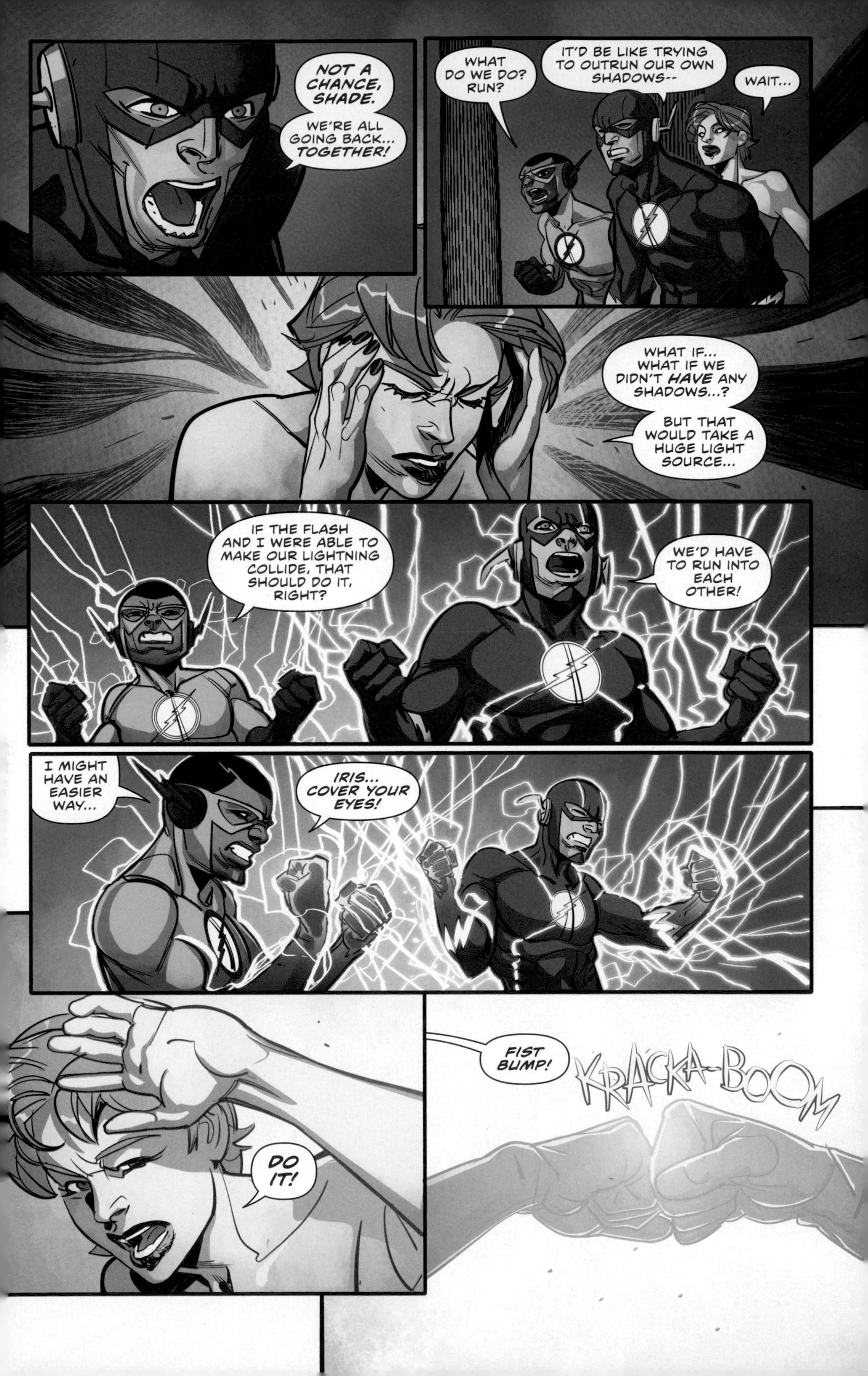

NOT A CHANCE, SHADE.
WE'RE ALL GOING BACK... TOGETHER!
WHAT DO WE DO? RUN?
IT'D BE LIKE TRYING TO OUTRUN OUR OWN SHADOWS--
WAIT...
WHAT IF... WHAT IF WE DIDN'T HAVE ANY SHADOWS...?
BUT THAT WOULD TAKE A HUGE LIGHT SOURCE...
IF THE FLASH AND I WERE ABLE TO MAKE OUR LIGHTNING COLLIDE, THAT SHOULD DO IT, RIGHT?
WE'D HAVE TO RUN INTO EACH OTHER!
I MIGHT HAVE AN EASIER WAY...
IRIS... COVER YOUR EYES!
DO IT!
FIST BUMP!
KRACKA-BOOM

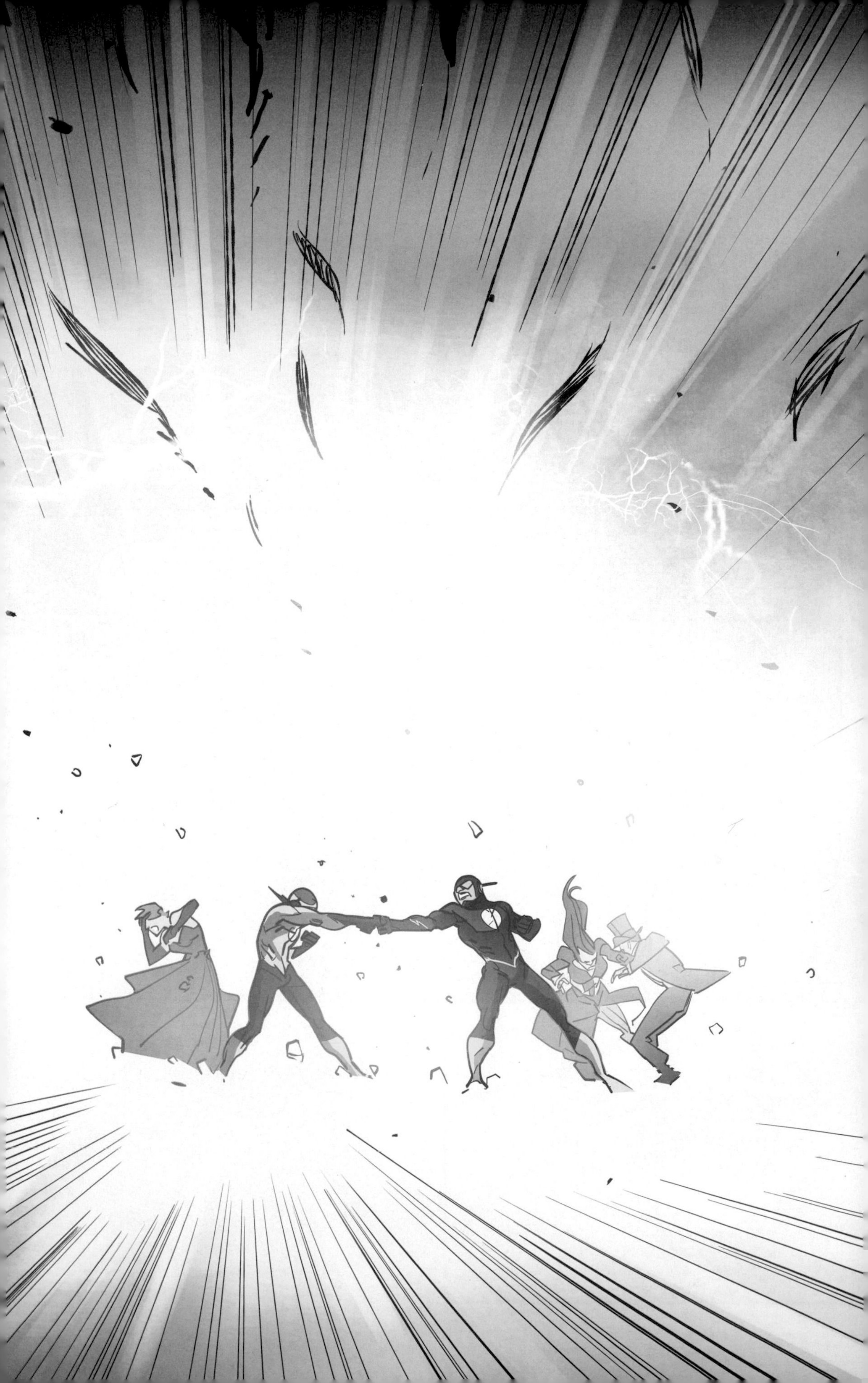

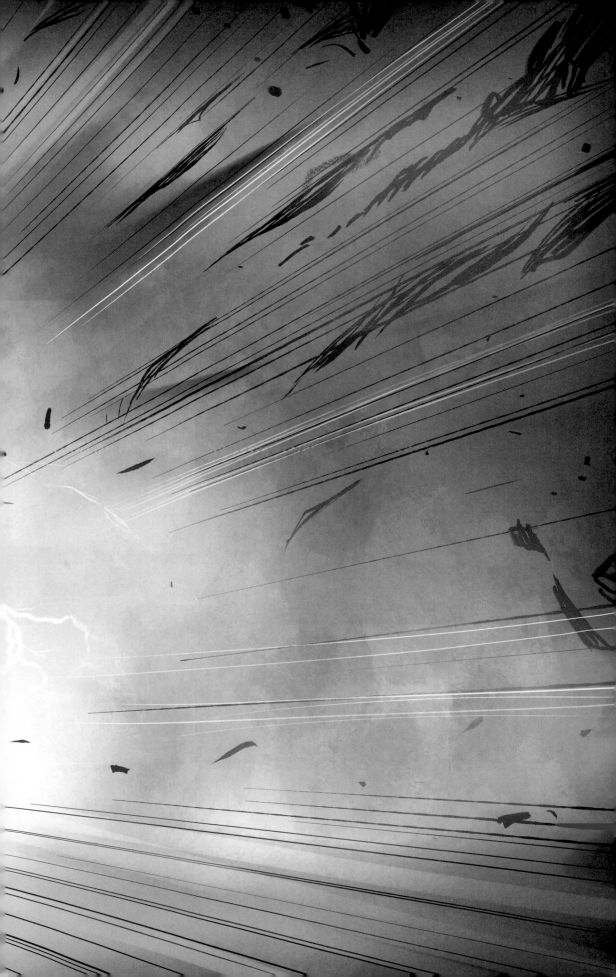

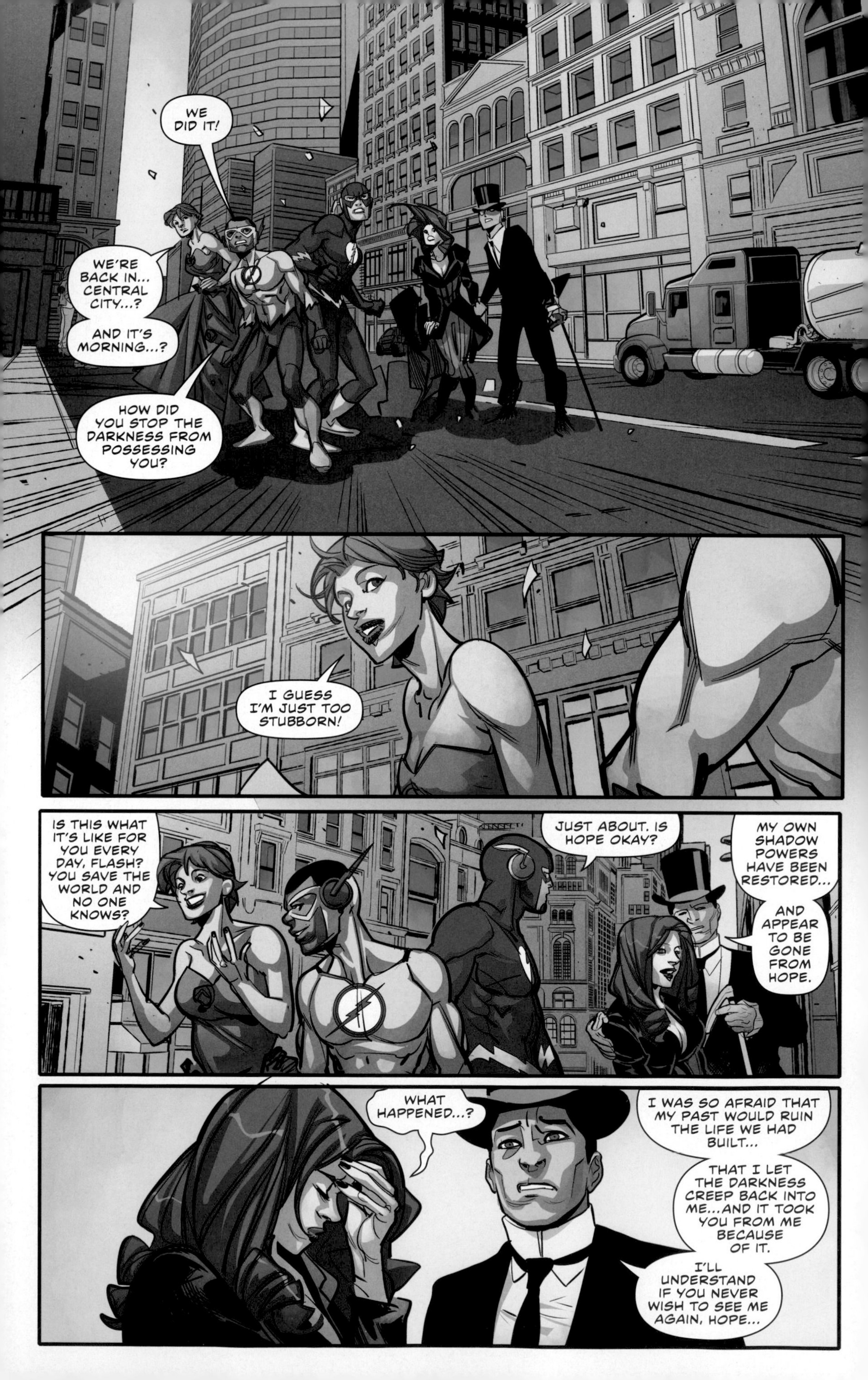
WE DID IT!
WE'RE BACK IN... CENTRAL CITY...?
AND IT'S MORNING...?
HOW DID YOU STOP THE DARKNESS FROM POSSESSING YOU?
I GUESS I'M JUST TOO STUBBORN!
IS THIS WHAT IT'S LIKE FOR YOU EVERY DAY, FLASH? YOU SAVE THE WORLD AND NO ONE KNOWS?
JUST ABOUT. IS HOPE OKAY?
MY OWN SHADOW POWERS HAVE BEEN RESTORED...
AND APPEAR TO BE GONE FROM HOPE.
WHAT HAPPENED...?
I WAS SO AFRAID THAT MY PAST WOULD RUIN THE LIFE WE HAD BUILT...
THAT I LET THE DARKNESS CREEP BACK INTO ME...AND IT TOOK YOU FROM ME BECAUSE OF IT.
I'LL UNDERSTAND IF YOU NEVER WISH TO SEE ME AGAIN, HOPE...

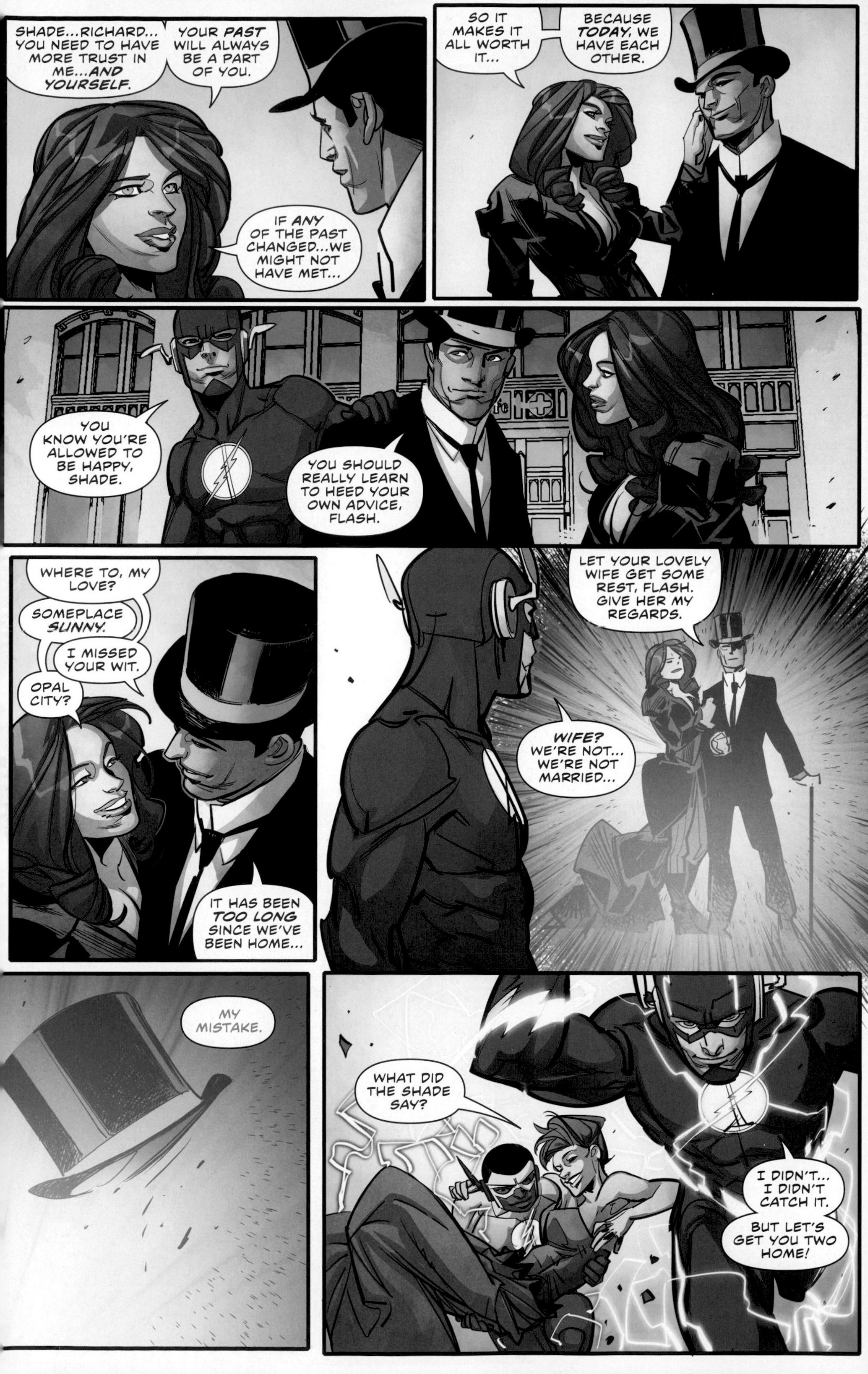
SHADE...RICHARD... YOU NEED TO HAVE MORE TRUST IN ME...AND YOURSELF.
YOUR PAST WILL ALWAYS BE A PART OF YOU.
IF ANY OF THE PAST CHANGED...WE MIGHT NOT HAVE MET...
SO IT MAKES IT ALL WORTH IT...
BECAUSE TODAY, WE HAVE EACH OTHER.
YOU KNOW YOU'RE ALLOWED TO BE HAPPY, SHADE.
YOU SHOULD REALLY LEARN TO HEED YOUR OWN ADVICE, FLASH.
WHERE TO, MY LOVE?
SOMEPLACE SUNNY.
I MISSED YOUR WIT.
OPAL CITY?
IT HAS BEEN TOO LONG SINCE WE'VE BEEN HOME...
LET YOUR LOVELY WIFE GET SOME REST, FLASH. GIVE HER MY REGARDS.
WIFE? WE'RE NOT... WE'RE NOT MARRIED...
MY MISTAKE.
WHAT DID THE SHADE SAY?
I DIDN'T... I DIDN'T CATCH IT.
BUT LET'S GET YOU TWO HOME!

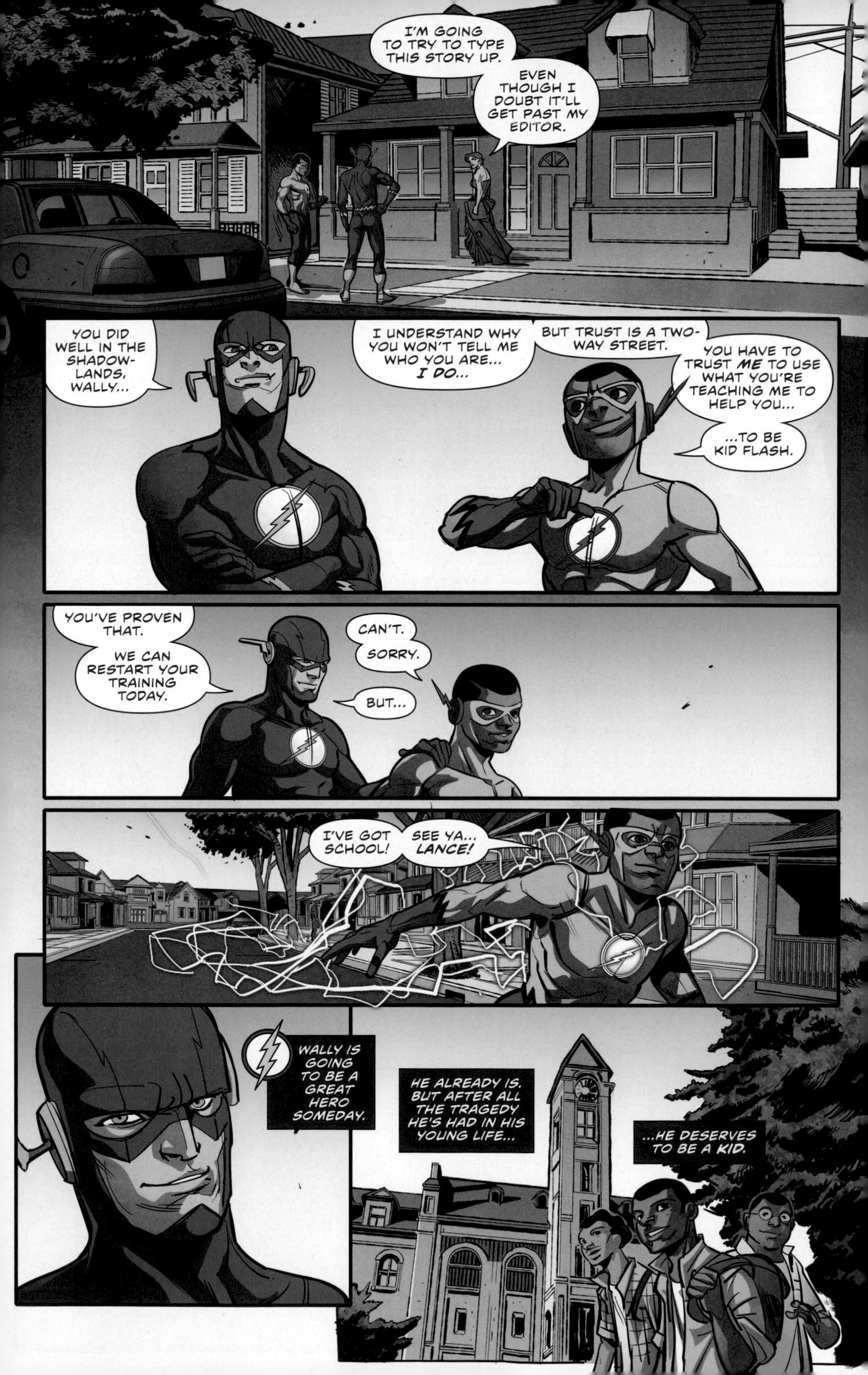
I'M GOING TO TRY TO TYPE THIS STORY UP.
EVEN THOUGH I DOUBT IT'LL GET PAST MY EDITOR.
YOU DID WELL IN THE SHADOW-LANDS, WALLY...
I UNDERSTAND WHY YOU WON'T TELL ME WHO YOU ARE... I DO...
BUT TRUST IS A TWO-WAY STREET.
YOU HAVE TO TRUST ME TO USE WHAT YOU'RE TEACHING ME TO HELP YOU...
...TO BE KID FLASH.
YOU'VE PROVEN THAT.
WE CAN RESTART YOUR TRAINING TODAY.
CAN'T.
SORRY.
BUT...
I'VE GOT SCHOOL!
SEE YA... LANCE!
WALLY IS GOING TO BE A GREAT HERO SOMEDAY.
HE ALREADY IS. BUT AFTER ALL THE TRAGEDY HE'S HAD IN HIS YOUNG LIFE...
...HE DESERVES TO BE A KID.

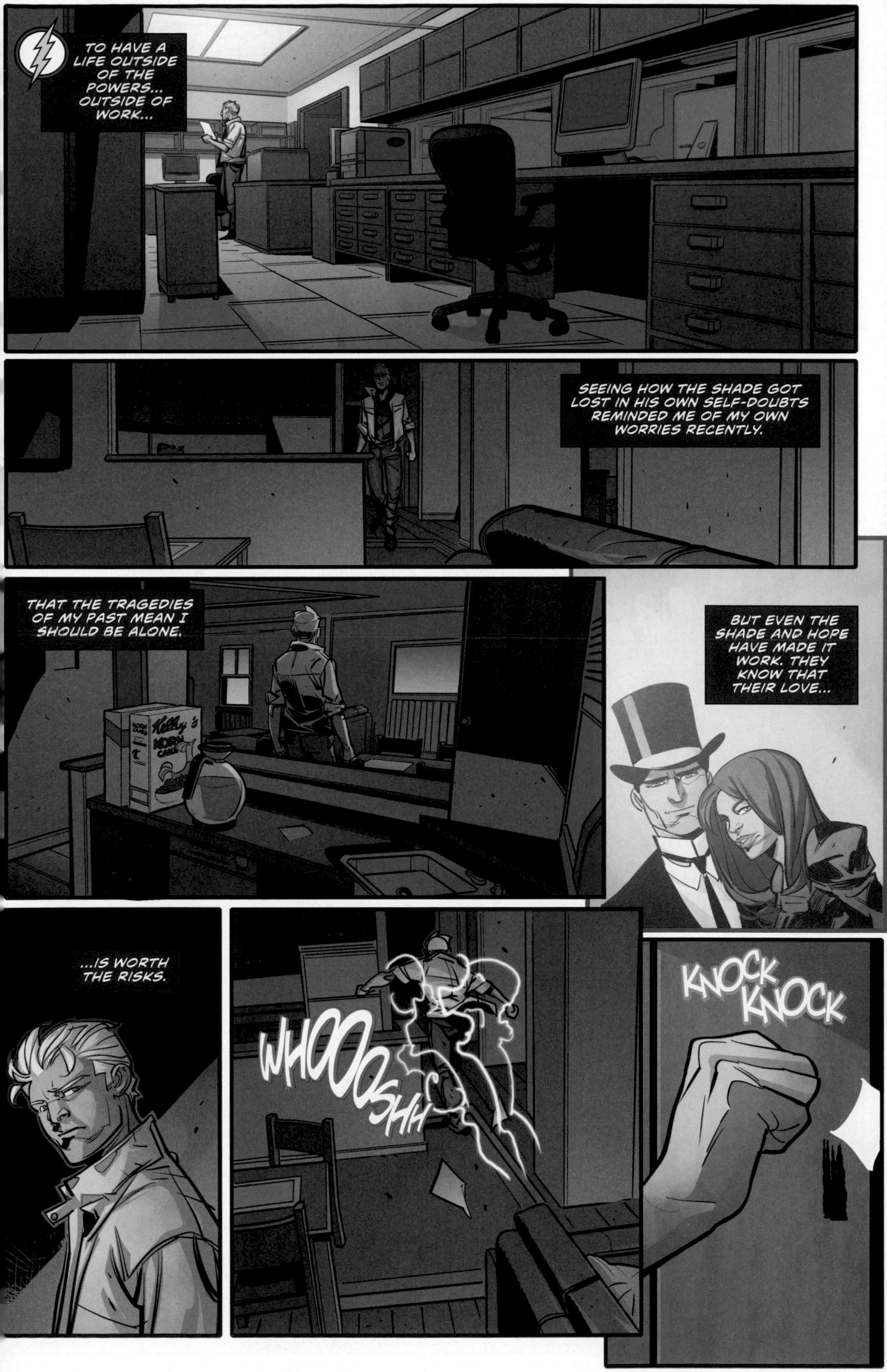

TO HAVE A LIFE OUTSIDE OF THE POWERS... OUTSIDE OF WORK...
SEEING HOW THE SHADE GOT LOST IN HIS OWN SELF-DOUBTS REMINDED ME OF MY OWN WORRIES RECENTLY.
THAT THE TRAGEDIES OF MY PAST MEAN I SHOULD BE ALONE.
BUT EVEN THE SHADE AND HOPE HAVE MADE IT WORK. THEY KNOW THAT THEIR LOVE...
...IS WORTH THE RISKS.
WHOOOOSHH
KNOCK KNOCK

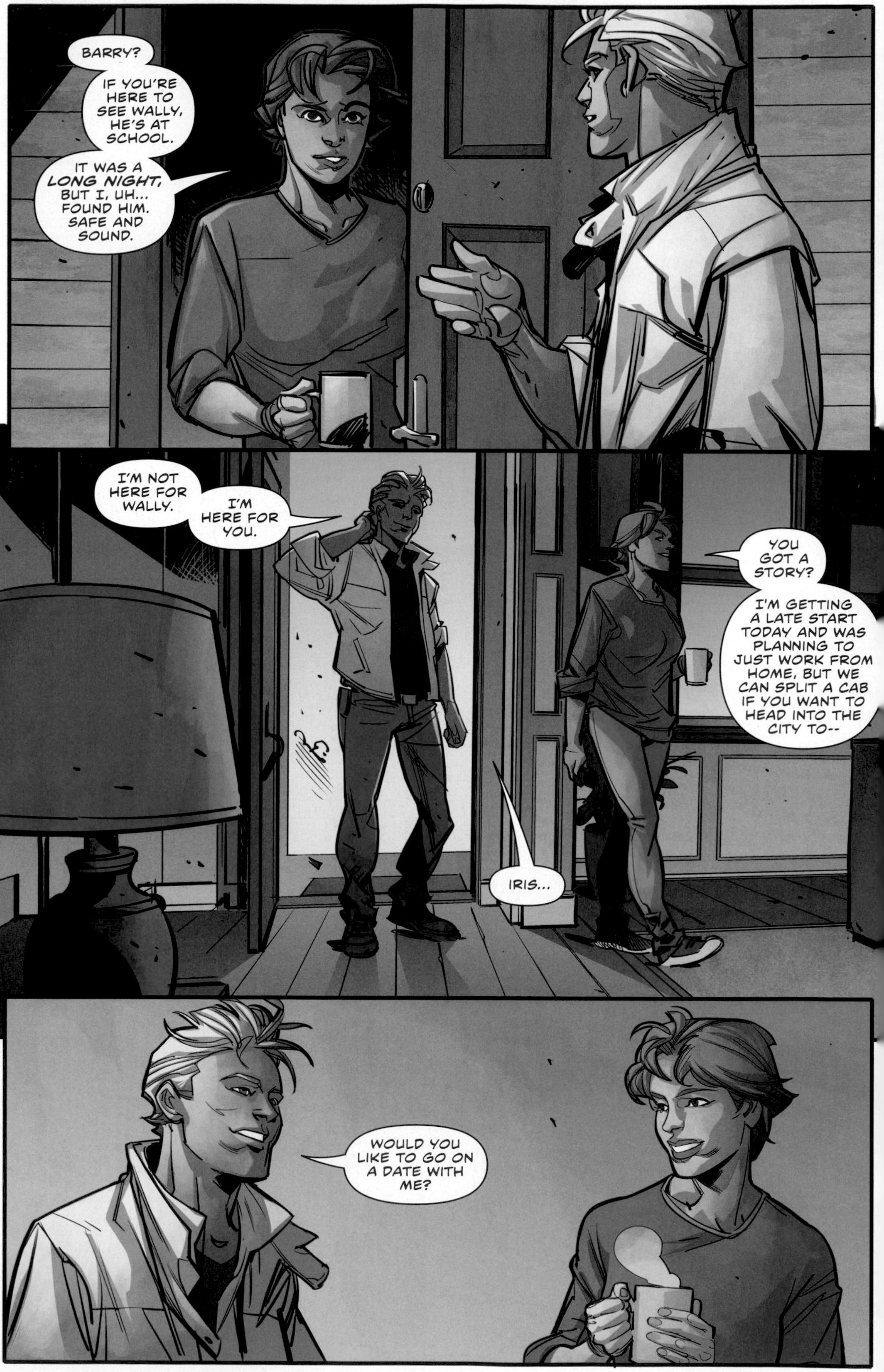
BARRY?
IF YOU'RE HERE TO SEE WALLY, HE'S AT SCHOOL.
IT WAS A LONG NIGHT, BUT I, UH... FOUND HIM. SAFE AND SOUND.
I'M NOT HERE FOR WALLY.
I'M HERE FOR YOU.
YOU GOT A STORY?
I'M GETTING A LATE START TODAY AND WAS PLANNING TO JUST WORK FROM HOME, BUT WE CAN SPLIT A CAB IF YOU WANT TO HEAD INTO THE CITY TO--
IRIS...
WOULD YOU LIKE TO GO ON A DATE WITH ME?

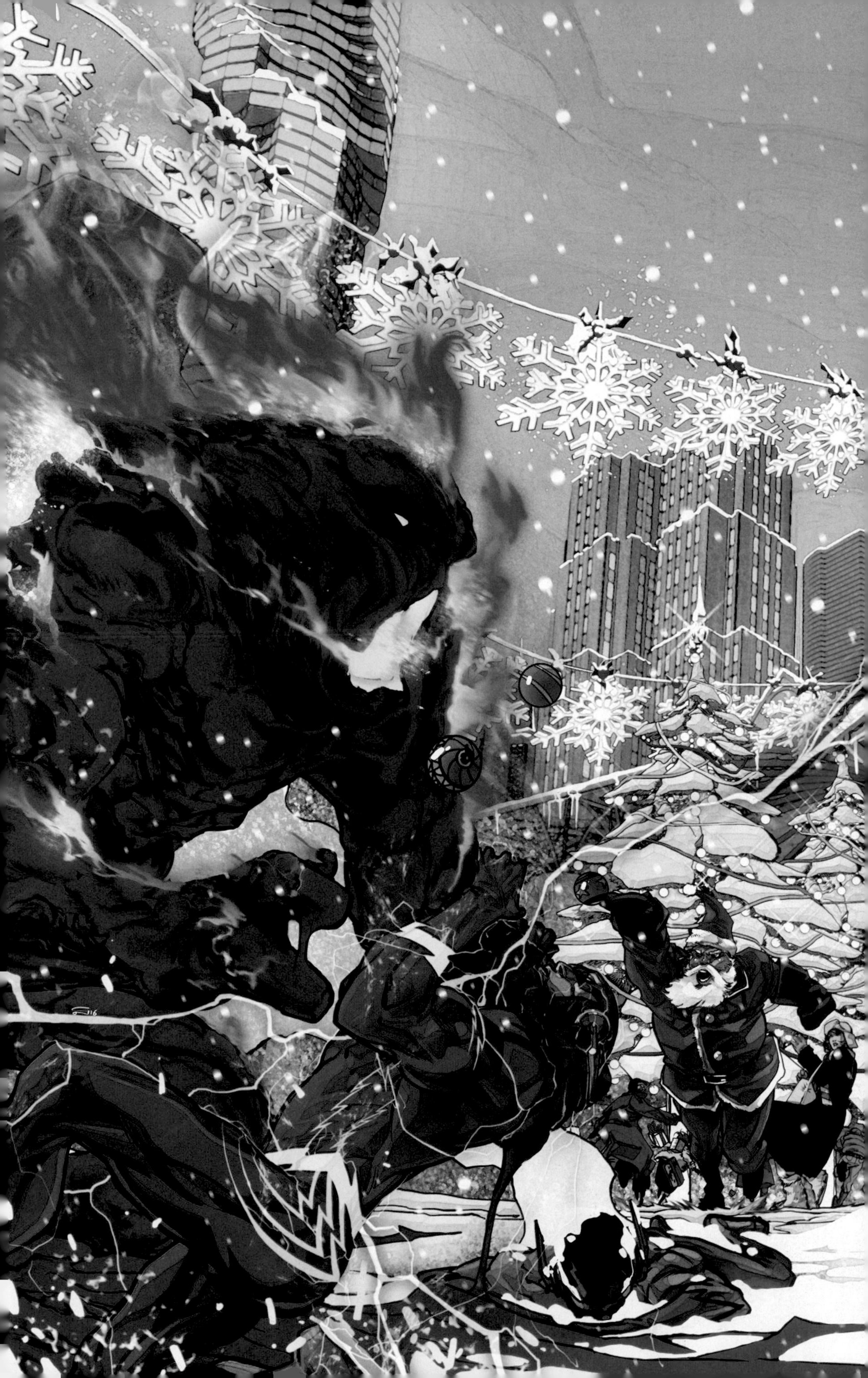

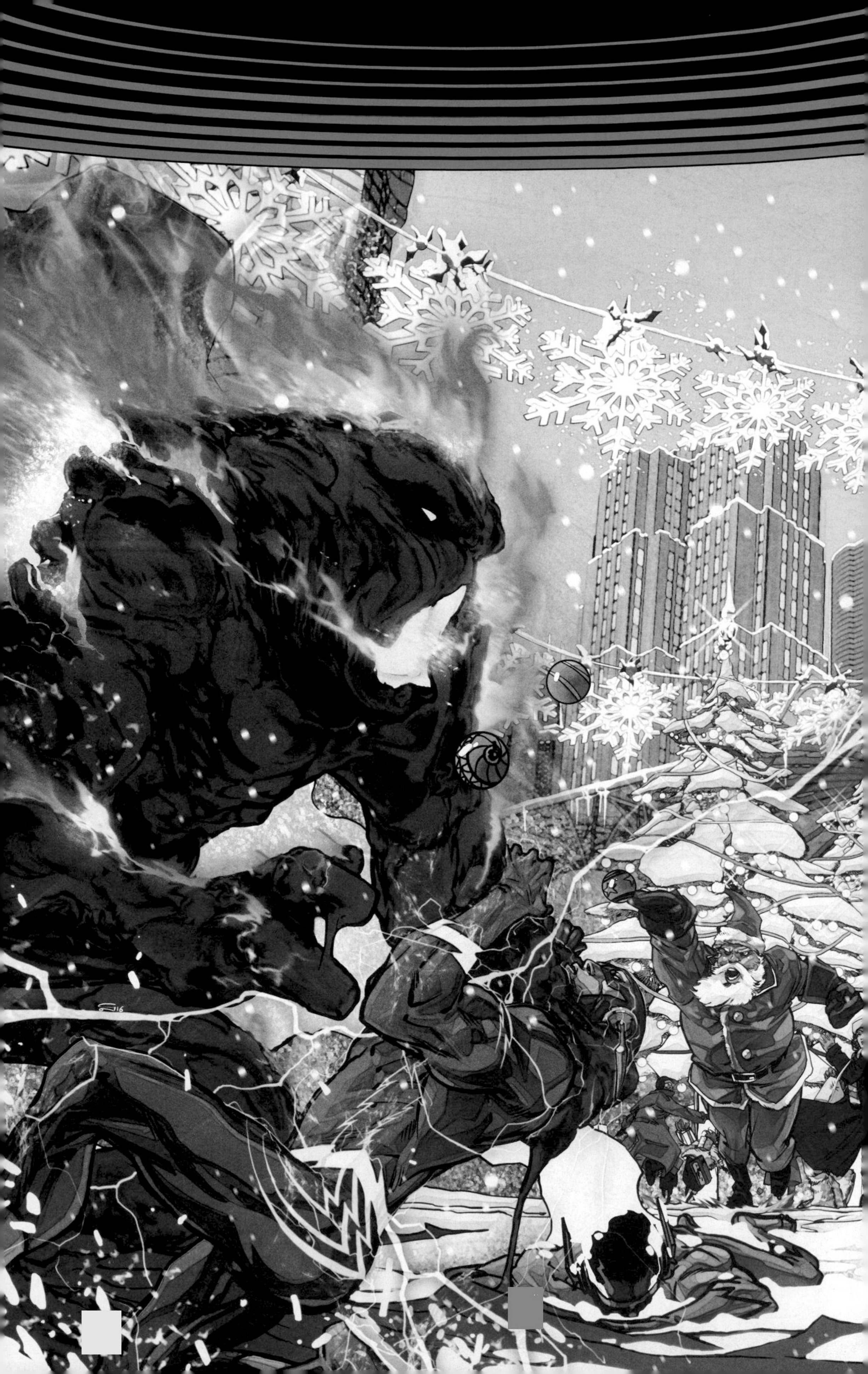

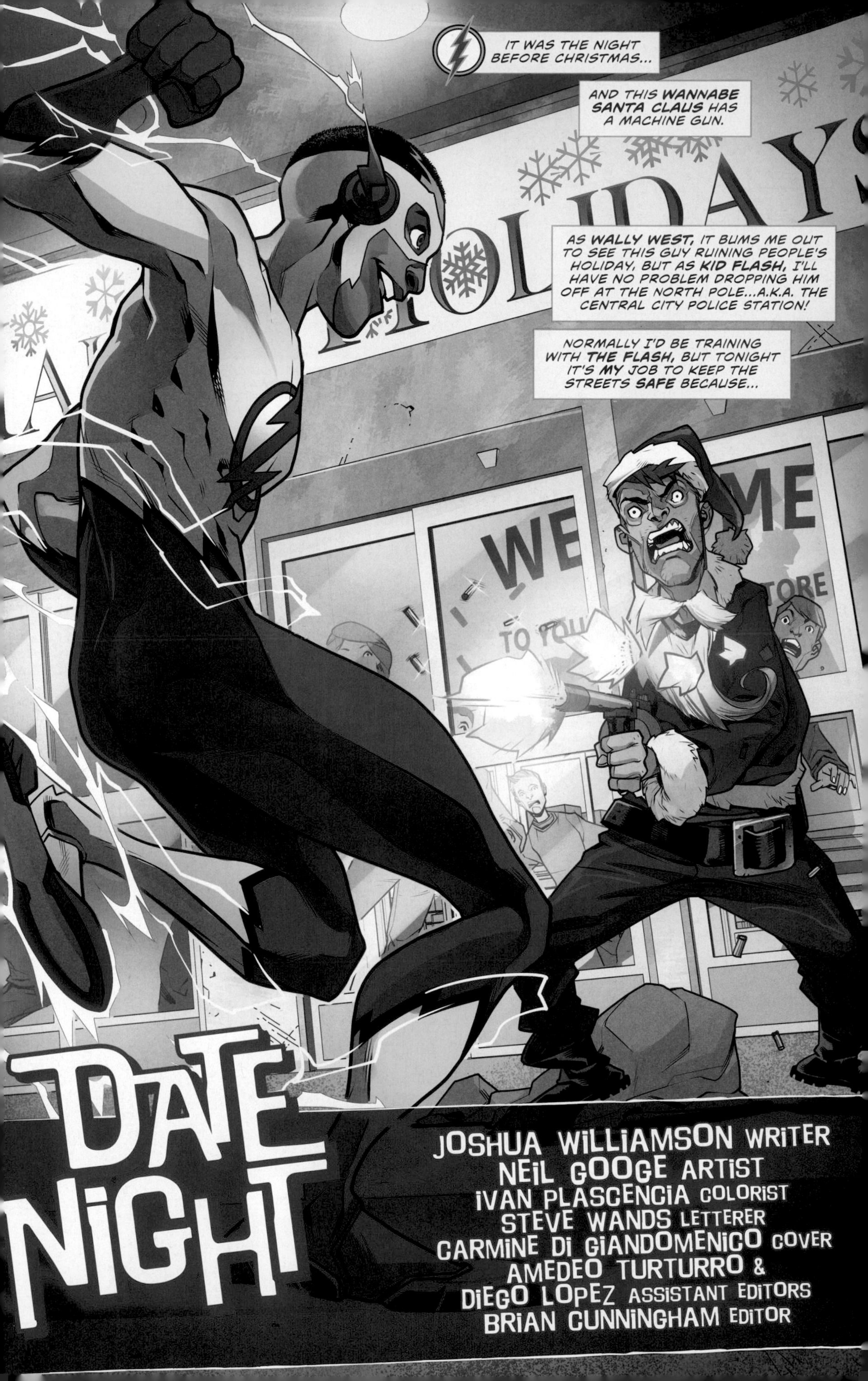
IT WAS THE NIGHT BEFORE CHRISTMAS...
AND THIS WANNABE SANTA CLAUS HAS A MACHINE GUN.
AS WALLY WEST, IT BUMS ME OUT TO SEE THIS GUY RUINING PEOPLE'S HOLIDAY, BUT AS KID FLASH, I'LL HAVE NO PROBLEM DROPPING HIM OFF AT THE NORTH POLE...A.K.A. THE CENTRAL CITY POLICE STATION!
NORMALLY I'D BE TRAINING WITH THE FLASH, BUT TONIGHT IT'S MY JOB TO KEEP THE STREETS SAFE BECAUSE...
DATE NIGHT
JOSHUA WILLIAMSON WRITER
NEIL GOOGE ARTIST
IVAN PLASCENCIA COLORIST
STEVE WANDS LETTERER
CARMINE DI GIANDOMENICO COVER
AMEDEO TURTURRO &
DIEGO LOPEZ ASSISTANT EDITORS
BRIAN CUNNINGHAM EDITOR

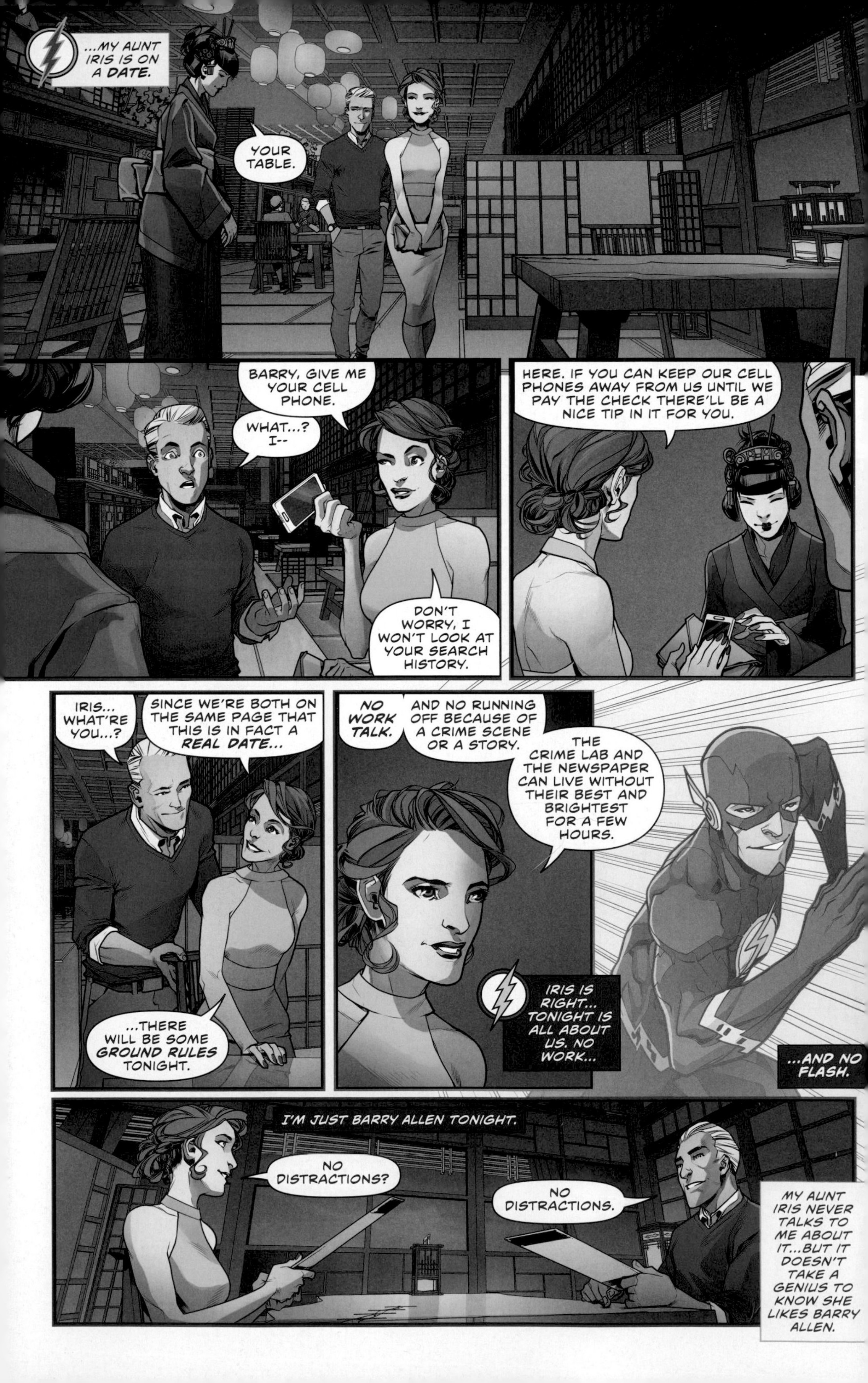
...MY AUNT IRIS IS ON A DATE.
YOUR TABLE.
BARRY, GIVE ME YOUR CELL PHONE.
WHAT...? I--
DON'T WORRY, I WON'T LOOK AT YOUR SEARCH HISTORY.
HERE. IF YOU CAN KEEP OUR CELL PHONES AWAY FROM US UNTIL WE PAY THE CHECK THERE'LL BE A NICE TIP IN IT FOR YOU.
IRIS... WHAT'RE YOU...?
SINCE WE'RE BOTH ON THE SAME PAGE THAT THIS IS IN FACT A REAL DATE...
...THERE WILL BE SOME GROUND RULES TONIGHT.
NO WORK TALK.
AND NO RUNNING OFF BECAUSE OF A CRIME SCENE OR A STORY.
THE CRIME LAB AND THE NEWSPAPER CAN LIVE WITHOUT THEIR BEST AND BRIGHTEST FOR A FEW HOURS.
IRIS IS RIGHT... TONIGHT IS ALL ABOUT US. NO WORK...
...AND NO FLASH.
I'M JUST BARRY ALLEN TONIGHT.
NO DISTRACTIONS?
NO DISTRACTIONS.
MY AUNT IRIS NEVER TALKS TO ME ABOUT IT...BUT IT DOESN'T TAKE A GENIUS TO KNOW SHE LIKES BARRY ALLEN.

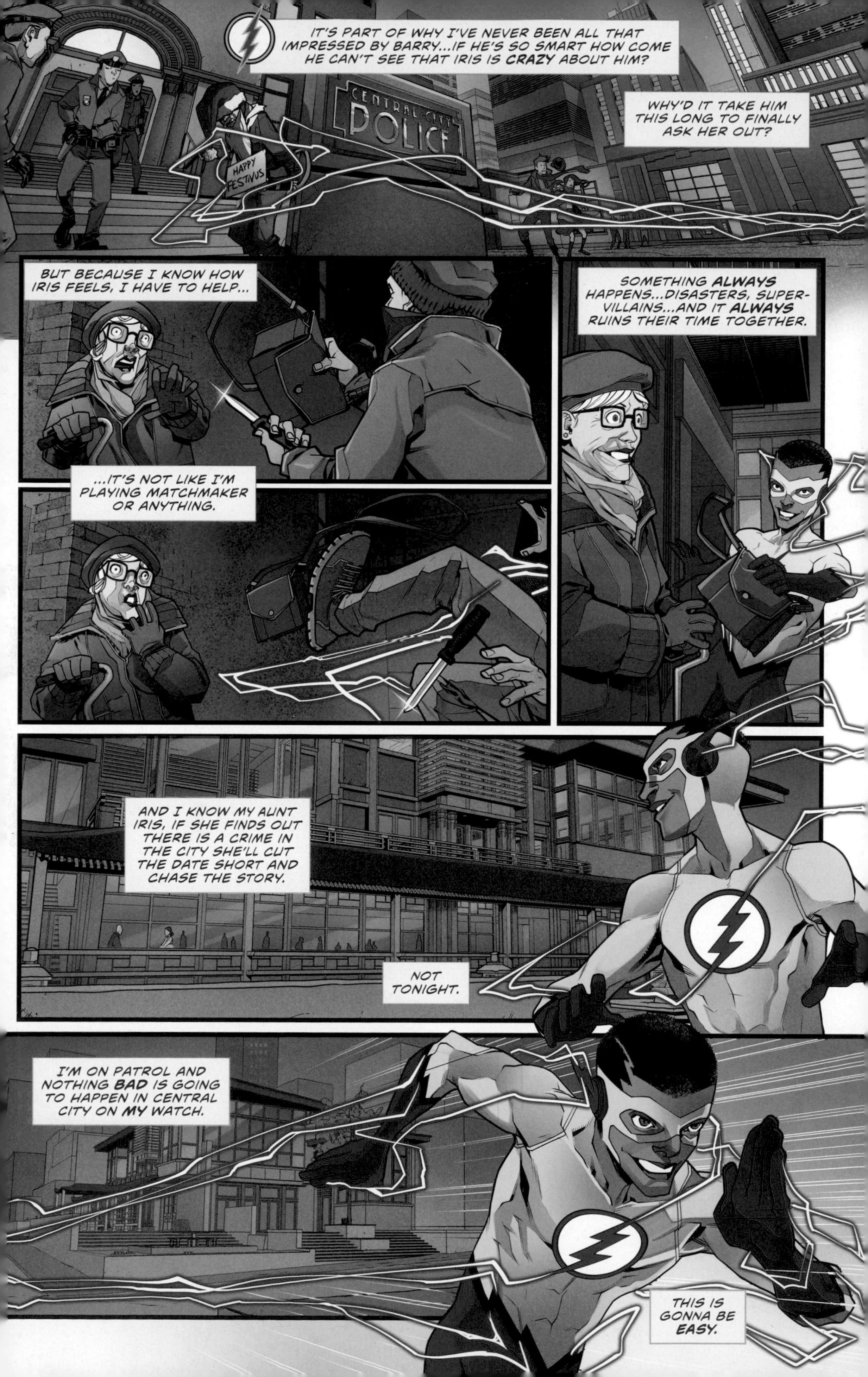
IT'S PART OF WHY I'VE NEVER BEEN ALL THAT IMPRESSED BY BARRY...IF HE'S SO SMART HOW COME HE CAN'T SEE THAT IRIS IS CRAZY ABOUT HIM?
CENTRAL CITY POLICE
HAPPY FESTIVUS
WHY'D IT TAKE HIM THIS LONG TO FINALLY ASK HER OUT?
BUT BECAUSE I KNOW HOW IRIS FEELS, I HAVE TO HELP...
...IT'S NOT LIKE I'M PLAYING MATCHMAKER OR ANYTHING.
SOMETHING ALWAYS HAPPENS...DISASTERS, SUPER-VILLAINS...AND IT ALWAYS RUINS THEIR TIME TOGETHER.
AND I KNOW MY AUNT IRIS, IF SHE FINDS OUT THERE IS A CRIME IN THE CITY SHE'LL CUT THE DATE SHORT AND CHASE THE STORY.
NOT TONIGHT.
I'M ON PATROL AND NOTHING BAD IS GOING TO HAPPEN IN CENTRAL CITY ON MY WATCH.
THIS IS GONNA BE EASY.

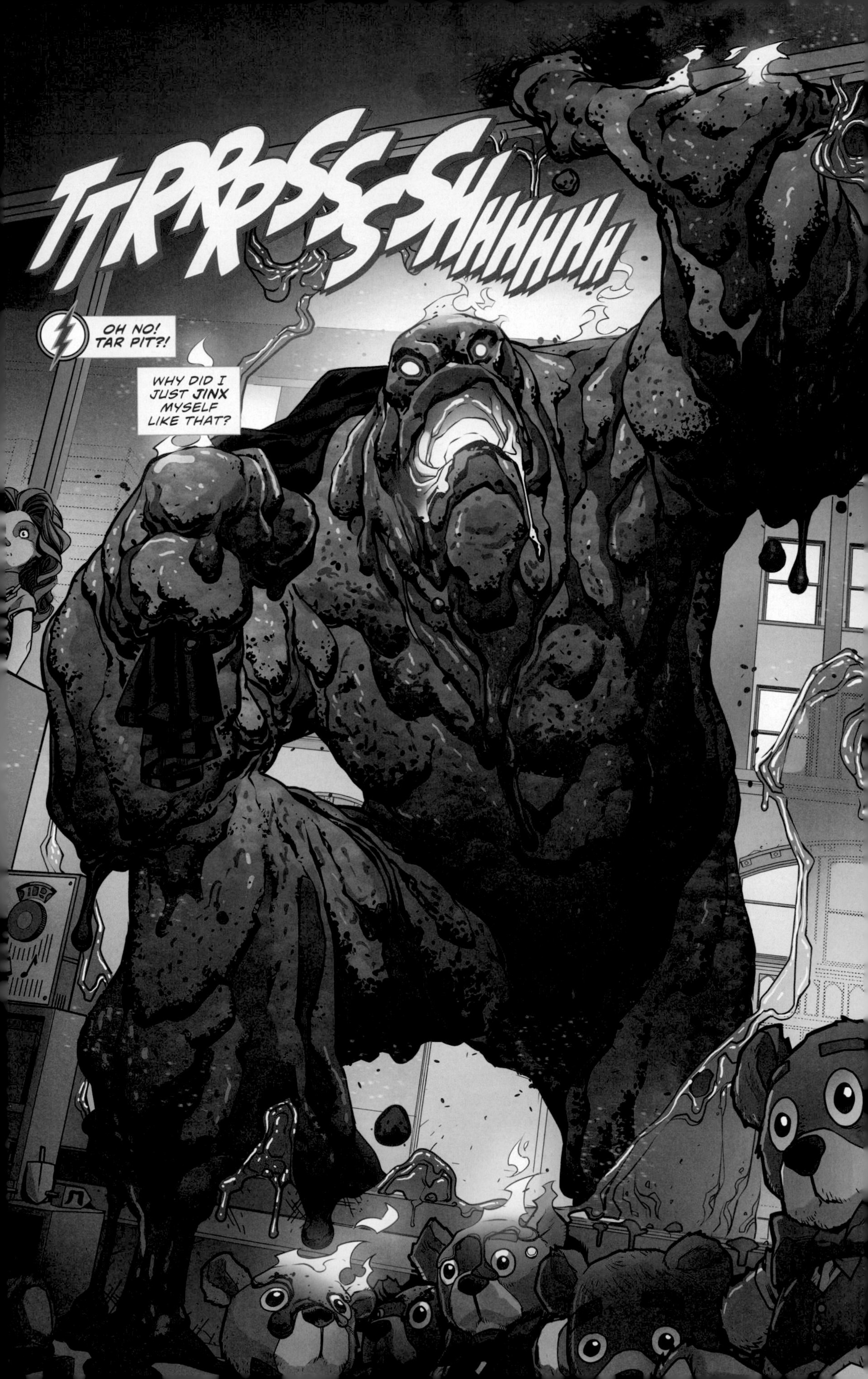

TTRRSS-SHHHHHH
OH NO! TAR PIT?!
WHY DID I JUST JINX MYSELF LIKE THAT?

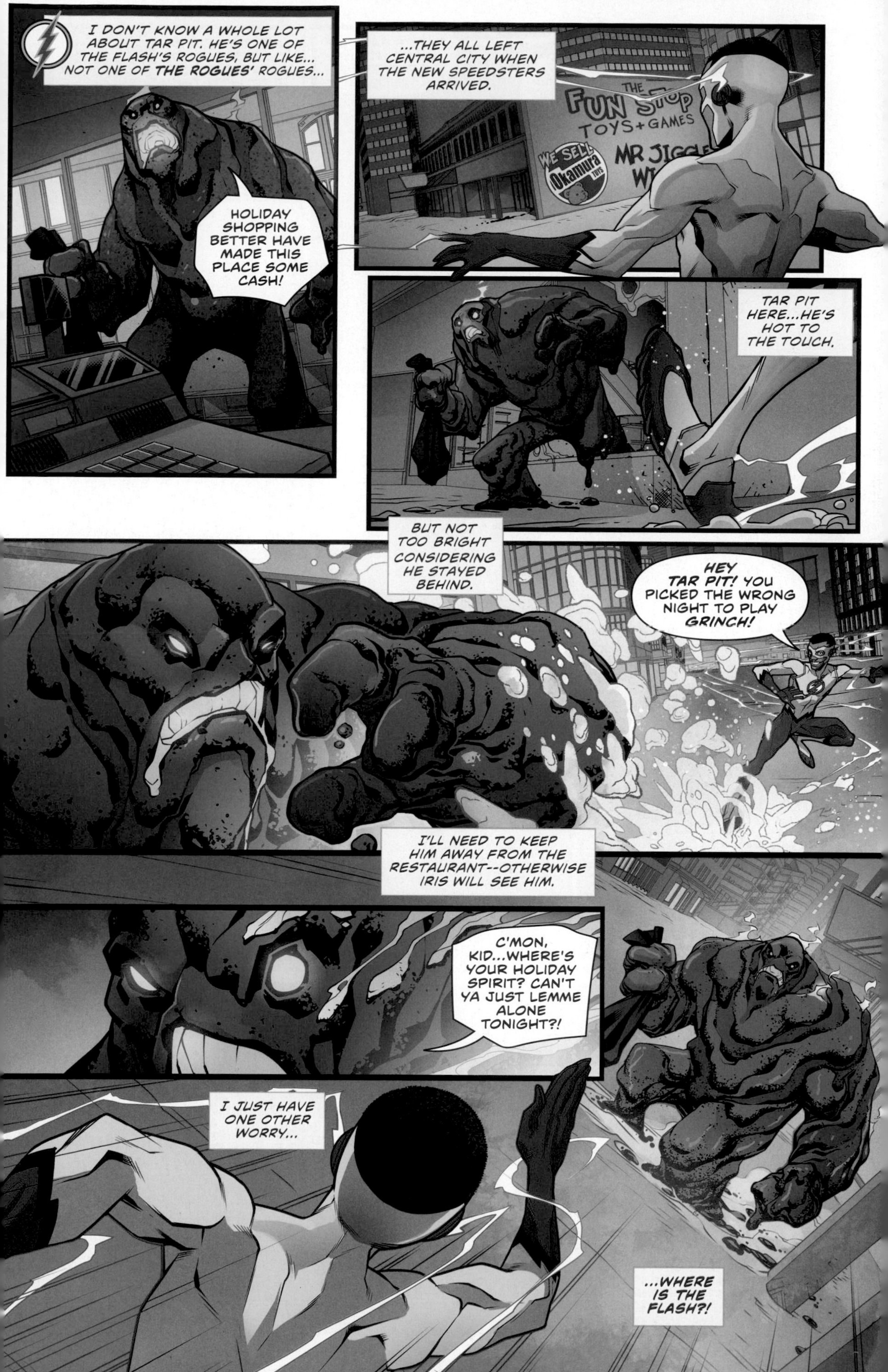
I DON'T KNOW A WHOLE LOT ABOUT TAR PIT. HE'S ONE OF THE FLASH'S ROGUES, BUT LIKE... NOT ONE OF **THE ROGUES'** ROGUES...
...THEY ALL LEFT CENTRAL CITY WHEN THE NEW SPEEDSTERS ARRIVED.
HOLIDAY SHOPPING BETTER HAVE MADE THIS PLACE SOME CASH!
THE FUN STOP TOYS + GAMES
WE SELL OKAMURA TOYS
TAR PIT HERE...HE'S HOT TO THE TOUCH.
BUT NOT TOO BRIGHT CONSIDERING HE STAYED BEHIND.
HEY TAR PIT! YOU PICKED THE WRONG NIGHT TO PLAY ***GRINCH!***
I'LL NEED TO KEEP HIM AWAY FROM THE RESTAURANT--OTHERWISE IRIS WILL SEE HIM.
C'MON, KID...WHERE'S YOUR HOLIDAY SPIRIT? CAN'T YA JUST LEMME ALONE TONIGHT?!
I JUST HAVE ONE OTHER WORRY...
...WHERE IS ***THE FLASH?!***

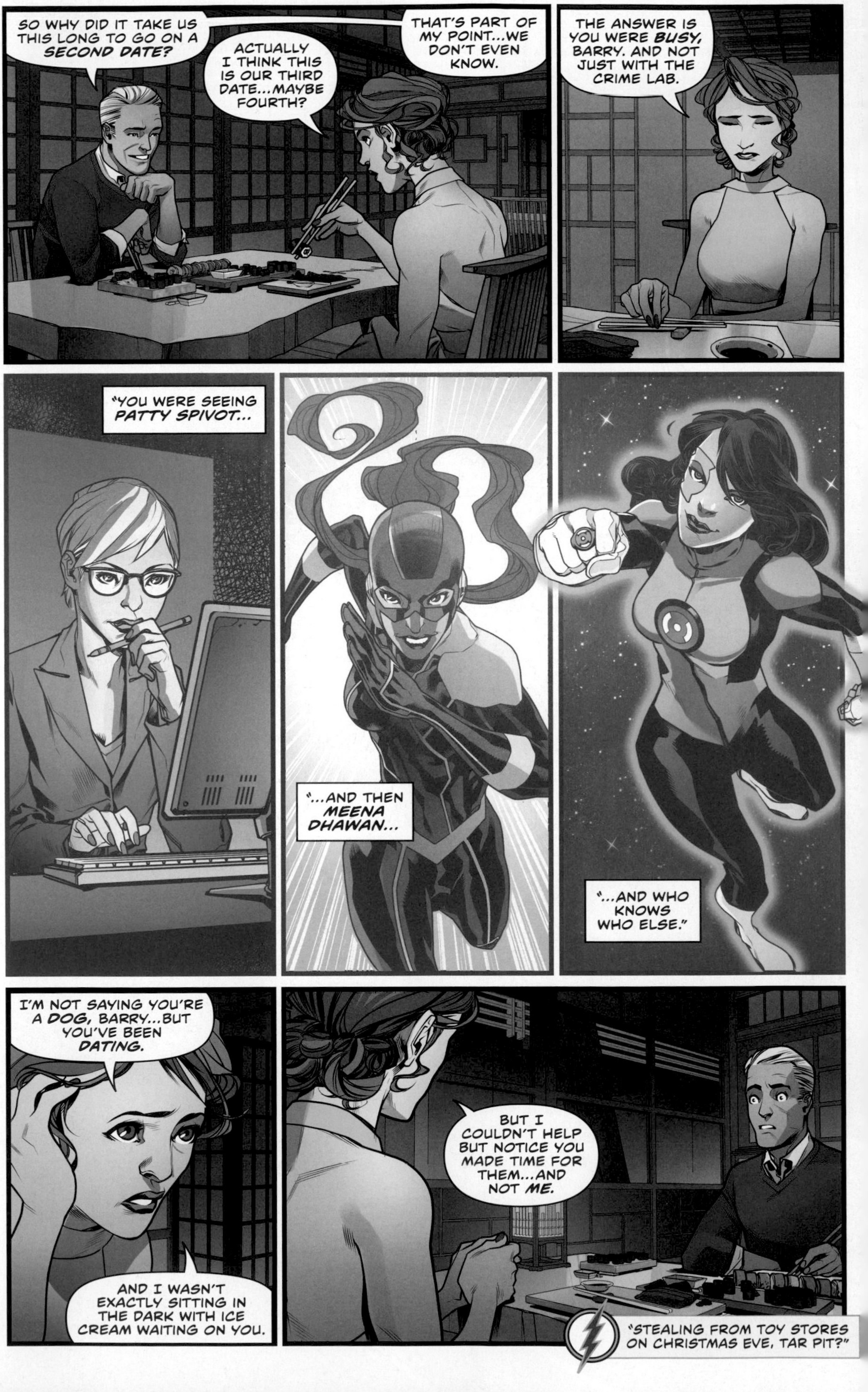
SO WHY DID IT TAKE US THIS LONG TO GO ON A SECOND DATE?
ACTUALLY I THINK THIS IS OUR THIRD DATE...MAYBE FOURTH?
THAT'S PART OF MY POINT...WE DON'T EVEN KNOW.
THE ANSWER IS YOU WERE BUSY, BARRY. AND NOT JUST WITH THE CRIME LAB.
"YOU WERE SEEING PATTY SPIVOT...
"...AND THEN MEENA DHAWAN...
"...AND WHO KNOWS WHO ELSE."
I'M NOT SAYING YOU'RE A DOG, BARRY...BUT YOU'VE BEEN DATING.
AND I WASN'T EXACTLY SITTING IN THE DARK WITH ICE CREAM WAITING ON YOU.
BUT I COULDN'T HELP BUT NOTICE YOU MADE TIME FOR THEM...AND NOT ME.
"STEALING FROM TOY STORES ON CHRISTMAS EVE, TAR PIT?"

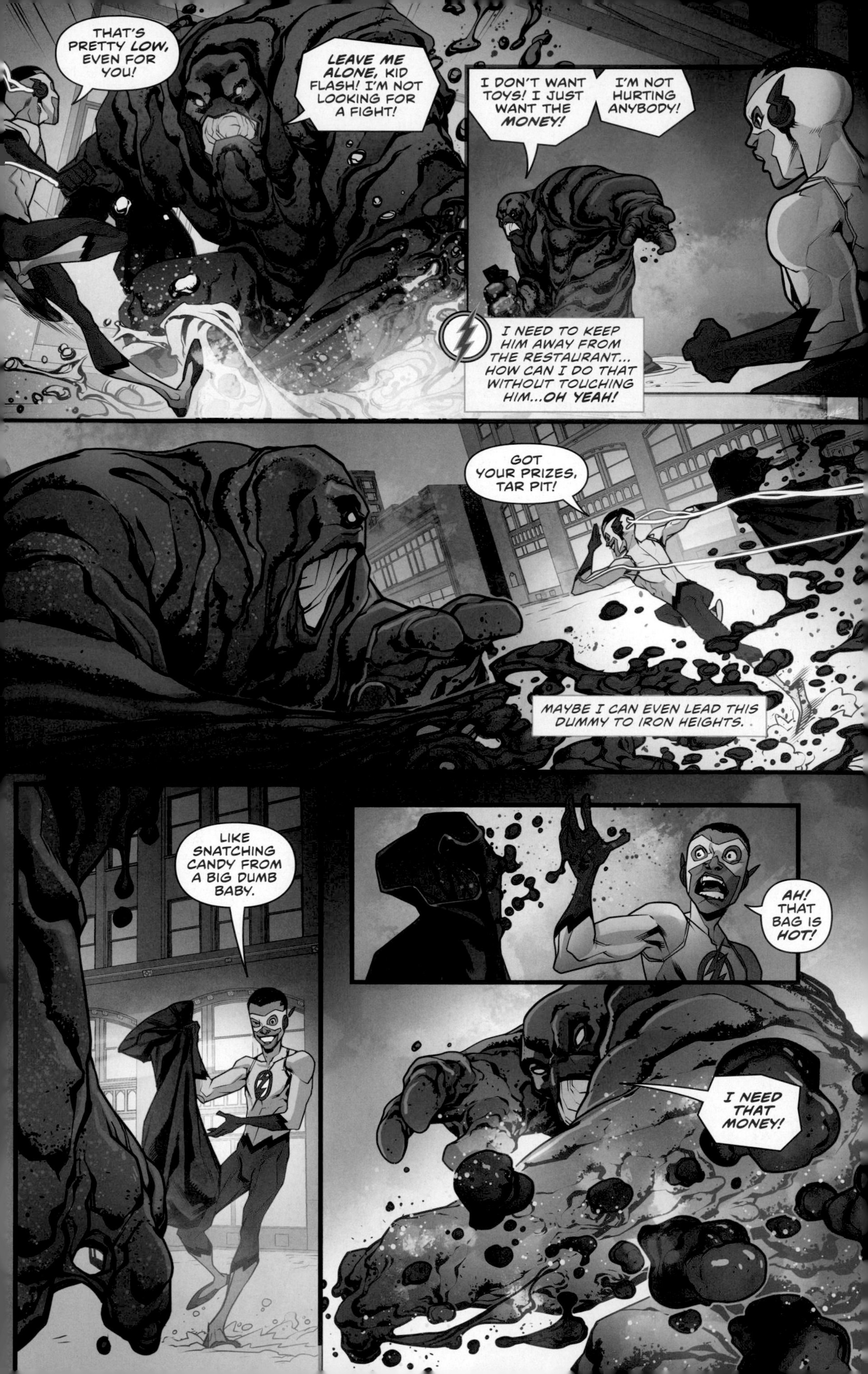

THAT'S PRETTY LOW, EVEN FOR YOU!
LEAVE ME ALONE, KID FLASH! I'M NOT LOOKING FOR A FIGHT!
I DON'T WANT TOYS! I JUST WANT THE MONEY!
I'M NOT HURTING ANYBODY!
I NEED TO KEEP HIM AWAY FROM THE RESTAURANT... HOW CAN I DO THAT WITHOUT TOUCHING HIM...OH YEAH!
GOT YOUR PRIZES, TAR PIT!
MAYBE I CAN EVEN LEAD THIS DUMMY TO IRON HEIGHTS.
LIKE SNATCHING CANDY FROM A BIG DUMB BABY.
AH! THAT BAG IS HOT!
I NEED THAT MONEY!

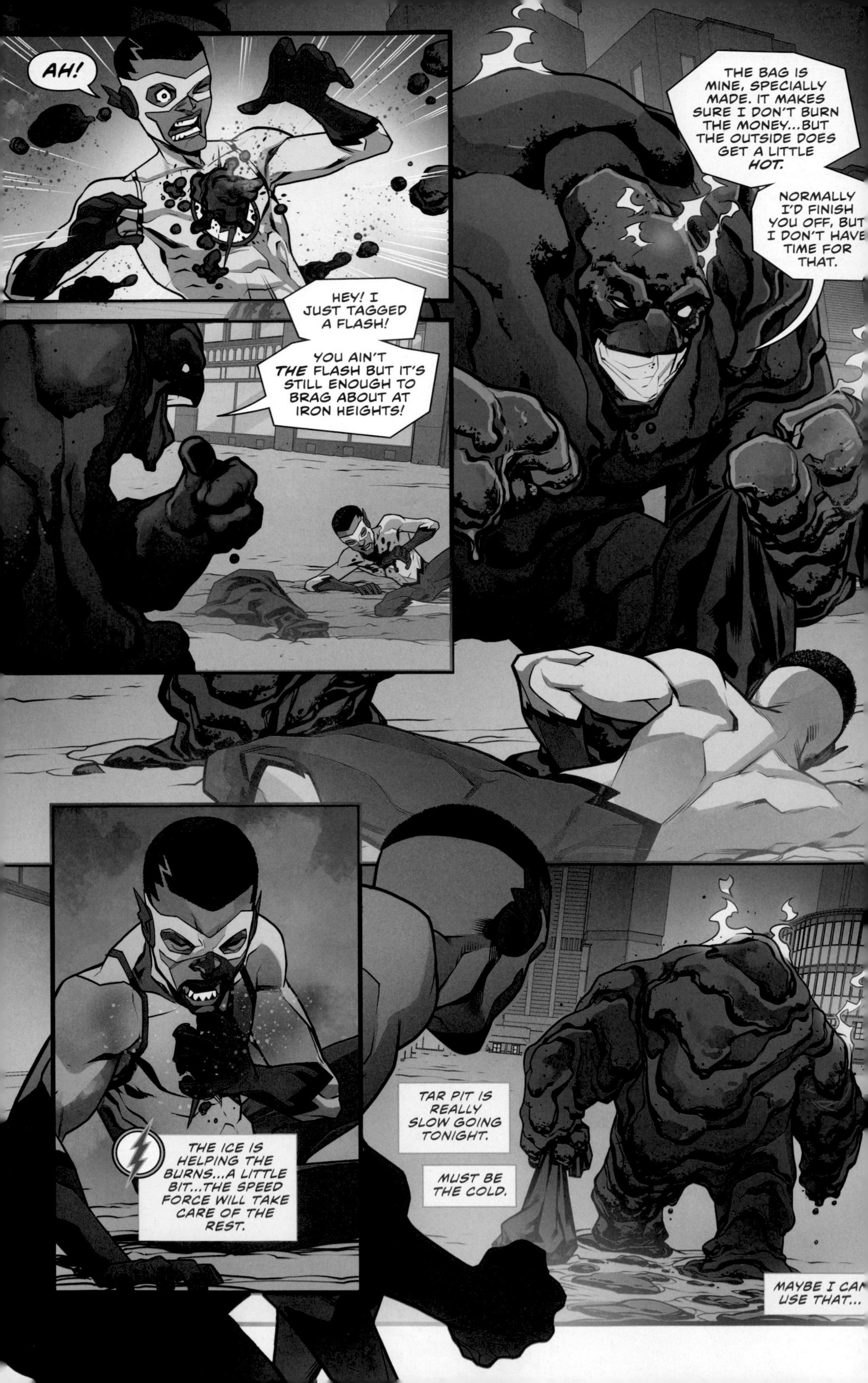
AH!
THE BAG IS MINE, SPECIALLY MADE. IT MAKES SURE I DON'T BURN THE MONEY...BUT THE OUTSIDE DOES GET A LITTLE HOT.
NORMALLY I'D FINISH YOU OFF, BUT I DON'T HAVE TIME FOR THAT.
HEY! I JUST TAGGED A FLASH!
YOU AIN'T THE FLASH BUT IT'S STILL ENOUGH TO BRAG ABOUT AT IRON HEIGHTS!
THE ICE IS HELPING THE BURNS...A LITTLE BIT...THE SPEED FORCE WILL TAKE CARE OF THE REST.
TAR PIT IS REALLY SLOW GOING TONIGHT.
MUST BE THE COLD.
MAYBE I CAN USE THAT...

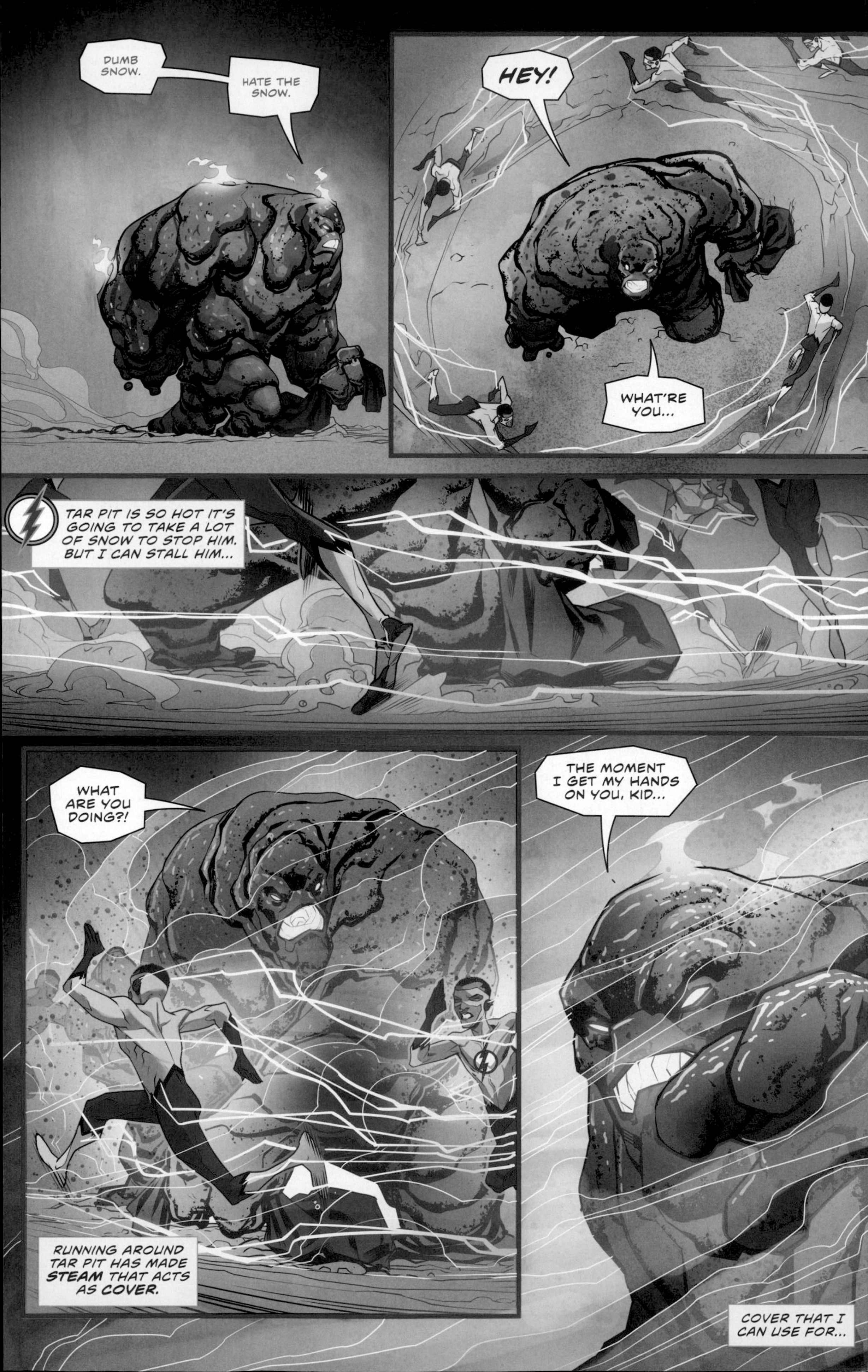

DUMB SNOW.
HATE THE SNOW.
HEY!
WHAT'RE YOU...
TAR PIT IS SO HOT IT'S GOING TO TAKE A LOT OF SNOW TO STOP HIM. BUT I CAN STALL HIM...
WHAT ARE YOU DOING?!
RUNNING AROUND TAR PIT HAS MADE STEAM THAT ACTS AS COVER.
THE MOMENT I GET MY HANDS ON YOU, KID...
COVER THAT I CAN USE FOR...

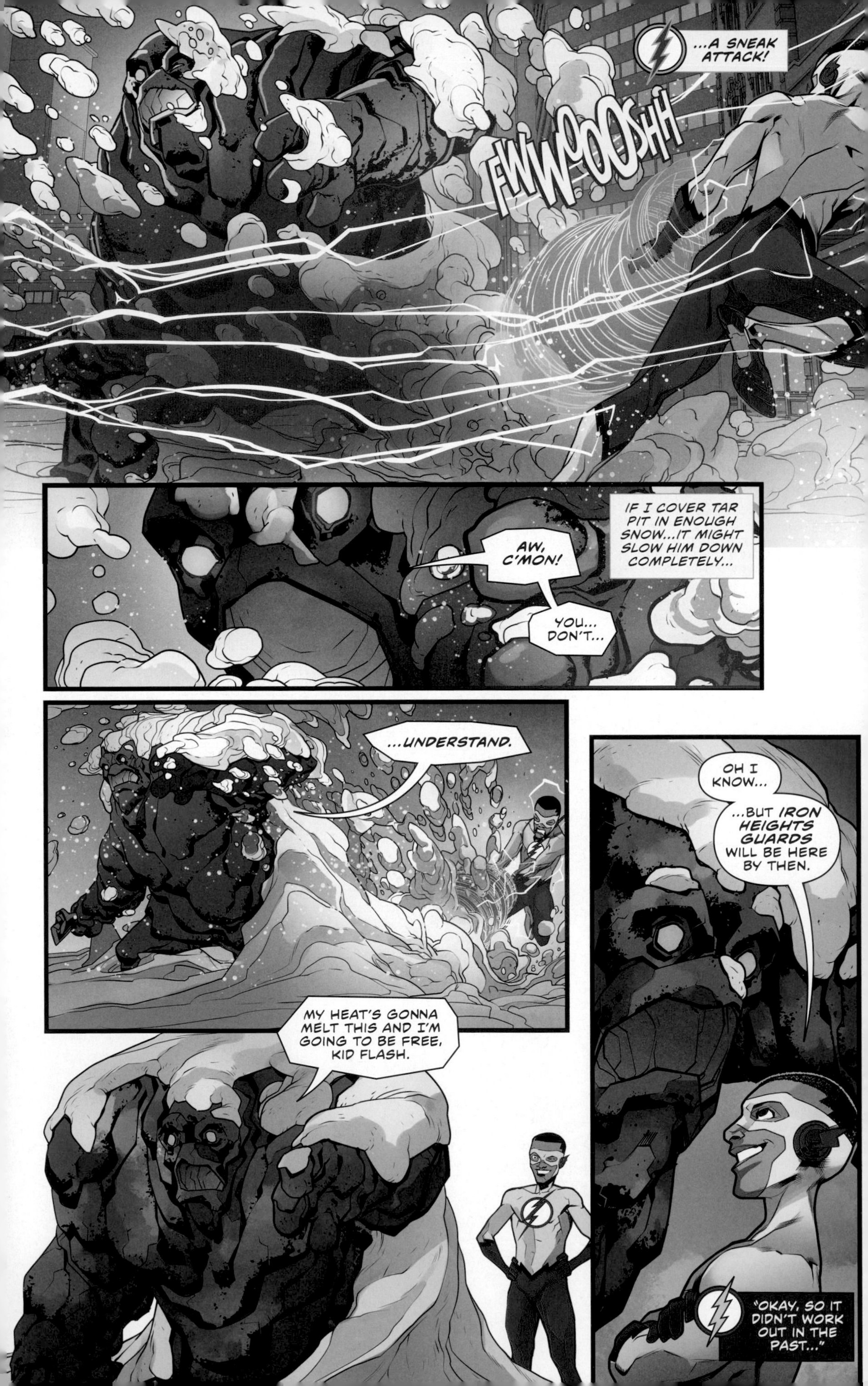
...A SNEAK ATTACK!
FWWOOOSHH
IF I COVER TAR PIT IN ENOUGH SNOW...IT MIGHT SLOW HIM DOWN COMPLETELY...
AW, C'MON!
YOU... DON'T...
...UNDERSTAND.
MY HEAT'S GONNA MELT THIS AND I'M GOING TO BE FREE, KID FLASH.
OH I KNOW...
...BUT IRON HEIGHTS GUARDS WILL BE HERE BY THEN.
"OKAY, SO IT DIDN'T WORK OUT IN THE PAST..."

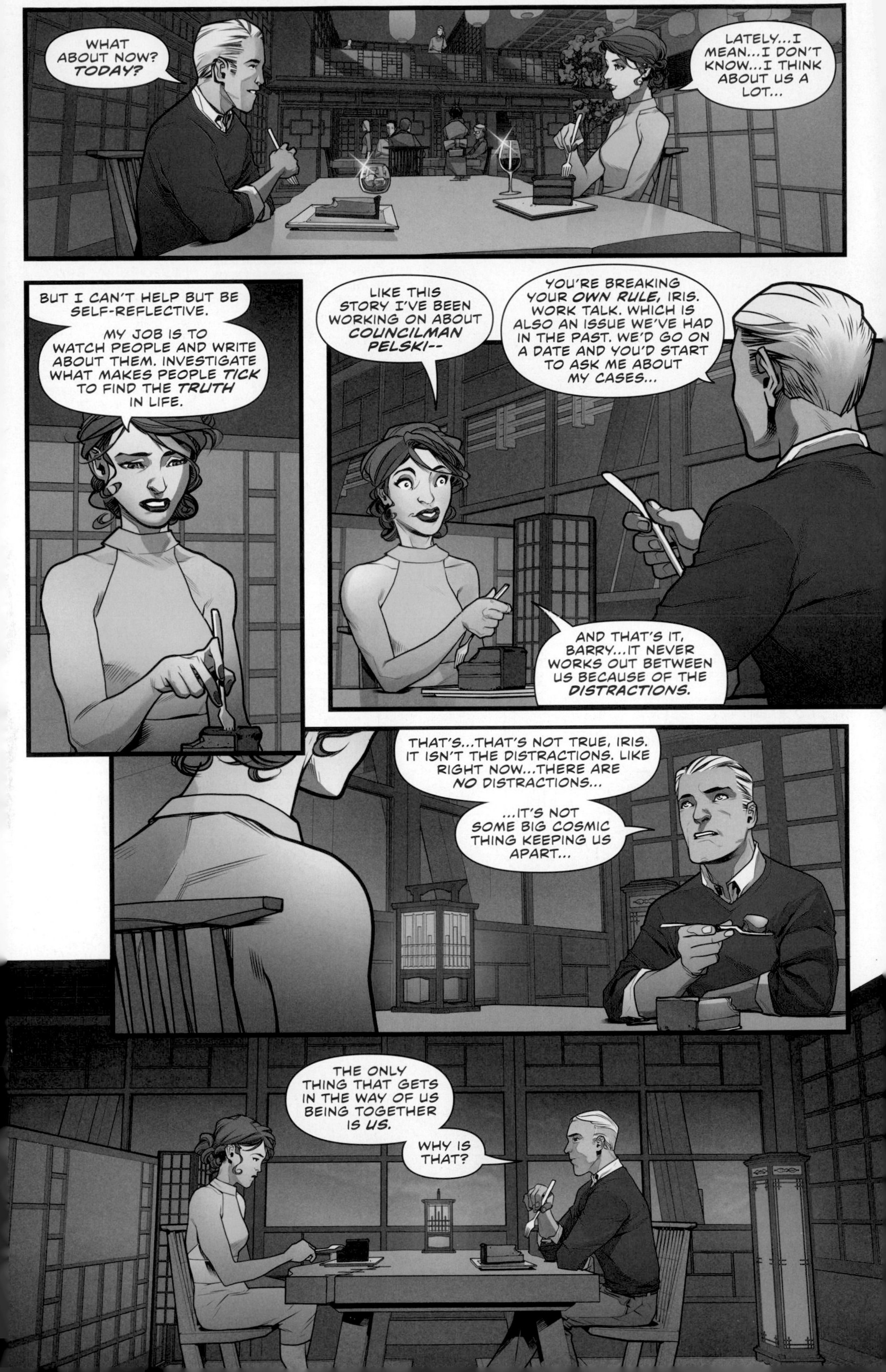
WHAT ABOUT NOW? *TODAY?*
LATELY...I MEAN...I DON'T KNOW...I THINK ABOUT US A LOT...
BUT I CAN'T HELP BUT BE SELF-REFLECTIVE.
MY JOB IS TO WATCH PEOPLE AND WRITE ABOUT THEM. INVESTIGATE WHAT MAKES PEOPLE *TICK* TO FIND THE *TRUTH* IN LIFE.
LIKE THIS STORY I'VE BEEN WORKING ON ABOUT *COUNCILMAN PELSKI--*
YOU'RE BREAKING YOUR *OWN RULE,* IRIS. WORK TALK. WHICH IS ALSO AN ISSUE WE'VE HAD IN THE PAST. WE'D GO ON A DATE AND YOU'D START TO ASK ME ABOUT MY CASES...
AND THAT'S IT, BARRY...IT NEVER WORKS OUT BETWEEN US BECAUSE OF THE *DISTRACTIONS.*
THAT'S...THAT'S NOT TRUE, IRIS. IT ISN'T THE DISTRACTIONS. LIKE RIGHT NOW...THERE ARE *NO* DISTRACTIONS...
...IT'S NOT SOME BIG COSMIC THING KEEPING US APART...
THE ONLY THING THAT GETS IN THE WAY OF US BEING TOGETHER IS *US.*
WHY IS THAT?

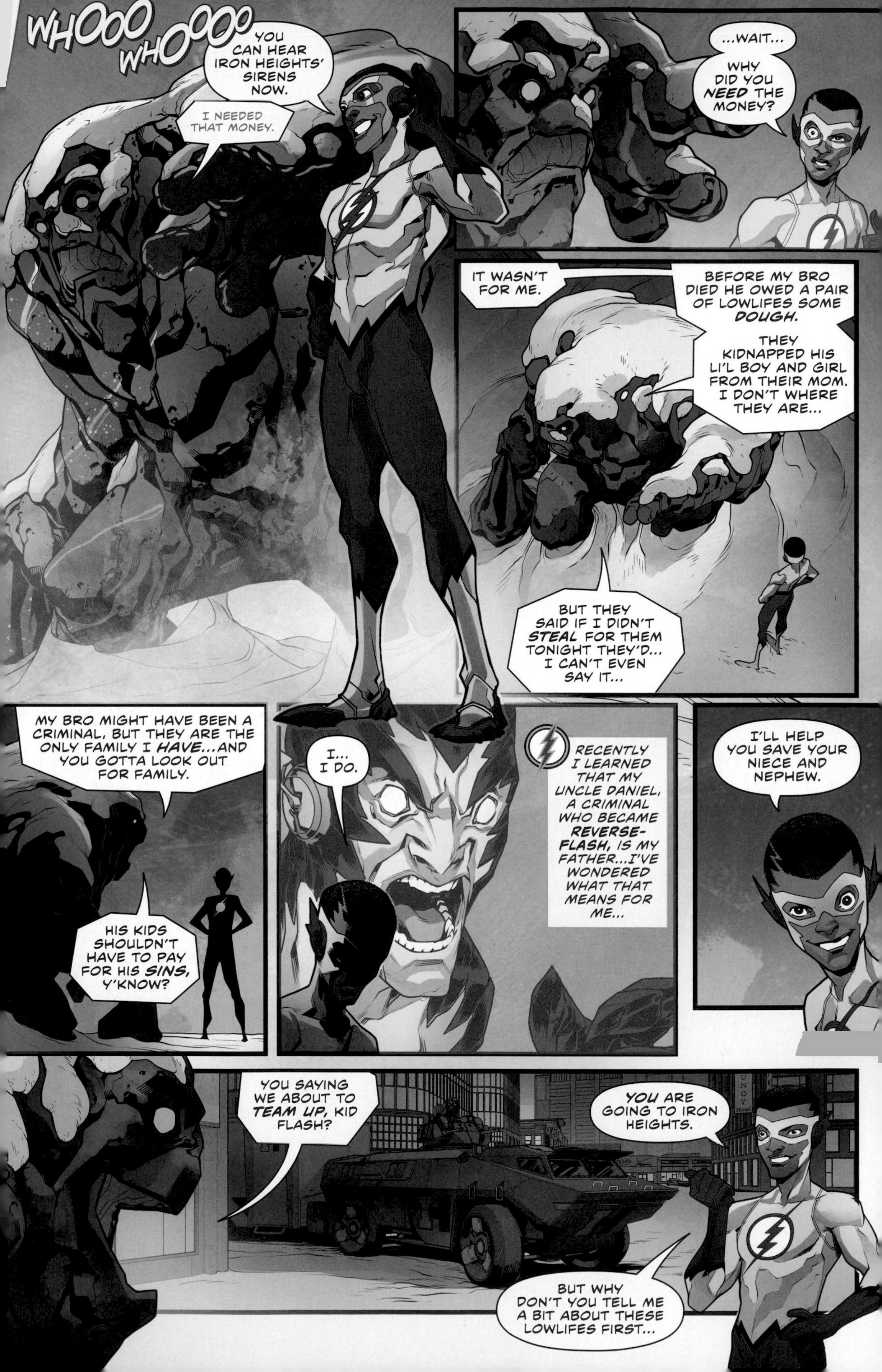
WHOOO WHOOOO
YOU CAN HEAR IRON HEIGHTS' SIRENS NOW.
I NEEDED THAT MONEY.
...WAIT...
WHY DID YOU NEED THE MONEY?
IT WASN'T FOR ME.
BEFORE MY BRO DIED HE OWED A PAIR OF LOWLIFES SOME DOUGH.
THEY KIDNAPPED HIS LI'L BOY AND GIRL FROM THEIR MOM. I DON'T WHERE THEY ARE...
BUT THEY SAID IF I DIDN'T STEAL FOR THEM TONIGHT THEY'D... I CAN'T EVEN SAY IT...
MY BRO MIGHT HAVE BEEN A CRIMINAL, BUT THEY ARE THE ONLY FAMILY I HAVE...AND YOU GOTTA LOOK OUT FOR FAMILY.
HIS KIDS SHOULDN'T HAVE TO PAY FOR HIS SINS, Y'KNOW?
I... I DO.
RECENTLY I LEARNED THAT MY UNCLE DANIEL, A CRIMINAL WHO BECAME REVERSE-FLASH, IS MY FATHER...I'VE WONDERED WHAT THAT MEANS FOR ME...
I'LL HELP YOU SAVE YOUR NIECE AND NEPHEW.
YOU SAYING WE ABOUT TO TEAM UP, KID FLASH?
YOU ARE GOING TO IRON HEIGHTS.
BUT WHY DON'T YOU TELL ME A BIT ABOUT THESE LOWLIFES FIRST...

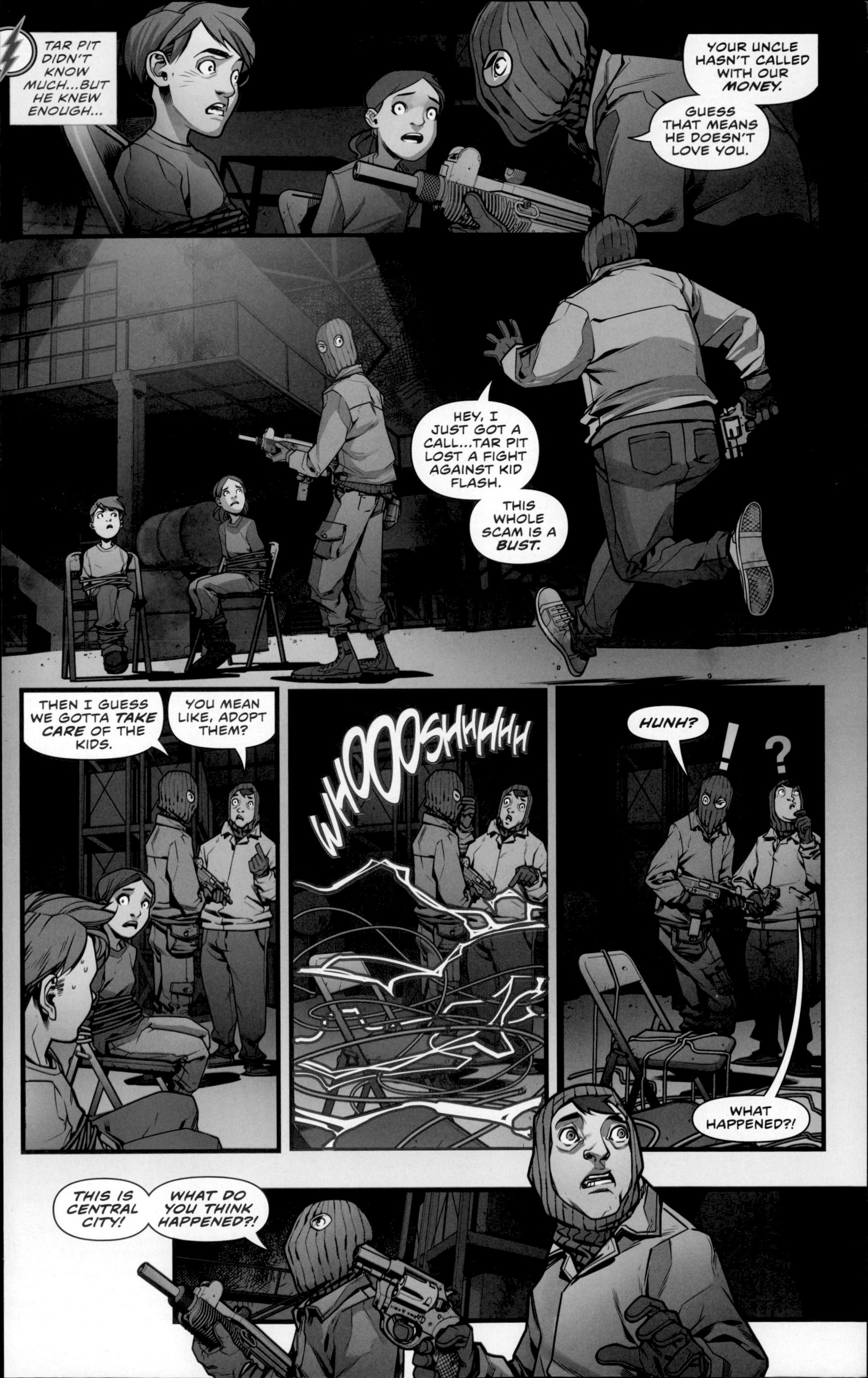

TAR PIT DIDN'T KNOW MUCH...BUT HE KNEW ENOUGH...
YOUR UNCLE HASN'T CALLED WITH OUR MONEY.
GUESS THAT MEANS HE DOESN'T LOVE YOU.
HEY, I JUST GOT A CALL...TAR PIT LOST A FIGHT AGAINST KID FLASH.
THIS WHOLE SCAM IS A BUST.
THEN I GUESS WE GOTTA TAKE CARE OF THE KIDS.
YOU MEAN LIKE, ADOPT THEM?
WHOOOSHHHHH
HUNH?
!
?
WHAT HAPPENED?!
THIS IS CENTRAL CITY!
WHAT DO YOU THINK HAPPENED?!

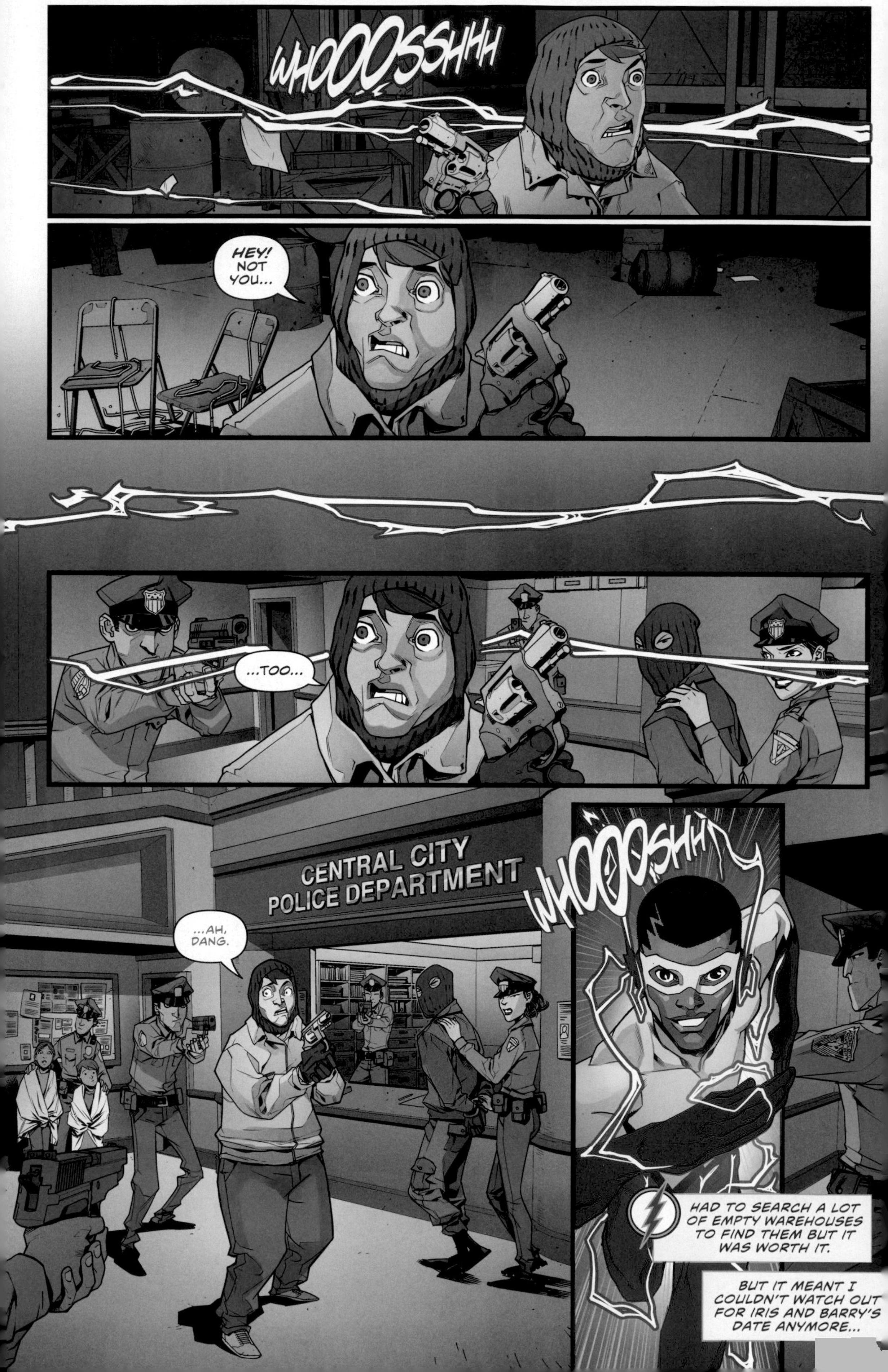
WHOOOOSSHHH
HEY! NOT YOU...
...TOO...
CENTRAL CITY POLICE DEPARTMENT
...AH, DANG.
WHOOOSHH
HAD TO SEARCH A LOT OF EMPTY WAREHOUSES TO FIND THEM BUT IT WAS WORTH IT.
BUT IT MEANT I COULDN'T WATCH OUT FOR IRIS AND BARRY'S DATE ANYMORE...

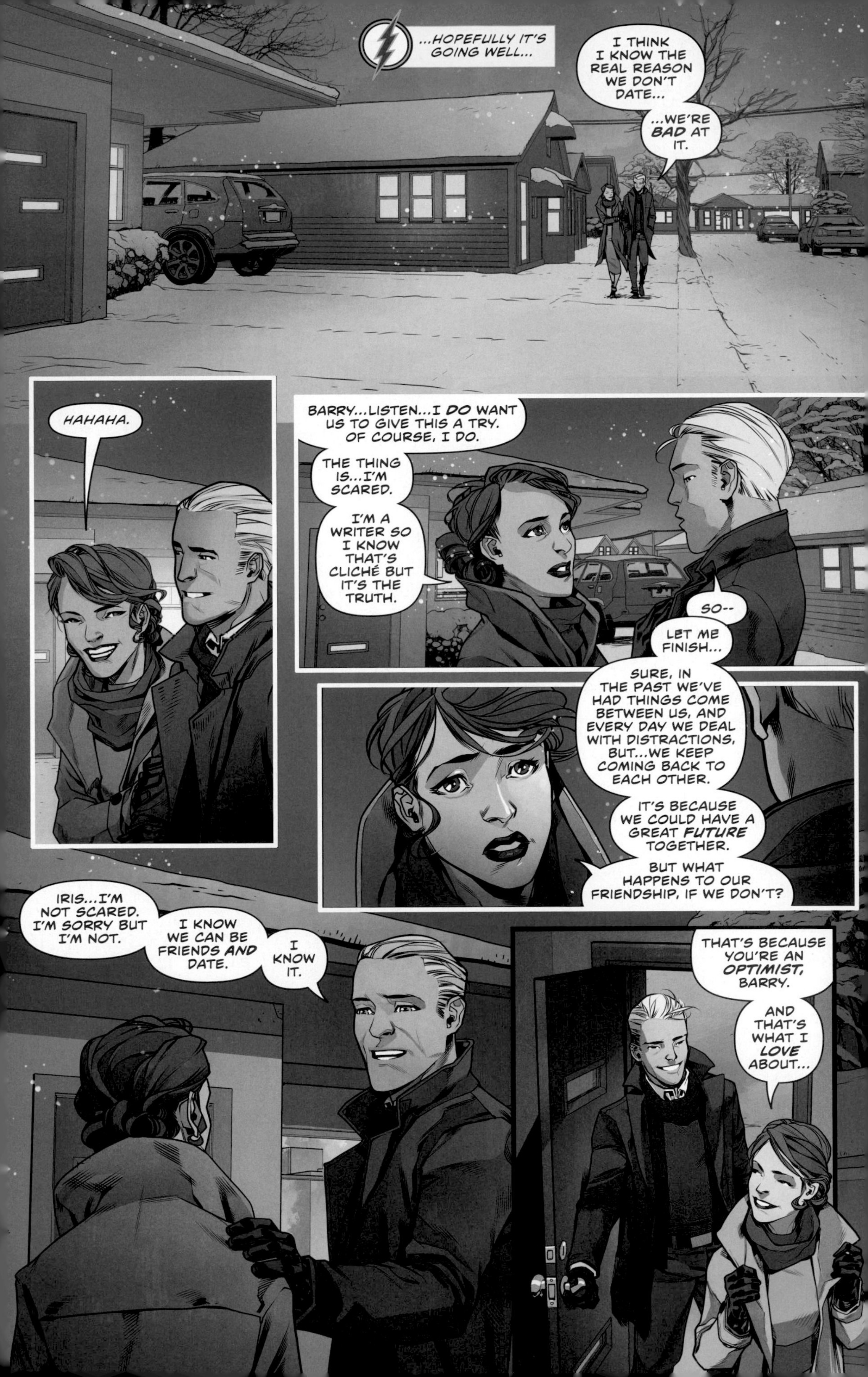
...HOPEFULLY IT'S GOING WELL...
I THINK I KNOW THE REAL REASON WE DON'T DATE...
...WE'RE BAD AT IT.
HAHAHA.
BARRY...LISTEN...I DO WANT US TO GIVE THIS A TRY. OF COURSE, I DO.
THE THING IS...I'M SCARED.
I'M A WRITER SO I KNOW THAT'S CLICHÉ BUT IT'S THE TRUTH.
SO--
LET ME FINISH...
SURE, IN THE PAST WE'VE HAD THINGS COME BETWEEN US, AND EVERY DAY WE DEAL WITH DISTRACTIONS, BUT...WE KEEP COMING BACK TO EACH OTHER.
IT'S BECAUSE WE COULD HAVE A GREAT FUTURE TOGETHER.
BUT WHAT HAPPENS TO OUR FRIENDSHIP, IF WE DON'T?
IRIS...I'M NOT SCARED. I'M SORRY BUT I'M NOT.
I KNOW WE CAN BE FRIENDS AND DATE.
I KNOW IT.
THAT'S BECAUSE YOU'RE AN OPTIMIST, BARRY.
AND THAT'S WHAT I LOVE ABOUT...

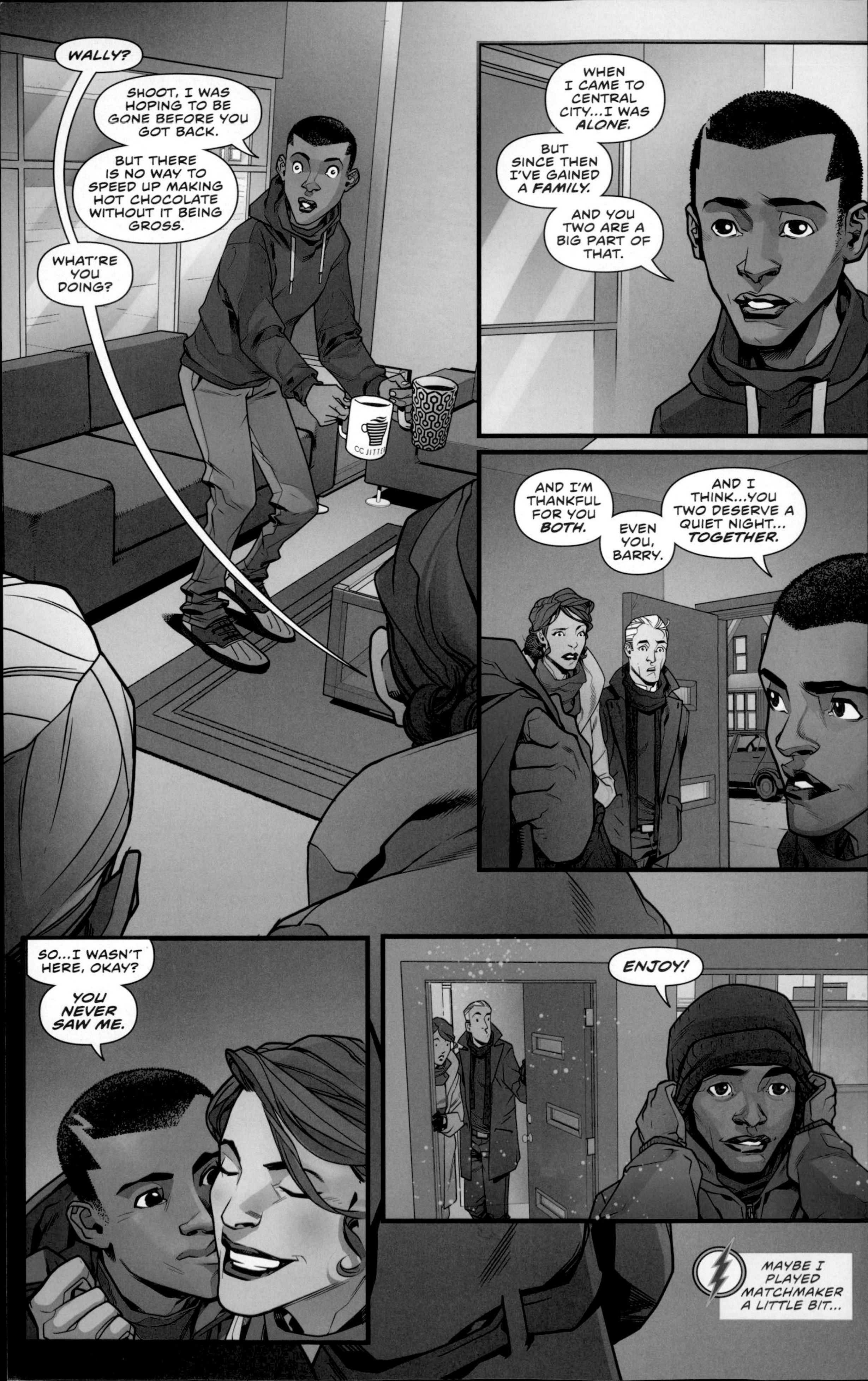
WALLY?
SHOOT, I WAS HOPING TO BE GONE BEFORE YOU GOT BACK.
BUT THERE IS NO WAY TO SPEED UP MAKING HOT CHOCOLATE WITHOUT IT BEING GROSS.
WHAT'RE YOU DOING?
CC JITTERS
WHEN I CAME TO CENTRAL CITY...I WAS ALONE.
BUT SINCE THEN I'VE GAINED A FAMILY.
AND YOU TWO ARE A BIG PART OF THAT.
AND I'M THANKFUL FOR YOU BOTH.
EVEN YOU, BARRY.
AND I THINK...YOU TWO DESERVE A QUIET NIGHT... TOGETHER.
SO...I WASN'T HERE, OKAY?
YOU NEVER SAW ME.
ENJOY!
MAYBE I PLAYED MATCHMAKER A LITTLE BIT...

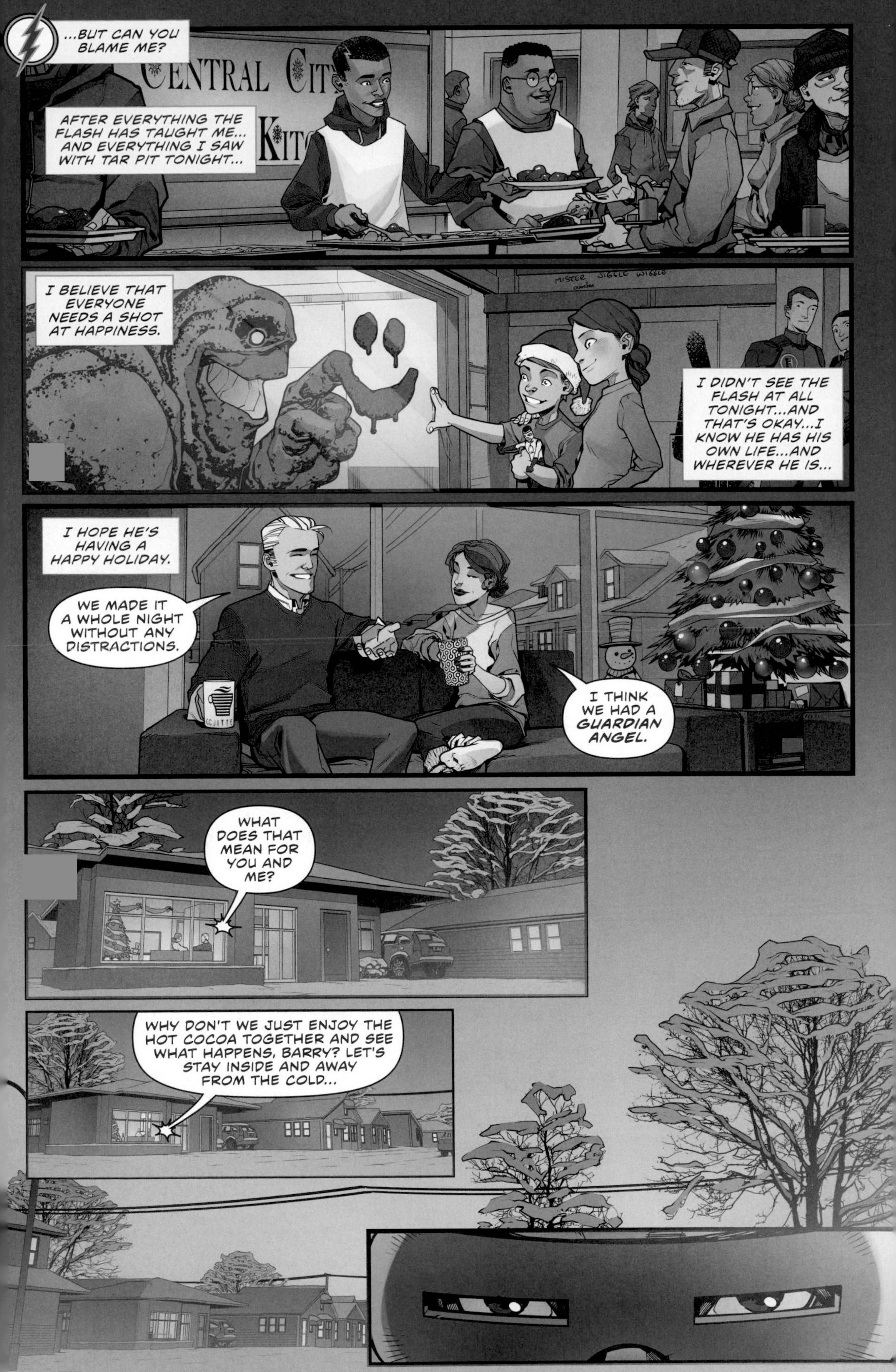
...BUT CAN YOU BLAME ME?
CENTRAL CITY
KITC
AFTER EVERYTHING THE FLASH HAS TAUGHT ME... AND EVERYTHING I SAW WITH TAR PIT TONIGHT...
I BELIEVE THAT EVERYONE NEEDS A SHOT AT HAPPINESS.
MISTER JIGGLE WIGGLE
I DIDN'T SEE THE FLASH AT ALL TONIGHT...AND THAT'S OKAY...I KNOW HE HAS HIS OWN LIFE...AND WHEREVER HE IS...
I HOPE HE'S HAVING A HAPPY HOLIDAY.
WE MADE IT A WHOLE NIGHT WITHOUT ANY DISTRACTIONS.
I THINK WE HAD A GUARDIAN ANGEL.
WHAT DOES THAT MEAN FOR YOU AND ME?
WHY DON'T WE JUST ENJOY THE HOT COCOA TOGETHER AND SEE WHAT HAPPENS, BARRY? LET'S STAY INSIDE AND AWAY FROM THE COLD...

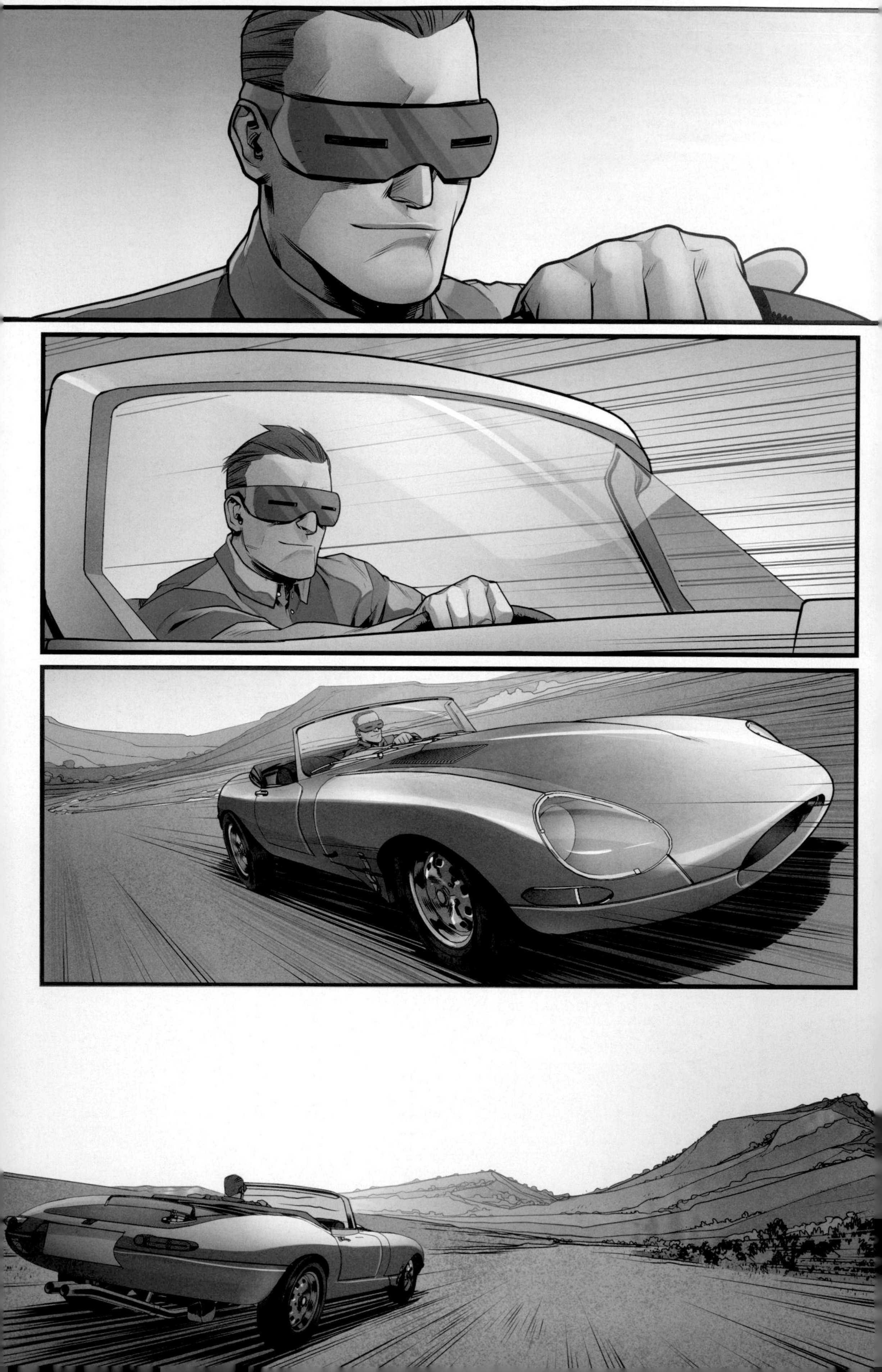

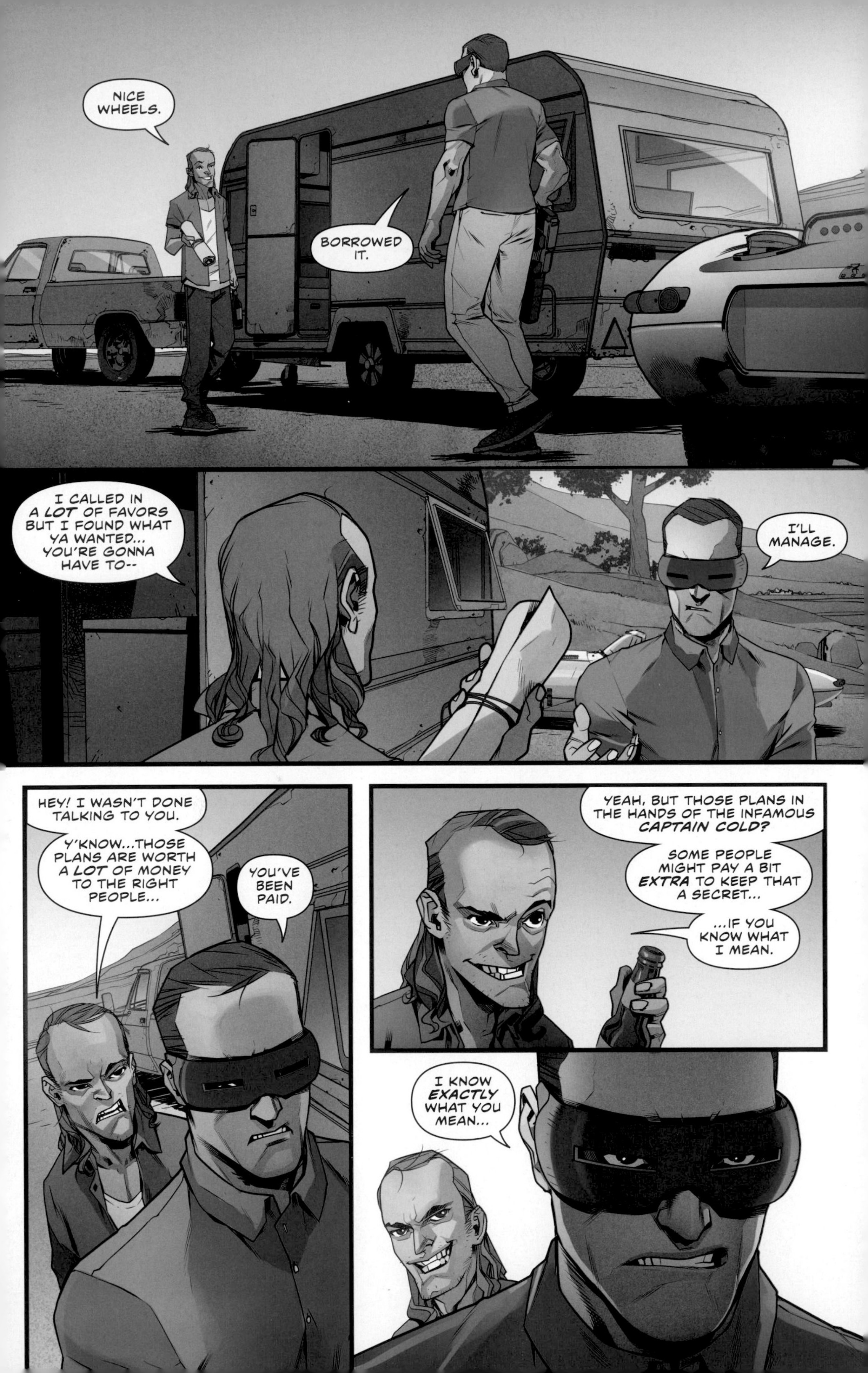
NICE WHEELS.
BORROWED IT.
I CALLED IN A LOT OF FAVORS BUT I FOUND WHAT YA WANTED... YOU'RE GONNA HAVE TO--
I'LL MANAGE.
HEY! I WASN'T DONE TALKING TO YOU.
Y'KNOW...THOSE PLANS ARE WORTH A LOT OF MONEY TO THE RIGHT PEOPLE...
YOU'VE BEEN PAID.
YEAH, BUT THOSE PLANS IN THE HANDS OF THE INFAMOUS CAPTAIN COLD?
SOME PEOPLE MIGHT PAY A BIT EXTRA TO KEEP THAT A SECRET...
...IF YOU KNOW WHAT I MEAN.
I KNOW EXACTLY WHAT YOU MEAN...

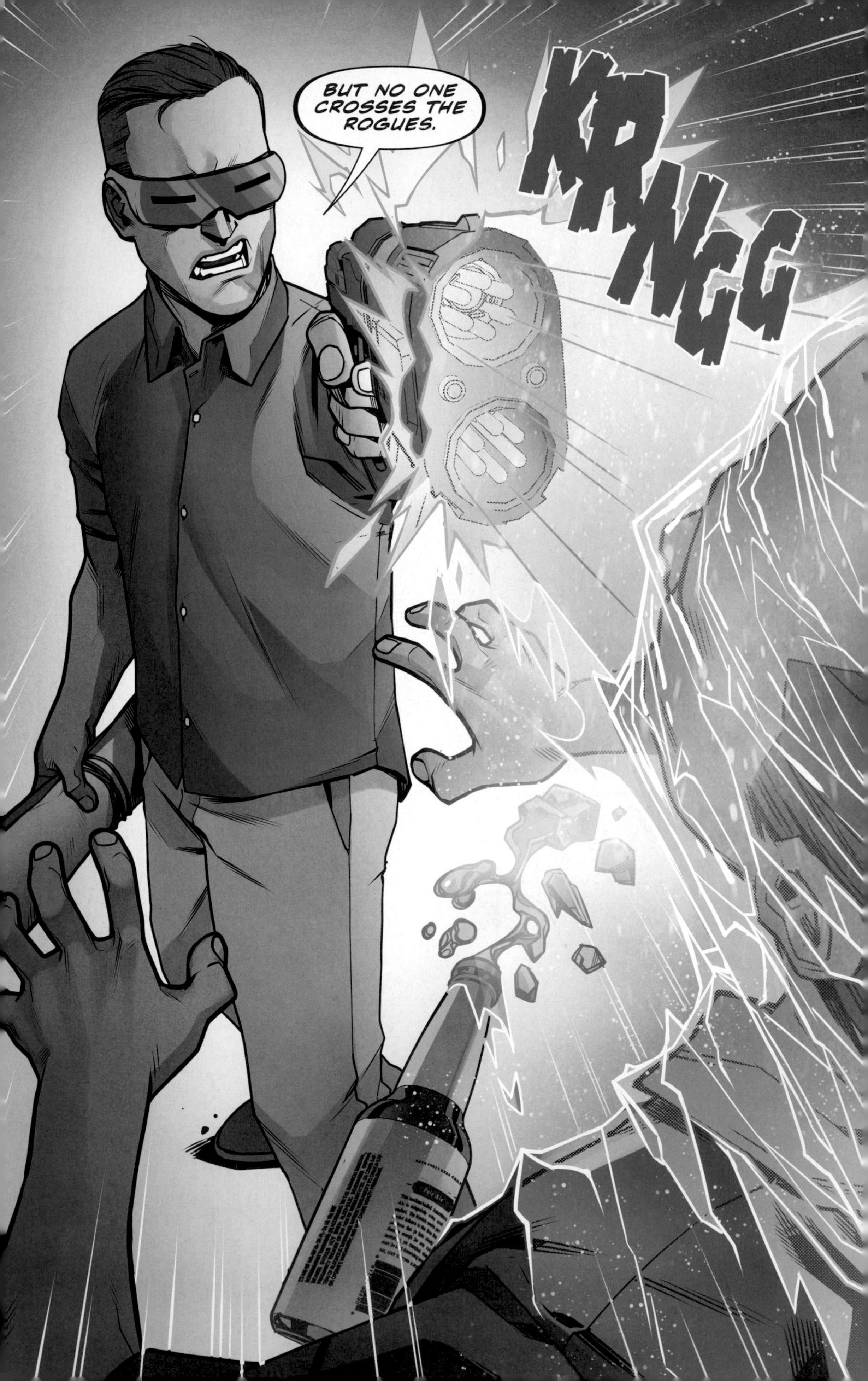
BUT NO ONE CROSSES THE ROGUES.
KRNGG

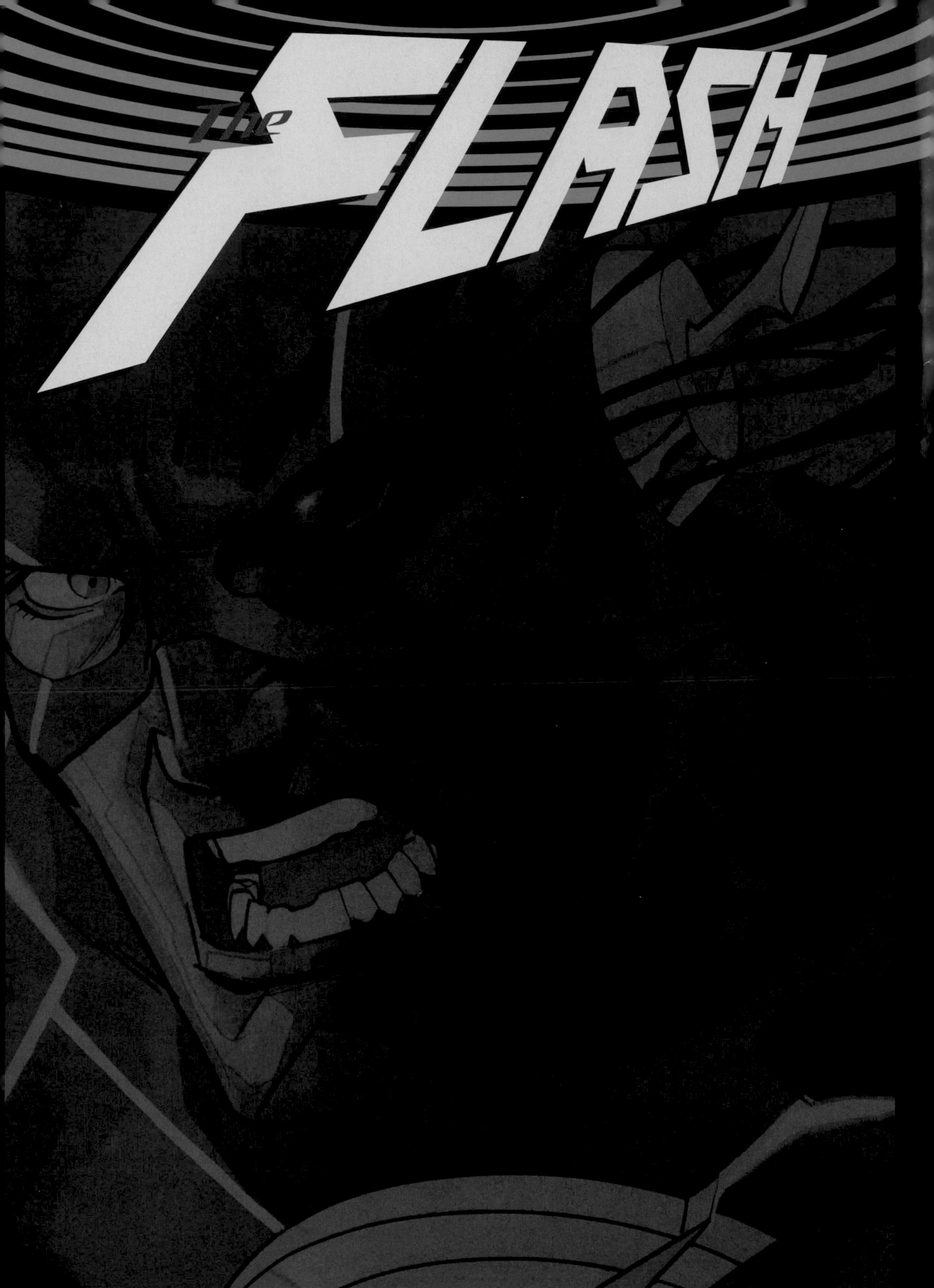
The FLASH

VARIANT COVER GALLERY

THE FLASH #9 variant cover by DAVE JOHNSON

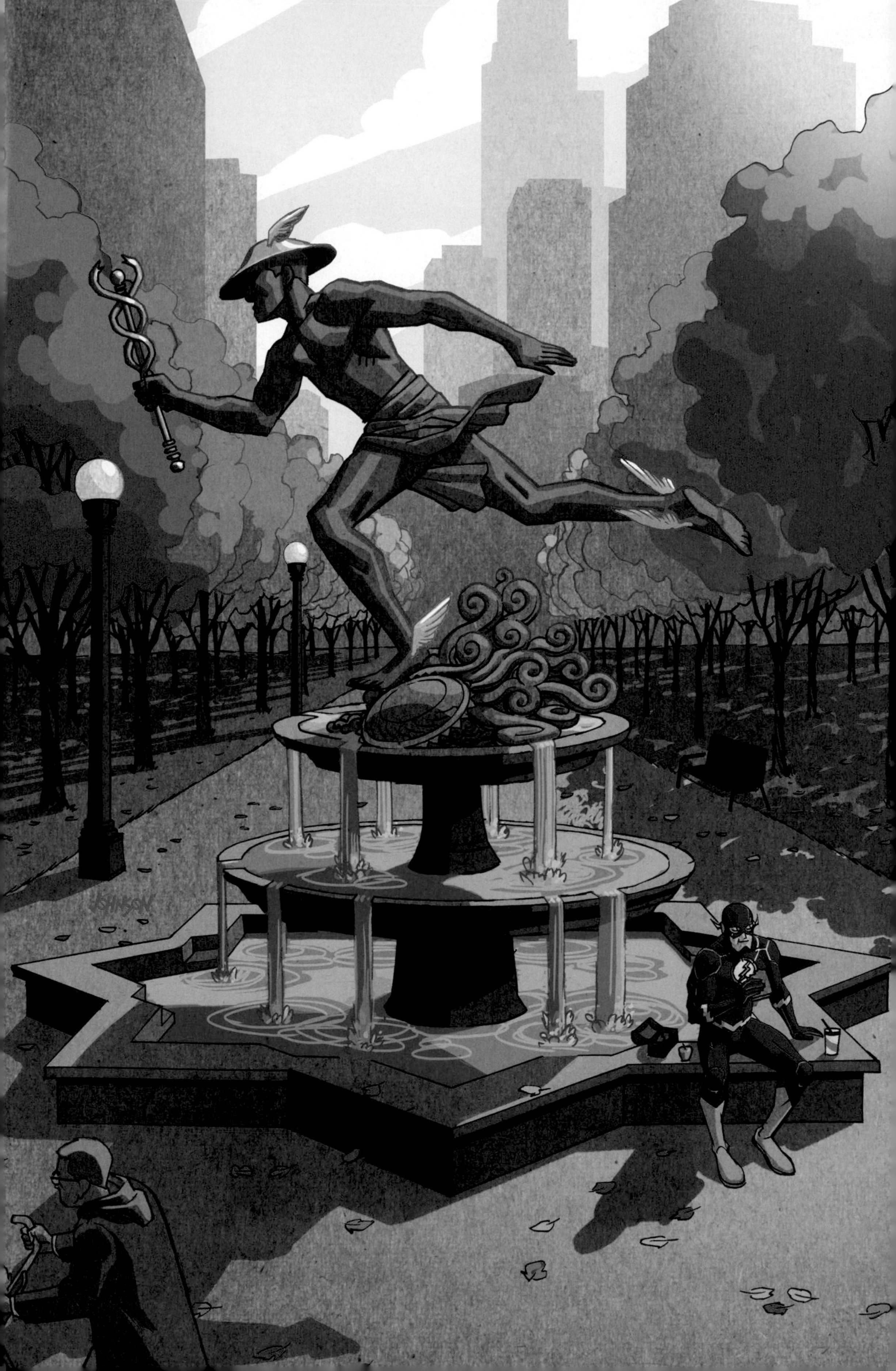
JOHNSON

THE FLASH #18 variant cover by DAVE JOHNSON

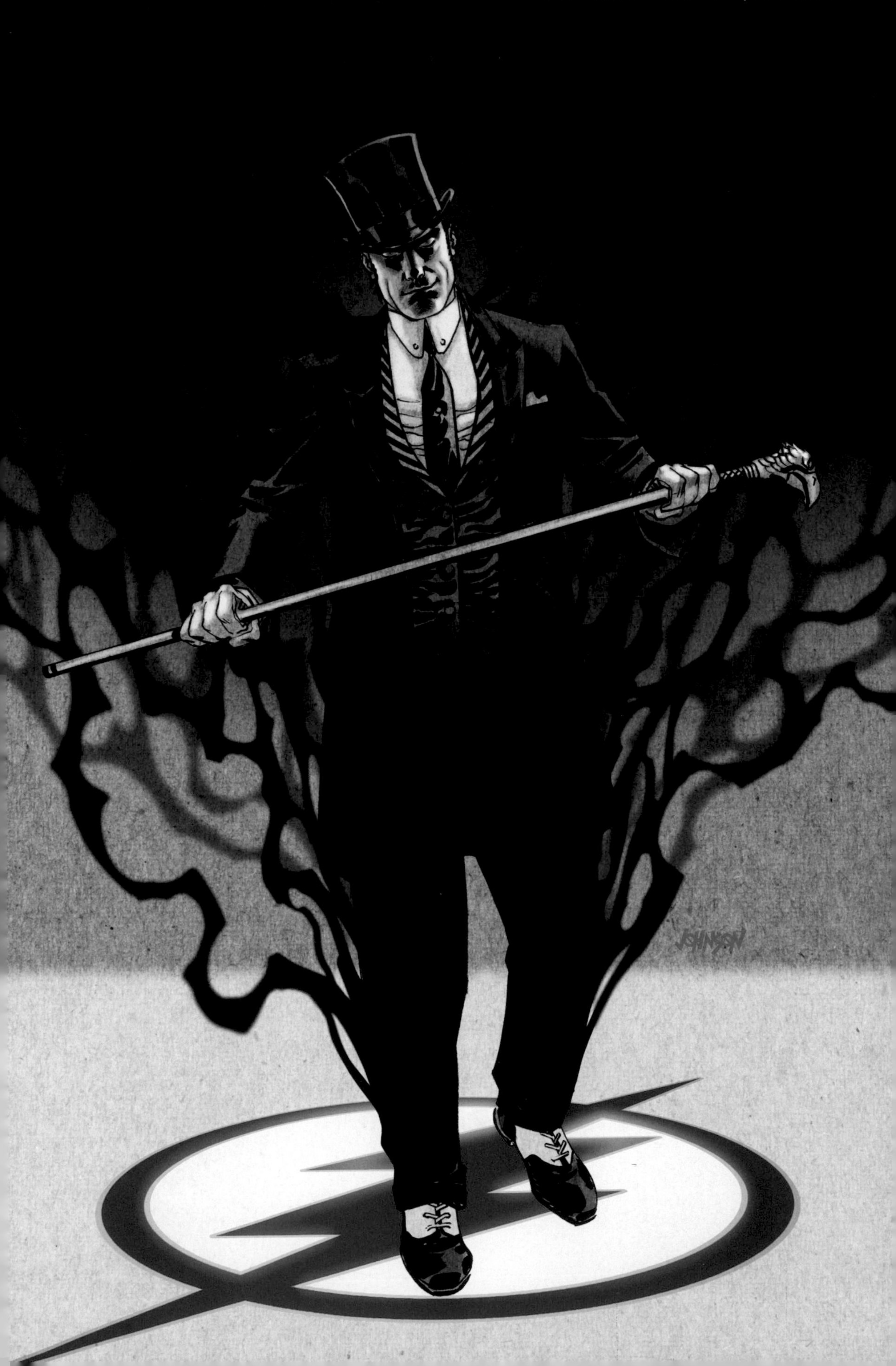
JOHNSON

THE FLASH #11 variant cover by DAVE JOHNSON

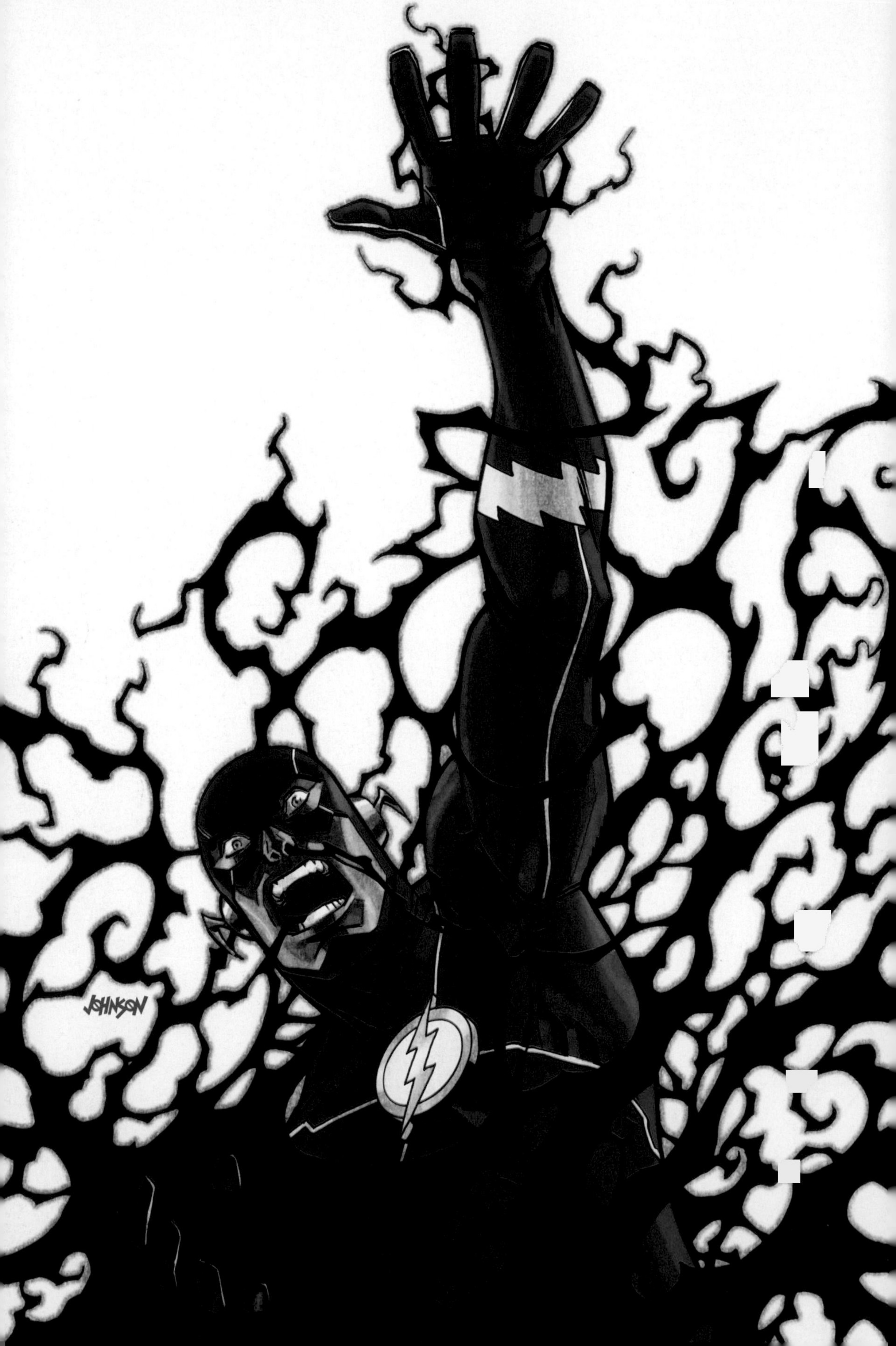
JOHNSON

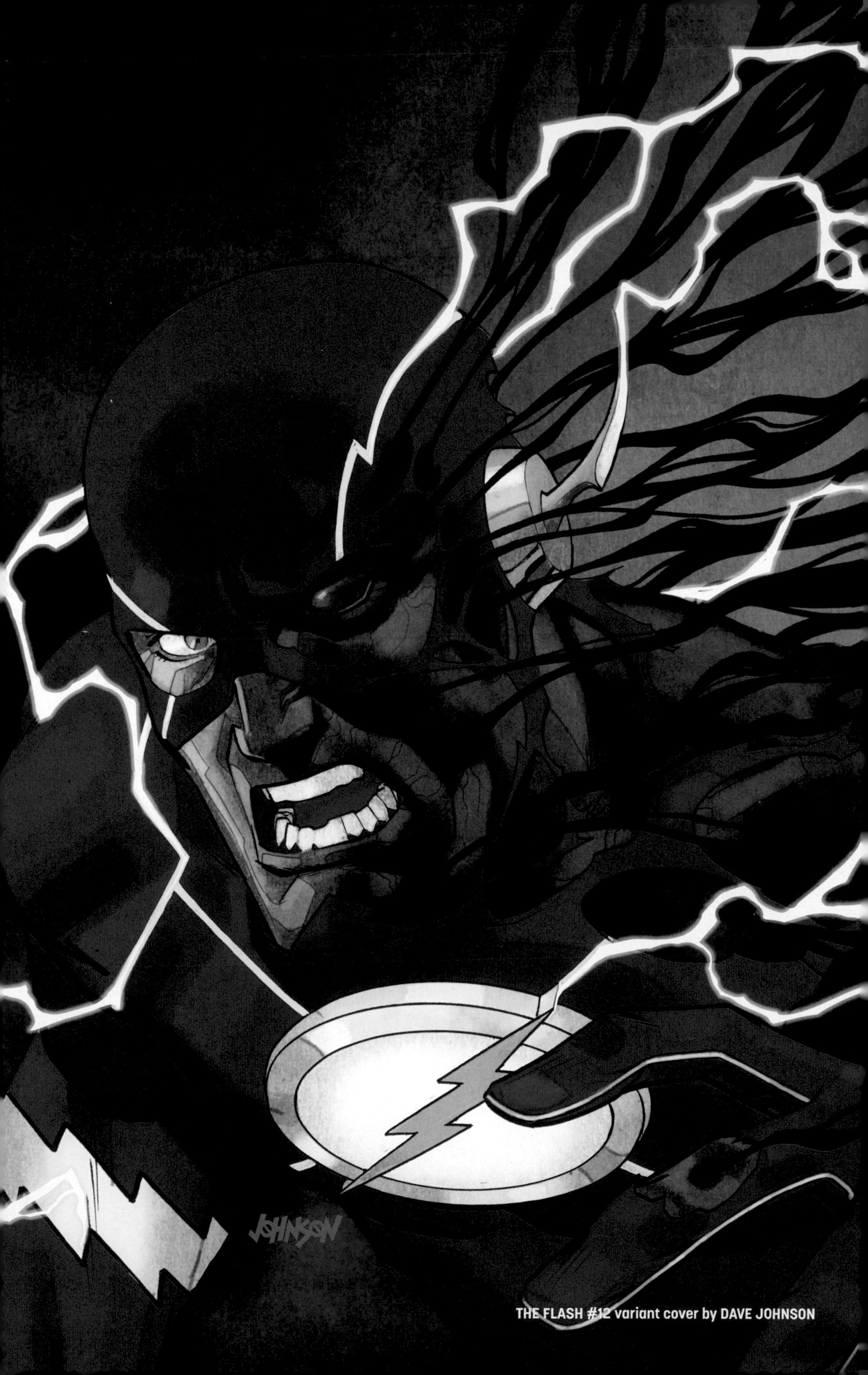
JOHNSON

THE FLASH #12 variant cover by DAVE JOHNSON

THE FLASH #13 variant cover by DAVE JOHNSON

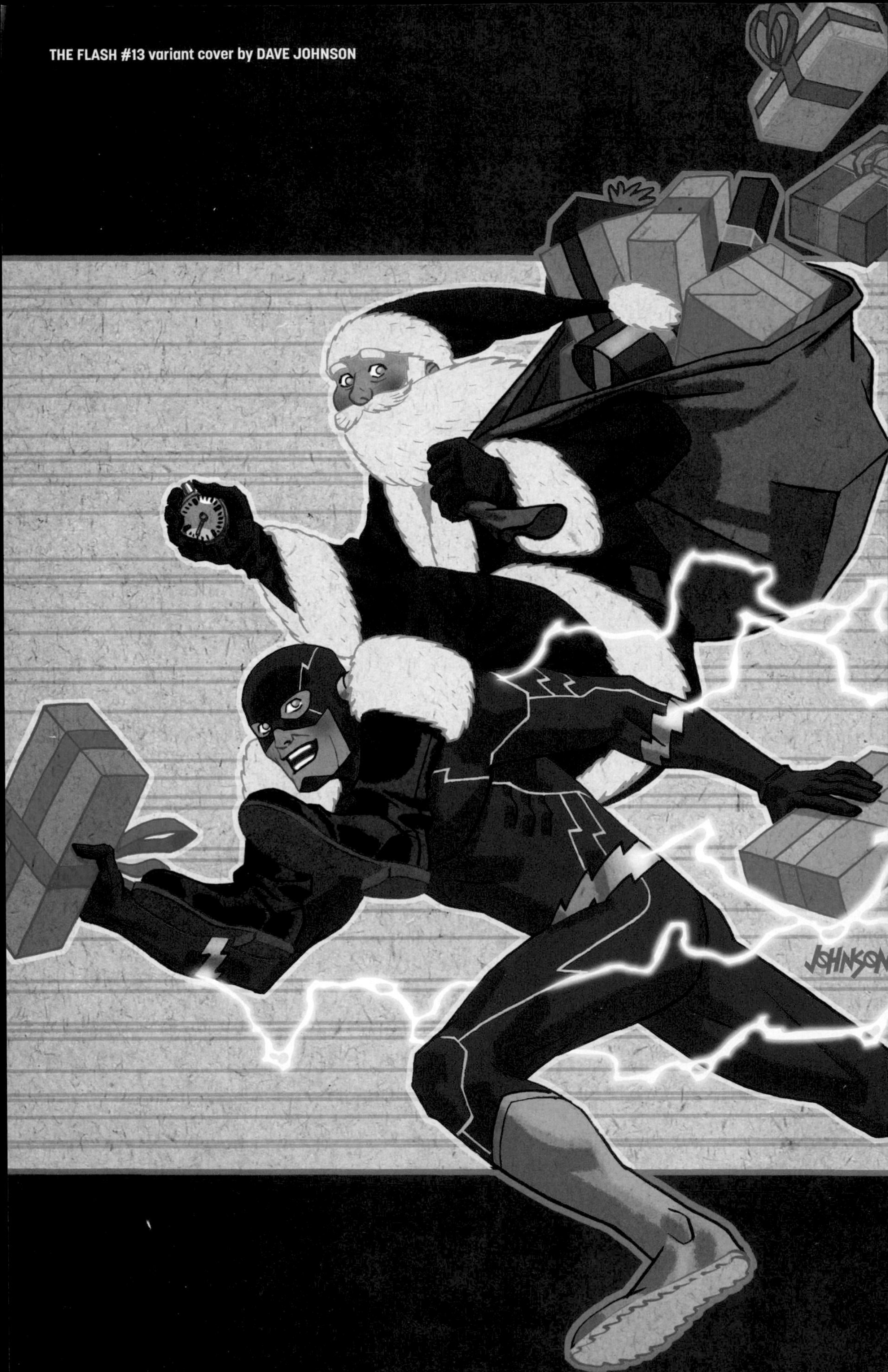

THE FLASH #9 PENCILS
by JORGE CORONA

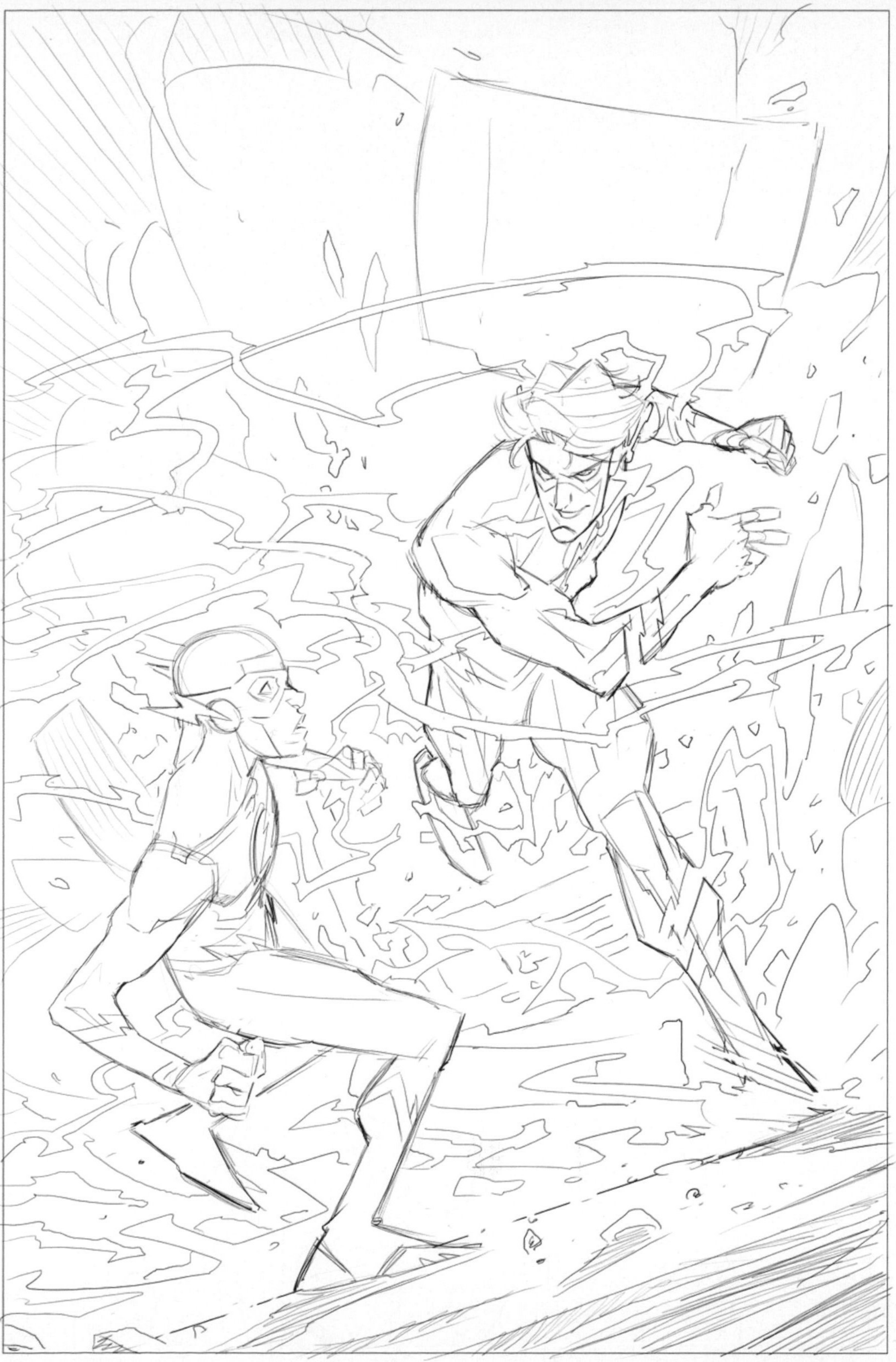

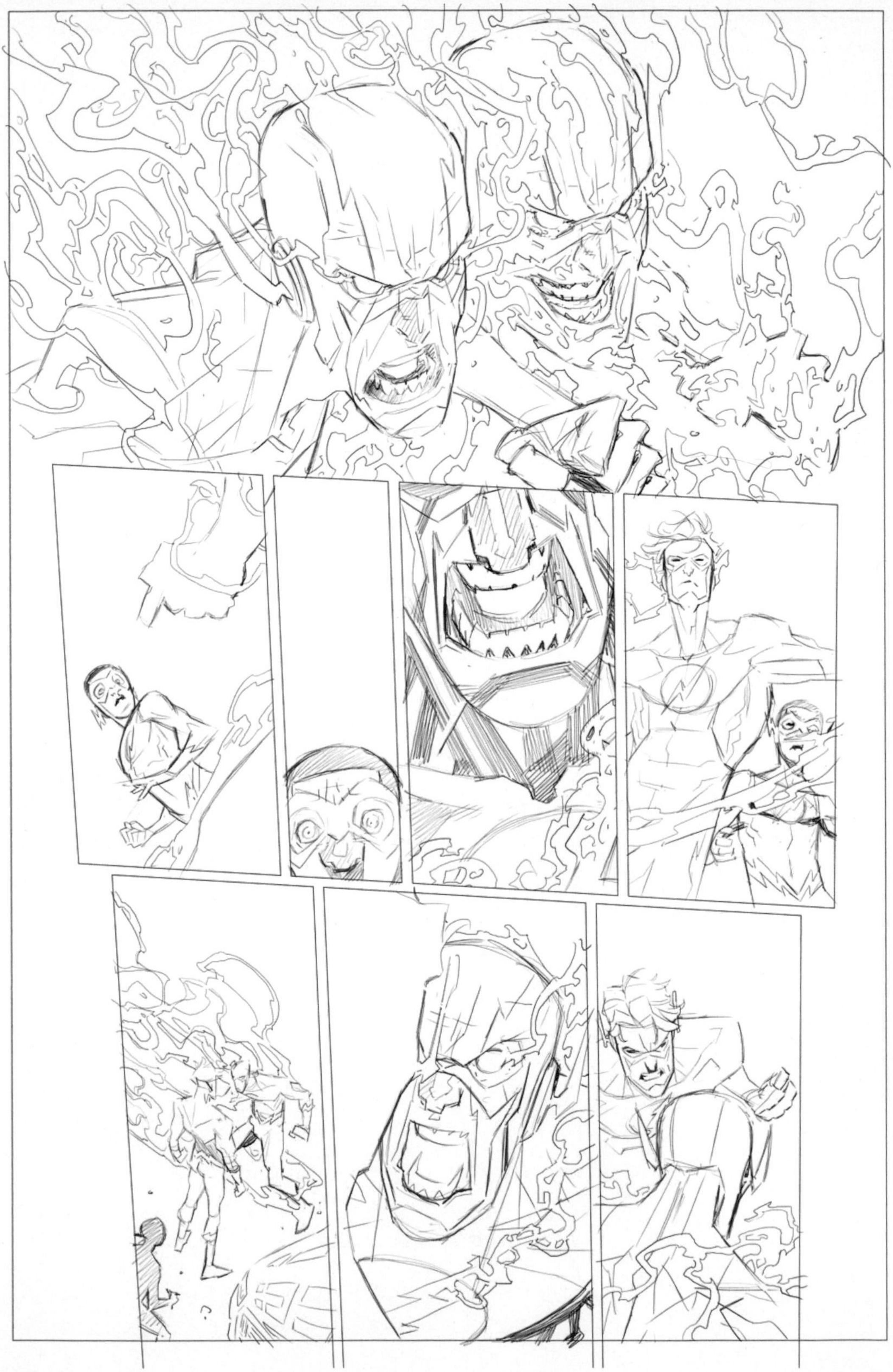

THE FLASH #10 PENCILS
by FELIPE WATANABE

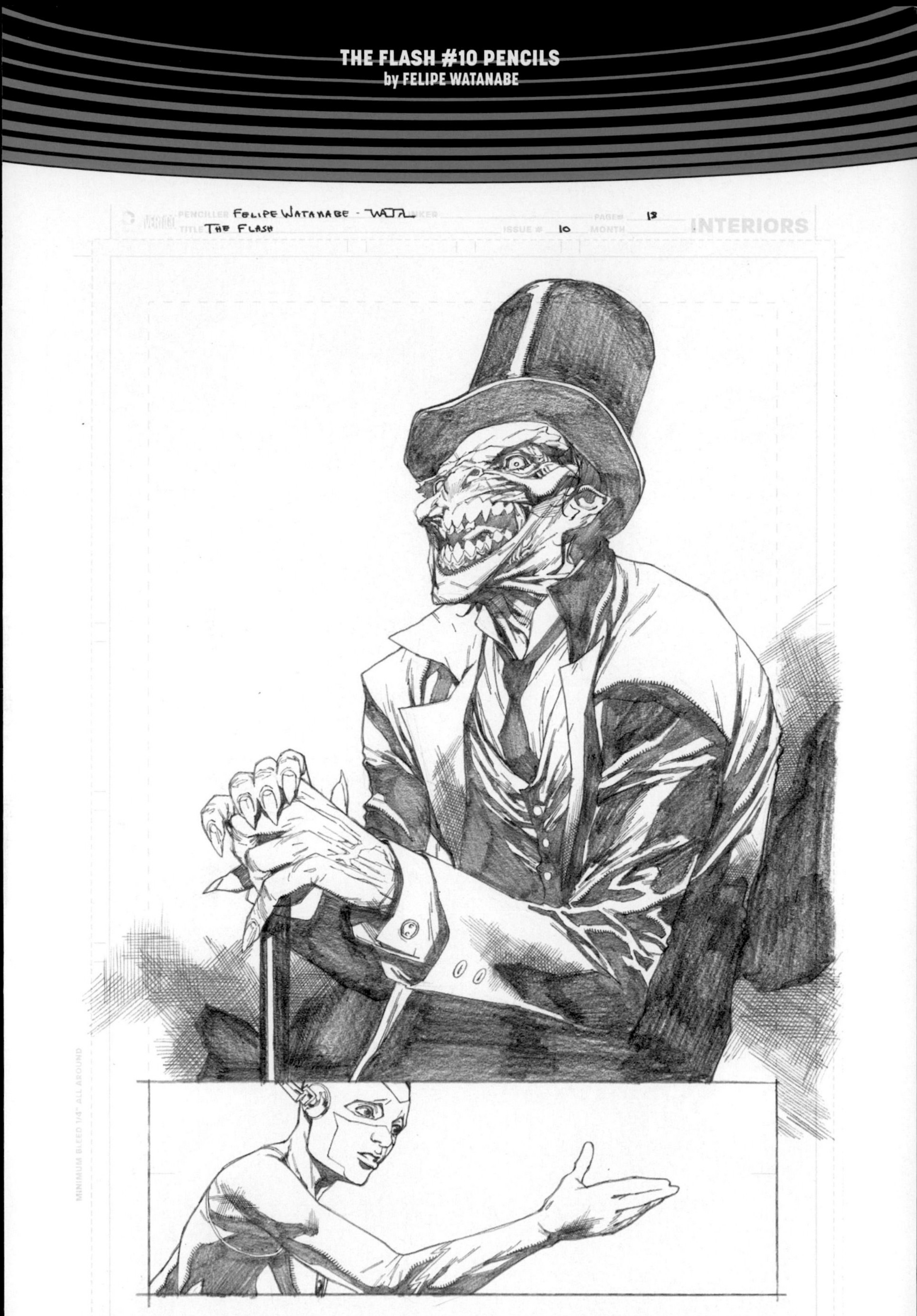
PENCILLER FELIPE WATANABE
TITLE THE FLASH
ISSUE # 10
PAGE # 13
INTERIORS
MINIMUM BLEED 1/4" ALL AROUND
DOUBLE PAGE SPREAD: CUT AS SHOWN, ABUT PAGE EDGES, TAPE ON BACK, DO NOT OVERLAP

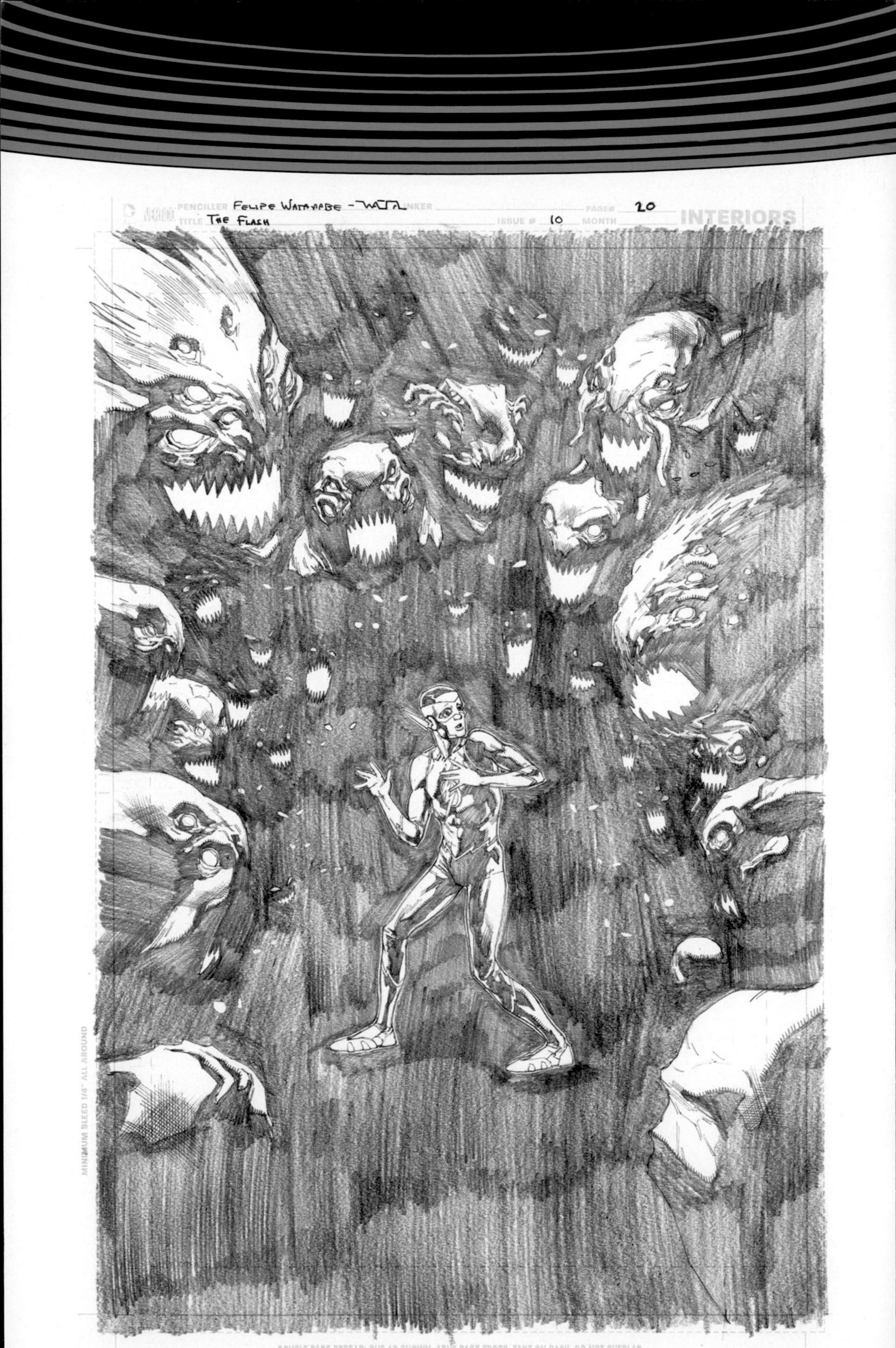
PENCILLER Felipe Watanabe
PAGE# 20
TITLE The Flash
ISSUE # 10
INTERIORS
MINIMUM BLEED 1/4" ALL AROUND
CUT RIGHT-HAND PAGE AT THIS LINE
DOUBLE PAGE SPREAD: CUT AS SHOWN, ABUT PAGE EDGES, TAPE ON BACK, DO NOT OVERLAP
CUT LEFT HAND PAGE AT THIS LINE

THE FLASH #12 PENCILS
by DAVIDE GIANFELICE

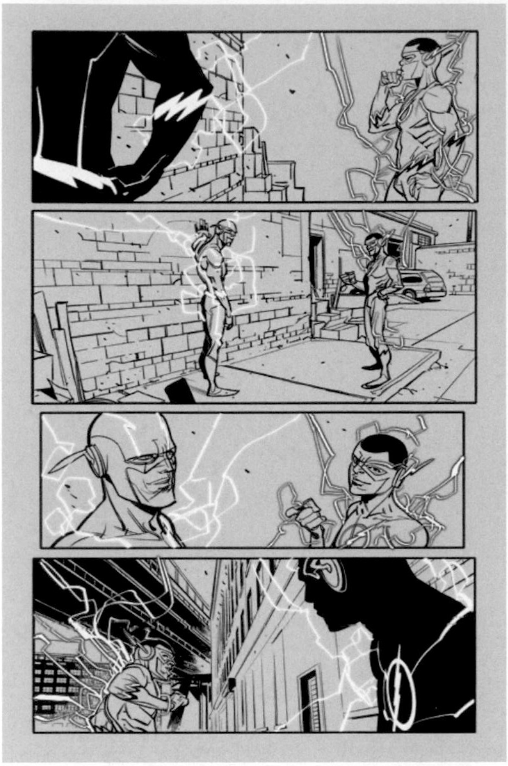

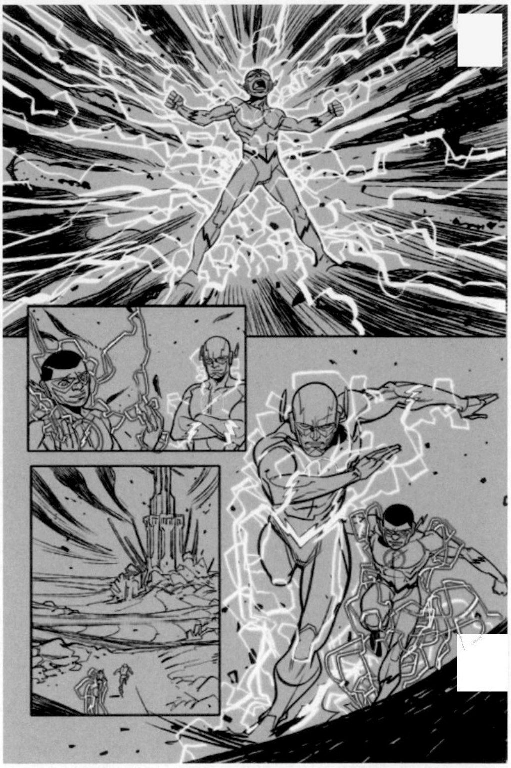

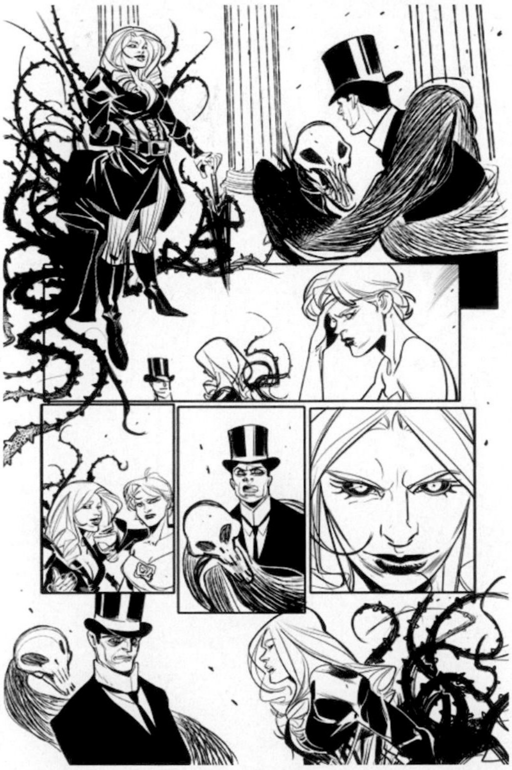

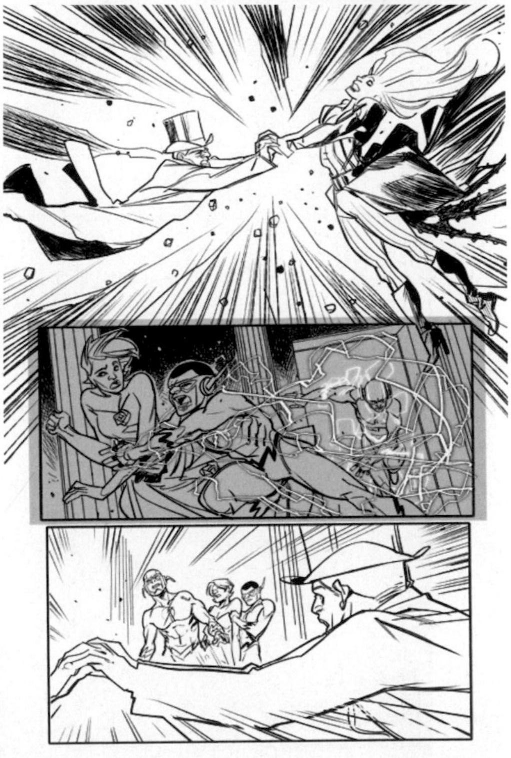

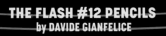

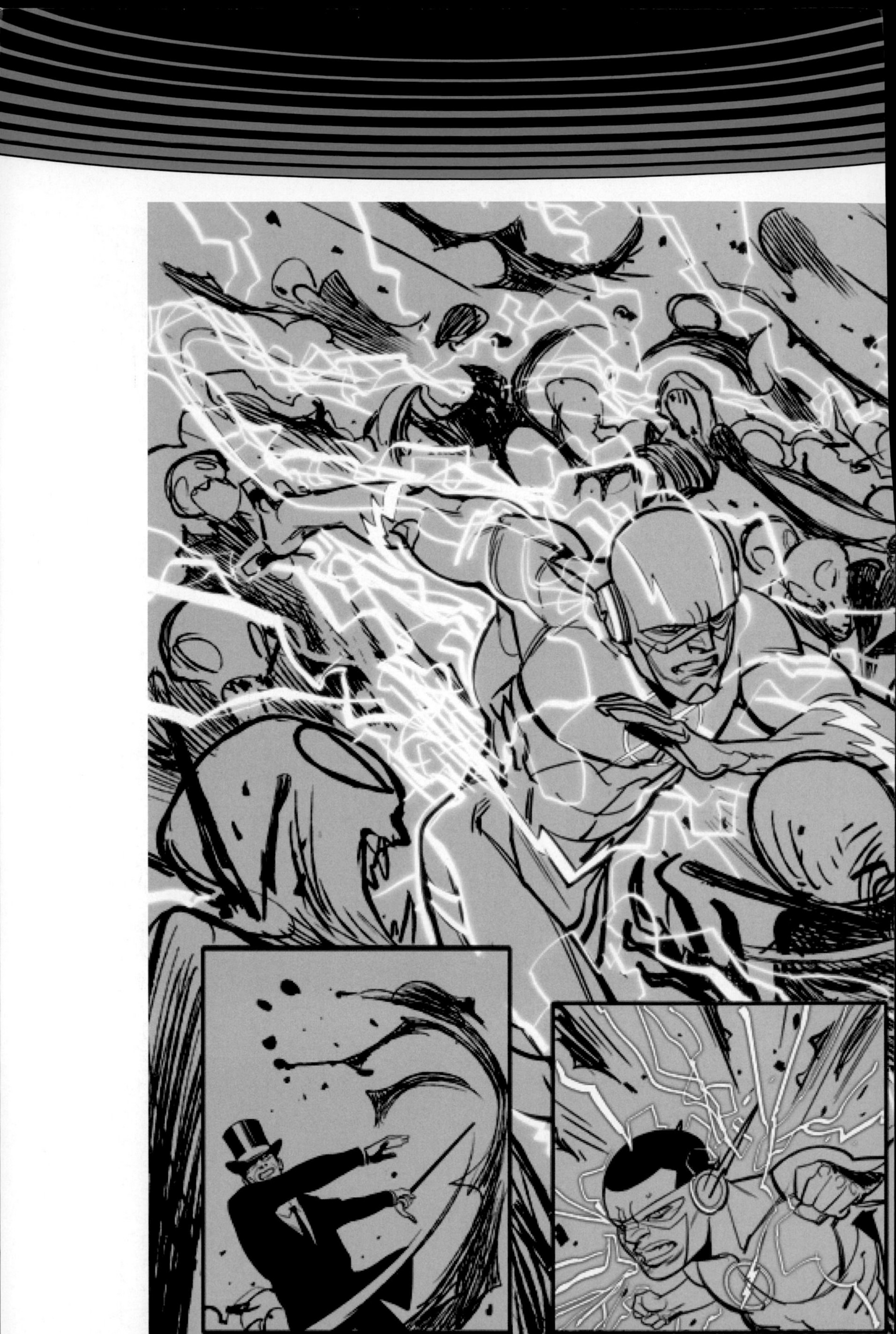

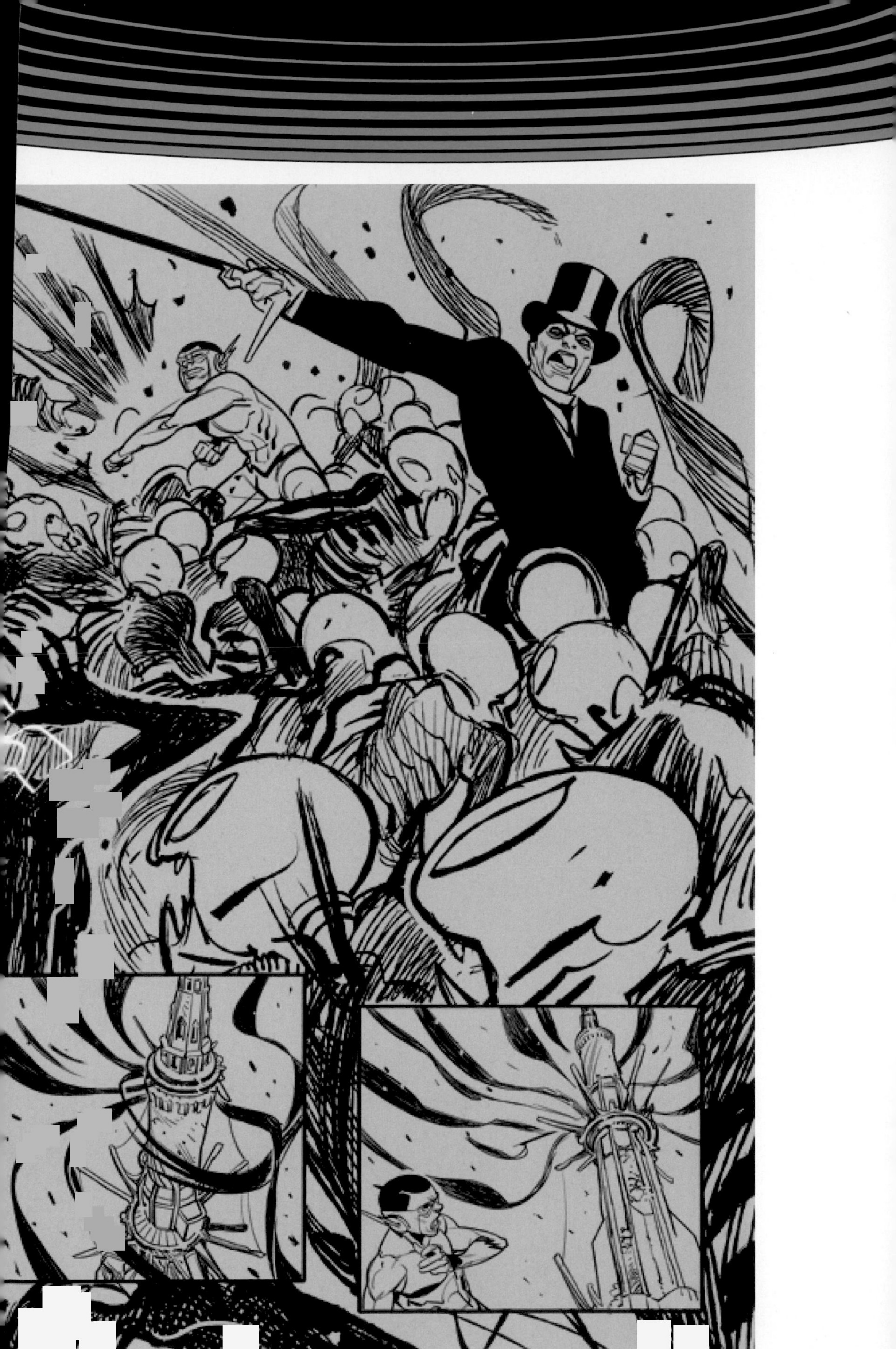

THE FLASH #13 PENCILS
by NEIL GOOGE

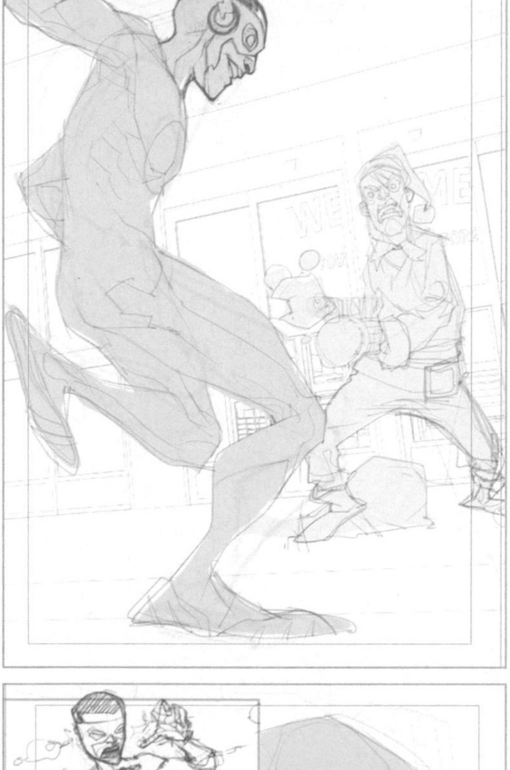

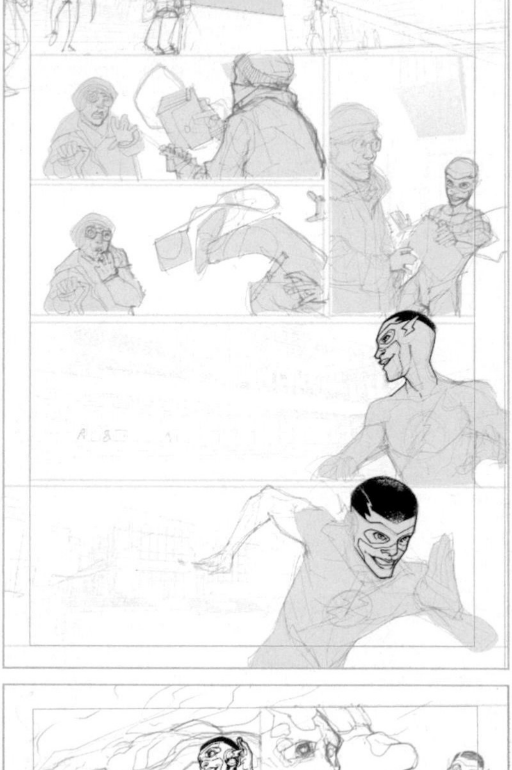

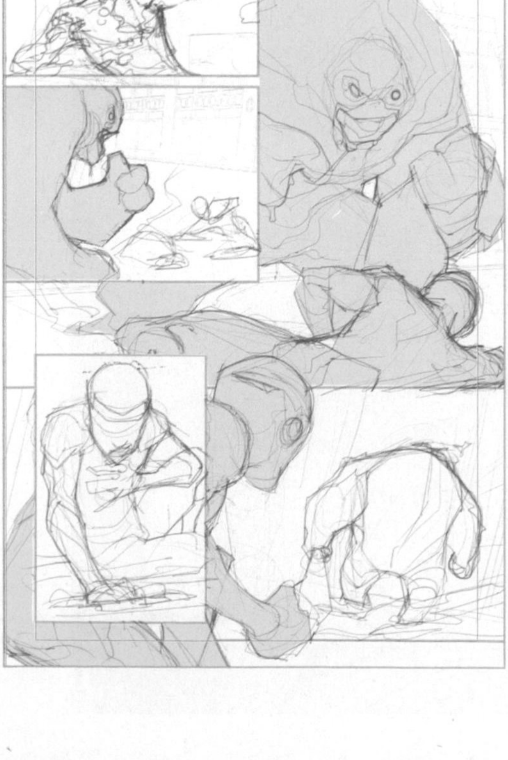

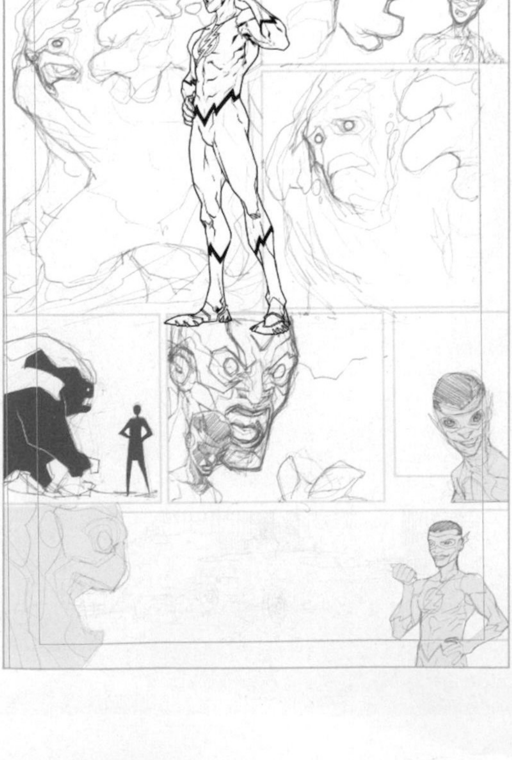

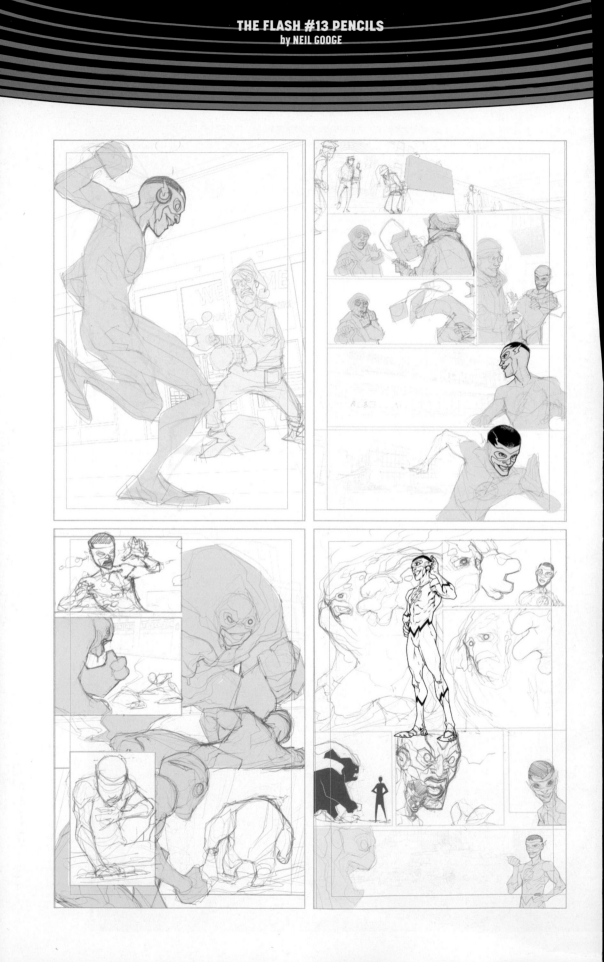